THE CENTRE IS BLACK

THE CENTRE IS BLACK

M. G. N. KAHENDE

JANUS PUBLISHING COMPANY
London, England

First published in Great Britain 2000
by Janus Publishing Company Limited,
76 Great Titchfield Street,
London W1P 7AF

www.januspublishing.co.uk

**A CIP catalogue record for this book
is available from the British Library.**

ISBN 1 85756 438 3

Phototypeset in 11.5 on 13.75 Century Schoolbook
by Keyboard Services, Luton, Beds

Cover design Hamish Cooper

Printed and bound in Great Britain

Acknowledgments

My special thanks go to my children, Wanjiru, Njoroge
and Timothy;
To Nyambura Gikonyo, Annie Nyambura 'Gachungwa',
Muthoni Gichema, Wanjiru Ndungu, Julie Njuguna,
Wanjiru Munene, and especially Margaret Nyandia for the
creation of 'Nzinga'.

Dedicated to all those who have sacrificed so much to set
Africa free.
And
To those who believe in the future and greatness of Africa.

Contents

1

The Song of My People

In heaven there are long queues of desperate souls waiting to be allocated human bodies, so they can come to live on earth. Some will never get a chance before the day of judgement, the day of Armageddon. How disappointed they will be! Not I. Call me Everywhere, the impatient soul that jumped the queue and sneaked to earth before my turn. I was not scared to enter and live in a dark and watery womb for nine months, not at all! I am not of the stock of cowards. I would gladly have been born of woman had my chances been better. Unfortunately, I was at the tail end of the queue and my chances of landing here pretty slim.

Secondly, I had harboured for long a burning desire to be a citizen of Kuzania, but judging by the disproportionately large numbers heading to India and China, I feared I might land there, too. That would have broken my heart. My singular wish was to live in Kuzania, the origin of man, home to the garden of Eden, the centre theatre of battles between good and evil; past, present and future; the land that the Good Lord created as a living symbol of His majesty and perfection.

I came here in the form of a free bodiless soul but, once

in a while, I co-lodge in a human body as I fancy. Maybe my illegal and hurried flight was a miscalculation but it is too late to change that now. I am the lost and forgotten soul, missing in action, self-exiled, a prisoner of conscience in Kuzania. Such is my unenviable plight. I have been here for donkeys years, for countless seasons, and I guess I will still be here when life ceases on earth, as my return to heaven is not guaranteed. I am a rebel but of the benevolent kind, like Robin Hood.

I have a sacred duty to tell you the story of my people, the people of Kuzania. I do not exist in the statistics of census, as they count bodies not souls. This is another of my handicaps, the unregistered citizen! But I am not stateless, I tell you, I am a citizen of Kuzania by naturalisation. Alas! My friend, listen to my story.

The citizens of Kuzania have weak bodies and weak souls and the way things are going they are threatened with extinction. Soon, they will be as dead as dodos barring a miracle and, yet, it is they who hold the key to the ultimate salvation of man in the final battle between good and evil, the Armageddon!

Should I tell you the story in a song? How I would like to sing for you the song of my people, a tune so cacophonous it would offend your faculties. It is the song of a people trapped in the labyrinths of despondency and despair, so forlorn they have become subhuman. But I can't sing the song for you because I have long lost my voice. My lungs are punctured and I gasp for breath. My voice comes in whispers, drowned in the grumbling of my empty stomach. My tongue is tied with fear, fear of the most repressive organs of state power ever known to man. Weak, hungry, breathless, voiceless and scared, how can I tell you the story of my people in a song?

Just look at my face! Do you see the furrowed contortions

over wasted skin? They were once my laughter lines when life had meaning. These ribs you count from a distance like the exposed grills of a glass window once held powerful muscles supported by steel sinews. Below them this hollow of deflation was once a full belly. This white dry tongue once had wonderful tales to tell with a deep resounding voice, glorious tales of the heroism and wealth of my people. There were many songs to sing, songs of joy.

I beg you, do not turn away from my ghostly state. I need your help. I swear, I was once pleasing to behold and, if we strike rapport, it could very well lead to my restoration and your own salvation. I am not beyond repair, though the therapy might be lengthy and my restoration, the African renaissance!

You look pale and unsure! Why? Maybe I have talked too much and as a result grown pale and haggard. Am I not fit for the job? Listen, I have an old dear friend whose name is Agu, a wonderful and trustworthy man. He is stronger than I am ... how we have withered in Kuzania!

Nibble, nibble, time gnaws away life by the minute. For those with no guts, the end is sooner. The weather eats away limestone and granite in different fashion. The softer goes faster. Agu is of the granite type and, although aged, not much of him has been chipped away. He is about or just over one hundred years old, though he looks seventy. With gasps of breath, with the remains of my once melodious voice, I will implore him to tell you the story of our people. You must listen. I will stand by to fill in the gaps created by his human frailty.

*

Age takes away pangs of pain, and calamities can be borne ever more calmly and boldly. Tear glands run dry when the softness in the heart is no more. News of disasters and tragedies are received with less pain, with only a bead of sweat on the forehead. Age gives one a constitution as hard as granite. It is the blessing of seasoned fortitude.

Agu the centenarian, the prophet, the seer, the sage, was the very epitome of solidified calmness. In his life he had been a witness to legions of heinous, torturous tragedies both natural and man-made. The latter were the most painful to bear. They did not cease and each season they increased in frequency, fury and grotesqueness. His disposition shielded him like a great fortress, though it suffered many scars. Were it not for his numbness in the face of the onslaught on the soul of his people, he would have become past tense long ago, gone to the nether world with a broken heart. His was a gift from above and it served him well, the very best one could wish for. It gave him hope that all was not lost in Kuzania, though succeeding governments had lost direction and turned their fangs and venom on the very people they were supposed to serve and protect. The word 'why?' had defied his protective shield. It hung menacingly on his dishevelled lips, as a parasite fixes itself inextricably on a host. At eventide when the calm tropical wind blows the sun to sleep, the chill would make his lips quiver involuntarily and the word would issue forth, 'why?', 'why?', 'why?', as trees swayed.

It was a question that weighed on him heavily as he desperately sought solutions to the state of despair, which had become the bane of his people. The situation in Kuzania defied common sense and logic. Chaos, evil and sin had become the masters of the state, the creed of the political leadership. It was ten times worse than Sodom and Gomorrah.

Whether Everywhere had anything to do with it or not is of little concern here but, lately, in the still of the night, Agu had begun to receive messages from a celestial source. Each subsequent night the messages increased in duration, frequency, coherence and clarity. They were in answer to his question of 'why?' He absorbed the messages with his characteristic calmness and locked them in his granite-hard heart. The deep roots of the ailments molesting his people were being revealed. He was also assured that with great efforts the era of despair could be overcome but the struggle would be of a kind and magnitude hitherto unknown. It would involve the hearts and minds of the people in the struggle between good and evil, a struggle that had both heaven and hell participating by proxy.

From then on Agu wore a radiant smile and people wondered what miracle could have brought the brightness on his old face. He was rejuvenated, looking many years younger as though age had retreated in fear. He was happy for his people that at last a new story of joy and fulfilment would be told 'like the good old times,' he said to himself.

Innocence, pure sweet innocence...

Like the ageless, massive granite rocks around Kahindo Falls along Glitta River, Agu had become indestructible with age. He had become immortal, or almost so. His wisdom surpassed that of King Solomon, who did not live to be a hundred and who had died in the misery of madness, watched by his many wives. Agu did not suffer from the folly of Solomon playing around with countless women. His three wives had served him well.

They were all dead but his children, grandchildren and great-great-grandchildren looked after him to the best of their abilities.

Agu was seated on a three-legged traditional stool outside his hut, as was his custom at sunset. In the daytime he would walk around the slums mainly for exercise but at times offering counsel to those whose lives had ceased to have meaning. These were his people. The yellow rays of the setting sun seemed to bounce off his clean head like reflections off a mirror. The rays created a glow around his face. He looked saintly. Senility often afflicts the aged but it had chosen not to have anything to do with Agu. He was of sound mind, sharp in hearing but his eyes were not as powerful as they had once been. His teeth, too, had suffered. Originally thirty-two teeth in all, most had wasted away over the years, leaving a shaky, sketchy representation of four, with two on each jaw towards the front, and with gaps in between. His tongue ran over them repeatedly, giving him a sweet sensation at a time when nothing else in life did. He lamented that he no longer could do justice to a roast rib of a goat if he chanced on one. Meat was a rare commodity among the poor in Kuzania and he had nothing much to lament about in reality.

The evening confusion in the slums of Kawempe in the city of Glitta was at its highest. Tired remains of subhumans were moving in all directions, aimlessly. Still they kept on moving to and fro, like shadows, moving in circles. They all looked the same: sad, depressed, downcast, underfed, sick and haggard.

One distinguished figure had more life than the rest. It was the village drunkard, singing at the top of his voice, staggering from side to side, moving two steps forward and one backward, with each motion shouting, 'forward always, backward never', as he made unsure progress to another beer joint. He was belting out a discordant hymn that thanked God for 'such a wonderful world'. From what was known of him, he was sick, unemployed, wifeless and lived in a makeshift hovel constructed from discarded cartons and planks of wood. Why he had not died of pneumonia and mosquito bites was anybody's guess. He spent the day assisting brewers of illicit beer and his pay was a free gulp of the deadly stuff. Rumour also had it that he was the father of countless bastards from beer-brewing women. Agu watched him with pity as he passed by.

The drunkard was followed by a mob of urchins who teased him by imitating his steps and his tuneless voice as he sang. With great effort the drunkard would stop, turn around and fix a wild gaze on the children, threatening them with a beating. The children would retreat a step or two and giggle, holding to one another. With an obscene expletive the drunkard would turn around and resume his unsteady march, the children following still. Those watching him wondered what he had to thank the Lord for. Alcohol does not make one a good judge on any issue, personal or public. Agu saw in the man the very embodiment of the chaos and confusion in Kuzania.

Besides the drunkard, the roads were full of workers and jobseekers returning from the city of Glitta, 'the city in the sun'. Many of them had trekked the twenty-kilometre distance, as they could not afford the bus fare. Others had come by the minibuses, known as 'scuds'. Those walking had a higher probability of living to see another day, as the scuds were no more than suicide machines, the drivers high on Indian hemp.

The absence of any form of joy on the people's faces was of great concern to Agu. His people were drifting through

7

life like zombies until they were claimed by graves in premature death. To many, death was a release from the unbearable daily hardships of life, which yielded only agony and pain. It was only for prostitutes, who entertained foreigners as tourist attractions, the tycoons revelling in illegal business and the corrupt and insensitive politicians, that Kuzania was heaven. For the rest, Kuzania was hell. Agu knew that sooner or later, their heaven would come tumbling down, as was the case in Sodom and Gomorrah. Evil cannot wear the crown unchallenged for long. Theirs would be a sad end.

Kuzania had lost sense of direction and had decayed like so many other African countries. It had a myriad of vices that benefited the chosen few in the inner circle of state power – the politically correct. In days gone by prophets, seers and sages were the pillars of society. They were reservoirs of knowledge and wisdom, revered. This may still be so in other lands but not in Kuzania. Here it is the politicians who are in command. They have supplanted wisdom and common sense and put money and power in their place. Their policy statements do not concern themselves with national goals, national wealth or strategic interests. State House is not White House! It is the nerve centre of chaos and man-made disasters. The key debates include the survival of the regime by hook or by crook, promotion of tribal divisions and ethnic clashes, genocide starvation of non-supporters, perfection of assassination and torture, rigging of elections and the looting of national wealth.

It is the devil's command post, spewing death and destruction in the name of leadership. The political leadership in Kuzania marvels at its own ingenuity since it has survived many sham elections. The nation is reeling to breaking-point as the leaders continue to serve the evil hydras of money and power. A change is going to come – it has to.

Agu was born around 1890, the son of a traditional hunter and a rich man in livestock. He was born with a honeycomb in his mouth, not a silver spoon. For generations his clan had provided great warriors, prophets, hunters and blacksmiths. It was a great clan, which was respected by the whole tribe, like the monarchy. In that context Agu was a prince.

His test for leadership was to begin with circumcision. On the eve of the event he was seated in the kraal, or village with his age mates, putting final touches to the ornaments to be worn after circumcision and healing. There were head gears made from buffalo hides, lion skins, leopard skins, monkey skins and cow hides, depending on how enterprising and lucky individuals had been in the final hunt. There were armbands, leg bands and metal ornaments for different parts of the body. The kraal smelt of sweat from the bodies of the enterprising boys to be initiated into manhood the following morning. The human odour was infused with the smell of half-dry animal skins. Agu's luck, strength and sharpness with weapons had yielded a lion skin and ostrich feathers. His ornaments were by far the most prized of the lot. Lesser mortals had decorations of impala and dik-dik skins with pheasant and chicken feathers. Upon healing they would constitute the next group of front-line warriors, releasing their immediate seniors to get married. The front-line warriors were the pride of the tribe, who defended as well as raided for additional livestock. The survival and prosperity of the tribe depended on them.

With the advent of colonialism, life and roles had begun to change. The white man with his army had prohibited intertribal wars and animal raids. Land had been alienated by force from the tribes and livestock taken to feed the army of occupation. The protection of animals in national parks and the arrival of cheap cutlasses from abroad threw Agu's family out of business as hunters and blacksmiths.

Thus Agu's circumcision group was denied the chance to test its manhood. The abolition of slave-trade also lessened their role. Agu's tribe had played a great role in disorganising slave-trade by denying the raiders access to the hinterland. They were a proud lot. The kraal system had been created to protect the population from slave raiders. The same foreigners who foamed in the mouth preaching about salvation were the same stock of people who had no value for human life. The cardinal, the bishop and the imam were no different from the slave traders. Some raided the bodies, others raided the souls and in some cases they did both. Their single quest was the destruction of the black civilisation, making the black man a tool for their needs both on the continent and abroad. Slave-trade had been replaced by domestic slavery and Agu's people were conscripted labourers on white men's farms. Those not in the plantations were taxed heavily in some bizarre demand known as 'hut tax'. Tribal raids had ceased but in their place a bigger war was looming. It was a war that called on tribes not to fight each other but to unite to drive out the aliens. In the meantime boys had to be circumcised to be men.

Very early the following morning Agu and his age mates were marched to the river, stark naked. There was a pool of water, next to Kahindo Falls on Glitta River, that had always been the theatre of the operation. The boys sat in the chilly water for thirty minutes to numb their bodies to the sharpness of the knife. They emerged from the pool and stood in single-file, their heels dug in the muddy soft-ness of the ground. With clenched fists they waited in turn for the knife. The circumciser stood in front of them, sharpening his knife on a stone. He looked at them in the eye, each in turn. There they stood, their eyes fixed unblinking on the far horizon, waiting to be declared men. The circumciser ended his bizarre dance and set about his seasonal speciality, removing excessive fore-skins from distended penises in the chill of the morning.

Agu was first in line because of his family standing. It conferred on him the leadership of the group. In the past leadership would have translated itself in organising and motivating the front-line warriors. Now it had no meaning, except perhaps if the fight against the foreigners should materialise. It would be a different fight and perhaps the front-line warriors would play no more than a subordinate role. The era of swords, spears, bows and arrows was gone. Agu was going to inherit a leadership with no responsibility, a most hollow honour.

Hovering over the circumcision ceremony were swarms of hawks. They would swoop down and collect the discarded skins after the people had left. Theirs was an early-morning breakfast treat.

A witch-doctor who lived in the caves near the falls would also join the hawks, challenging them to the skins. He would throw stones and other objects at the hawks to scare them off. If by chance he killed any of the birds, he carried it with the skins back to his cave. Neither the bones nor the feathers of the bird would ever leave the cave. To what use he put them remained a mystery.

The worth of Agu and his age-group who had now been initiated to manhood was no more than that of discarded skins from penises. They were to fall prey to the wishes of colonisers, the missionaries and any other 'witch-doctor' with a need for them. The soul of Africans was drifting in worthlessness, with forced labour, hut tax and peasant farming in marginal lands. The subjugation and dehumanisation were the beginning of a long journey to despondency and despair. The songs they sang were alien hymns and the gods they worshipped were alien, too. Frustration and anger did not unite the people but served only to underline their weakness. A new form of economic, social and religious stratification emerged. People became divided into the educated, the illiterate, the rich, the poor, believers, animists, Catholics, Protestants, Muslims and many other myriads of divisions. The tribe and the kraal system were battered from all angles and there was no counterforce to arrest the situation.

Agu's age-group therefore never played the traditional role expected of it. A new change had come to Kuzania, riding on the back of aliens. It was a change that spelt doom for a people who were once happy. The doom had stuck like a curse even after independence.

It was growing chilly and Agu took his three-legged stool and retreated to the warmth of his hut in the slums. His quivering lips were asking, 'Why?', 'why?', 'why?' There was no answer.

Agu ate dinner and retired to bed early. The unenviable plight of his people had become a throbbing pain. It occupied his thoughts throughout the day and was also the subject of his dreams when he slept. He knew that the problem lay with the political leadership in Kuzania, the demigods who lived like the gods of the Greeks on Mount Olympus, or in Happy Valley in Kuzania. As he lay on his bed his disquiet was almost tangible. He thought that the fate of man is unenviable. At best he lives like a monarch in an artificial world, drunk with power, enjoying animal comforts, wine, women and music. In that state he is as a mole out of its burrow. His vision of what is real is impaired. Empires come and go and monarchs are buried in graves in the avalanche of the dynamism of life. History will tell you of Romans and Turks and others who were swept away by the march of history. Why were the demigods in Kuzania so blind?

At his worst man is a beast; mischievous, treacherous, cruel and murderous, while at the same time weak, vulnerable and helpless. That is why someone once wrote that, 'life is nasty, brutish and short'. Nowhere was this the case more than in Kuzania. Here the vagaries of man are insurmountable. It is dumbfounding how confused the creature is when drunk with power. Man uses power against his fellow men. The oppressed are lost in docility for years and then one day, like animals awaking from hibernation, they rise up in rebellion and change the leadership with no guarantee for better results. It is a game of chance, like Russian roulette. And thus the see-saw confusion in the history of man continues.

Do you think the sad state of affairs in Kuzania can last for ever? Mr Tumbo, the minister for Commerce, thinks the status quo will last until kingdom come. They call him the people's representative.

The story of my people must change before kingdom come. They must have their soul restored with the renaissance. Their current plight is worse than that of beasts. If there is hope for mankind, it is Kuzania that holds the key. This is the birthplace of man and so it will be also the birthplace of his salvation.

Heavy in thought Agu drifted to sleep. Another day in his long life had gone, uneventfully.

*

The celestial vision came to Agu in the middle of the night. He saw the destruction of the twin evil cities of Sodom and Gomorrah by two celestial missiles, which looked like cruise missiles. They were fired from a UFO. They exploded like the bombs that destroyed Hiroshima and Nagasaki.

Agu wondered why the Good Lord had spared Kuzania for so long, as its level of evil evil had surpassed that of Sodom and Gomorrah; or was it that the Good Lord had never forgiven Kuzania for messing the garden of Eden? Was that the reason why God had left Kuzania to struggle on its own? For sure the struggle for independence was not a small Armageddon; it had been a big fight and Agu was a living witness to the heroic struggle of his people. The wind of change was hailed as the triumph of good over evil – or was it? Could it have been a change of tactic by the devil in which he had only changed guards, replacing white sentries with black ones? Had evil been cut away with the lowering of the colonial flag, only to regenerate itself like the tail of a lizard with the hoisting of the national flag at independence? If this was the case, and it certainly seemed so, where was the victory they had celebrated? However hard he searched he could not find anything to cheer about. 'The struggle continues...' he concluded.

His people had had wonderful dreams of independence. These dreams had been shaped and nurtured during the liberation struggle. They were supposed to blossom with independence but instead they had withered. People had hoped to come marching from the ruins of the past to build a new wonderful world. They were set to emerge from the pit of despair with vigour and determination and a new soul. They were yearning to play a key role in a brotherhood of man based on freedom, justice and mutual respect, as man rose to new heights of civilisation.

Somewhere along the line, they had missed the boat. They had dreamt too early. In a single swoop the twin-headed god of money and power had wrenched their dreams. Like the garden of Eden at creation, Kuzania at independence was the envy of the world. Endowed with great natural wealth – oil, gold and diamonds - Kuzania, it had been said, was going to be paradise on earth. Innocence, sweet pure innocence, the great mother of misery. Like the hawks and the witch-doctor fighting for the skin of penises near Kahindo Falls, greedy people swooped on Kuzania. Pestilence upon pestilence visited the nation. Its looted wealth was exported to world capitals while its people died from malnutrition, hunger and disease. There were attempted coup d'états, general insecurity, mismanagement of the economy, decay of institutions, rigging of elections, abuse of human rights, tribal clashes, immorality and devil worship. These were incessant and multiple assaults on the mind, the body and the souls of the citizens.

If mankind is to be saved, then the devil must be stopped in Kuzania, Agu concluded. A little wiser, though still confused, Agu drifted back to sleep, calmly as always, locking the secrets of the revelations in his granite-hard heart that celestial powers had chosen as their safe deposit. Agu was happy to carry the burden.

2

Dreams Betrayed

Old folks have many stories to tell, seldom about themselves. Just as one cannot stop the Nile from flowing to Cairo, one cannot stop old folks from telling tales.

On my part, it is unfair and outright cowardly to burden Agu with telling not just a tale but the long tragic history of our people. Old men don't tell long stories because it is exhausting and strength sapping. They don't have the heart for them. All, that is, except Agu. My decision to leave the centre stage to him was a wise one. Not only I, but celestial powers, too, have found favour in him. The Good Lord in heaven is on the prowl seeking out those who have outlived their usefulness on earth. He is like a hawk seeking young chicks. A long story could be just the exposure and another old man becomes past tense. That is another reason old folk tell short stories.

But the whims of the deities have built a shield of protection around Agu and he will not be gone before the story is told. I am relieved. In all my days – and I've been around for quite some while – never have I encountered one so blessed as Agu; not with wealth but with the higher qualities of man. Agu's disposition of selflessness, wisdom, courage, strength of mind and his devotion to the good of humanity will not go to waste. He is not just another old man and the story of my people is not just another story.

The history of man is general and the people of Kuzania in particular fascinated me even before I left heaven. Though the plight of man appears doomed, I have faith that man can be salvaged. People like Agu are the midwives of the crusade. The human race has hurtled towards a new millennium at break-neck speed, like meteorites, with no sense of purpose or direction. There are many dangers that lie ahead. The survival of man on earth for ever is not the issue; it is the good of man on earth that is the issue, the triumph of good over evil in the coming Armageddon. A new breed of man must rise from the present confusion and give the people a new soul, a new life, a new meaning. Without Agu such will not be possible. As Jesus Christ was the son of a poor carpenter in some desert village, so Agu, the old man in the slums, holds the key to the salvation of man from his follies. But it is his story, not mine...

From the prolonged drought the land lay so bare that the only green to be seen were swarms of giant flies feasting on carcasses and rot. The blazing sun had established itself as the master of the situation, scorching the earth to total submission. As if in an unholy alliance gales of dry wind were sweeping the country, spreading dust and disease. The whirling winds collected litter and roofs of houses and sent them in a spiral upwards only to deposit them elsewhere, like a tale of some strange dance.

The daily beat of the people slowed almost to a halt. There was a shortage of food, water and electricity throughout the land. Factories were grinding to a halt

17

and laying off workers. It was as if the end of the world had come riding on the back of the sun. In the slums, loosened soil had been carried by the wind and deposited on roofs. The corrugated-iron houses looked like an extension of the scorched, barren surroundings. People gathered and prayed for rain, not so much as to plant, since very few had any land, but as a relief from the harsh weather. While one can boldly brave hunger for a time, the people of Kuzania had no answer to the heat and dust.

It is an ill wind that blows nobody no good, though. In the ministry of Commerce, Hon. Tumbo, the people's representative, was busy signing contracts for relief food. The food was donated or bought duty-free in the name of 'Emergency Relief', but sold in the open market at exorbitant prices. The political bigwigs and their business associates were making a killing. Hon. Tumbo had seized the opportunity to amass money for his ambitious political campaign to State House as the next president of Kuzania.

Everything in Kuzania was governed by extremes from the weather, to politics, to the lives of its citizens. It was an unpredictable land, the land of the unimaginable, the unmanageable and the insoluble and yet this was the land that the Good Lord had created as a living symbol of His Majesty and perfection, in which the garden of Eden was planted, the original home of man.

It was Sunday morning and the population was milling to the church to confess its sins. Agu had none to confess and in all his days he had not attended the church once. He had not bowed to modern styles of worship but he was totally at peace with himself and with his maker, more so than the archbishop of Kuzania. He planned to take a walk to Kahindo Falls later in the day to bathe in the river and to sit by the breeze of the waterfall where he was circumcised.

There was a knock on the door. 'Come in,' he said. In came Shaka, the son of the late leader of the war for independence. He had graduated from high school and was now on the tarmac, jobless.

They sat by the fire with a pot of tea boiling on the traditional three-stone hearth.

'Have you found a job yet?' Agu asked.

'Not one I can be proud of with my level of education. I decided to join the gangs in construction sites mixing ballast and cement. It is not easy and the pay is peanuts. I guess it will keep my body and soul marching until I get something better.'

'My heart bleeds for you, my son. Out of your father's sacrifices, you deserved a scholarship!' Agu said in a voice betraying anger.

'It is all right, Great-grandpa, I believe things will change.'

Agu did not know whether Shaka was speaking about his unenviable plight or the general state of Kuzania.

As they drank tea, deep in thought, Shaka asked, 'You told me that a long time ago our people were happy, healthy and wealthy. What became of us?'

'It is a long story Shaka. It is the story of betrayal and greed. First came slave-trade and with it the dis-organisation of societies. African chiefs sold their able-bodied men for trinkets, cowrie shells, blankets and whisky. As a result whole communities were deci-mated. Production, commerce, social cohesion and the ability to defend ourselves were depleted. Then came colonialism and our people could not offer any meaningful resistance. We were subjugated and dehumanised. It was only the Ethiopians under their wise King Menelik II who defeated the colonisers because they had not sold their people in slavery.'

Agu took a sip of his tea and continued, 'Colonialism was a big curse. The white man with his commerce, civilisation, religion and brutal administration made slaves of us all. The soul of the black man was relentlessly assailed. In the end what was left of it was a fragmented shell. We were reduced to self-hate and total worthlessness, in a state of despair, sorrow and sadness.' The old man paused.

'But, Great-grandpa, wasn't the struggle for independence about our redemption and the restoration of black man's dignity and soul?' Shaka asked.

'True, it was, but only a few understood the extent of the damage and what needed to be done to restore the soul. Your father, and a few others like him, understood the magnitude of the problem. They were branded radicals and communists, betrayed by their own people and eliminated. Their betrayal denied the nation the chance to uproot the cancer eating our soul. It was the same in Congo when they killed Lumumba. It was the traitors to whom the mantle of leadership was bequeathed. They had been well grilled like robots on the need to maintain the status quo; that is, to continue serving foreign interests. That is why they are detached from the plight of the common man. As they say, you cannot serve God and Mammon at the same time. It is the reason our wealth finds its way to Switzerland rather than into our hands and banks. It is the reason you cannot get a scholarship or a job,' Agu explained further.

'We should then do away with them! They are not people's representatives but representatives of their stomachs and under foreign control! We should elect people who understand the need for restoration of the black soul, the need for renaissance!'

'Hush! Hush, young one. You have the fire of your father in your soul! I am gladdened. You are right but, unfortunately, once a system has been entrenched for decades and institutions put into place to protect it, it is almost indestructible unless the people unite to uproot it. Evil is deeply entrenched in Kuzania. In this country the voice of reason has no place and it is silenced most harshly. You automatically reap premature death.' Agu paused again.

'So how long are we going to be like this?' Shaka asked.

'Listen, every system carries with it seeds of its own destruction, as spies carry cyanide capsules. The system is ill defined and shaky, however strong it looks. The government has lost the support of the people and only rejuvenates itself through rigged elections. Its increasing brutality is alienating it from the international community. These are the cyanide capsules I have told you about. But I must warn you that every generation must rise and fight for what it deserves. No system yields power without a fight regardless of how impotent and irrelevant it has become. You saw how Mobutu tried to cling to power even beyond the eleventh hour!

'Today, many governments do not care how many people die from hunger, disease or police brutality. The people must stay constantly alert. Unfortunately for Kuzania our people have become docile and too weak from the onslaught. Nowhere is evil more entrenched

21

than here. This is the headquarters of evil on earth,' Agu concluded.

'Do you think Great-grandpa, that if we could muster all our efforts and move swiftly we could restore our soul?' Shaka asked.

The seriousness and maturity of Shaka surprised Agu. 'Of course, my boy, of course! Evil cannot prevail over good for ever. It will take a miracle but it can be done. I hope to see it before I become past tense!' Agu said with a radiant smile.

'Oh, Great-grandpa, do you know something I should know? How soon?' Shaka asked excitedly.

'Shaka, a young bull mounts a cow by the horns! Rashness only yields a painful fall. The evil hydra has many heads. It is futile to cut the heads. It is the heart of the beast we must go for, but you are too young!' Agu warned.

'No, Great-grandpa, I am old enough to sink my dagger in the heart of the hydra,' Shaka challenged.

'We shall see when the time comes. For now, keep looking for a decent job.'

Shaka knew it was time to go.

'Go in peace, my boy, and remember that no condition is permanent, however desperate the present might seem. We shall overcome,' concluded Agu.

'We shall overcome,' Shaka echoed the words of the old man with a big smile in his face.

Agu sat there, watching the fire, aware that Shaka would not rest until he had fully fathomed the story of his people. Later he picked his towel and headed for the river.

Agu passed by the withered plantations of maize that had yielded nothing for successive seasons. He noted that even the bananas and cassava had withered. He descended the boulders of the granite rocks to the pool. He took off his blanket and went into the water. For a long time he stayed there enjoying the coolness of the lukewarm water. Afterwards he lay on the rocks drying himself.

There were many stories told over Kahindo Falls, some most mysterious. The place derived its name from a legendary witch-doctor who once lived in a cave, round about the time Agu was circumcised. The most mysterious thing about the man was that he disappeared into thin air without a trace, never to be seen again. This was in the season of hailstorm, thunder and lightning.

The rainbow curved itself like a giant bow stretching from Watiti Valley to Kahindo Falls. When the rainbow descended on Kahindo Falls, the witch-doctor would take off his clothes and jump into the pool, illuminated by the kaleidoscope colours of the rainbow. He would beat the water with his hands and dance until the rainbow was gone. Very few people had the courage to watch Kahindo doing the rainbow dance. Afterwards he would continue his jig, jumping from boulder to boulder making shrieking sounds. In the final act of the drama he collected herbs, flowers and lizards. The herbs and flowers were of the poisonous type that even goats would not touch. People swore that he boiled it all up and drank the hideous broth. He was evil looking and scantily clad. At night, though, those in need paid him a visit for medicine to heal or to kill.

One day he descended into the pool to perform the rainbow dance and was never seen again. Some said he rode the rainbow and disappeared with it. Even if he had drowned, his body was never recovered.

Agu lay on the rocks he pondered what exactly had happened to Kahindo. Kuzania had many things that defied explanation.

That evening Agu's retreat to his hut was like the return of a general from an epic battle. Events in the day had given him unequalled satisfaction from his meeting with Shaka, the bath in the river to the memory of Kahindo and his rainbow dance. He had undergone a complete catharsis mentally, physically and spiritually. People he met stopped to stare at the halo on his face and the springy step in his walk. As a snake sheds its old skin to regain youthfulness, Agu had shed years. It felt good. Foremost he wanted to be alone, as events were pointing to renewed contacts with the celestial voice. He had a hunch that what would be revealed would have far-reaching bearings on his quest to save his people.

Darkness had began to envelop the land and with rain clouds starting to gather was threatening to be heavier still. There were signs that the long drought would soon be over, and its end would perhaps nudge people from the lethargy induced, among other things, by the scorching sun. Soon it would be the season when many things happen.

Agu's hut was warm from the wood fire, which had not completely died. He poked the ashes and glowing embers popped out. He pushed forward partly burnt stumps of firewood and added more. With a metallic pipe that rested close to the hearth, he blew the embers. The wood was dry and it immediately yielded to a yellow glow of flames. The flames reflected on the black soot on the hut wall, like gold paint. He lit the kerosene lamp and placed it on a log, which at times served as a seat. Agu's last wife died three years ago and, although he had teased his friends he would re-marry, deep inside he knew he did not have the heart or the energy to start a new relationship. He had a more important agenda in his hands. His solitary existence fitted perfectly with his mission, and secrecy was a precondition in such matters. Women, he knew, could never be trusted to keep secrets and in certain instances they had brought many a mighty man to ruin. There were Adam, Solomon and Samson who had come to regret the destructive powers vested in the beauty and softness of the opposite sex. He lay the matter to rest.

Agu warmed roasted arrowroots and sweet potatoes on the rekindled fire and ate them with fresh milk. All the while he was preoccupied with the events of the day and the promise of further contacts with the celestial voice. Out of impatience he retired early to bed. Maybe it was out of exhaustion after the walk or the soothing effects of the bath in the pool but Agu fell into sound sleep immediately he covered himself with a blanket. It was to be a long night like no other.

Agu could not tell for how long he had slept before the celestial voice came to him. For all he knew, the heavenly presence stayed in his room until the small hours of the morning. It spoke to him in a clear and commanding voice.

'You were once chosen by your people to lead front-line warriors. Over the years you have suffered the anguish of your unfulfilled responsibility. Brace yourself for what lies ahead because the time has come for you to lead new front-line warriors into battle. It is the battle between good and evil and Kuzania is the main theatre. Kuzania occupies a strategic place in the annals of celestial history. It was created with a special purpose. The following is the original history of Kuzania, which will show you how important the land and its people are. The people's suffering and tribulations are not an accident but critical in the epic battle between God and Satan, in the struggle between good and evil.'

The voice continued, 'Heaven was bliss for countless millenniums before undercurrents of discontent began to surface. It began with proposals to change this, modify that and do away with the other. The Good Lord, the master architect, was furious. He warned that things should be left the way he had designed them. Angered with the dissatisfaction of some of those around him, He decided to go on a long holiday far away. It was during the flight in His UFO that the idea of creating the earth and the garden of Eden struck Him. The garden of Eden would be His future holiday resort supplied by the rest of the earth. It was a brilliant idea. With the growing rumblings in Heaven, He also thought it would be an alternative home should things get out of hand:

'Out of the void, He created this galaxy. When the earth took shape He created the garden of Eden in the middle. At first the earth was one huge land mass; the separation came later. The land surrounding the garden was made with special care. First He created a coastline with spotless sandy beaches. It is the world-famous holiday resort you now call Mimosa. The coastline was given coral reefs and mangrove swamps to break the monotony of white sands and blue waters of the ocean. In the vastness of the ocean he stocked a prodigious abandon of creatures. It was beautiful to behold.

'Moving inland, he caused rolling, rising plains to be. He stocked the area with a vast array of wild animals both large and small. Far into the hinterland he caused highlands to rise progressively more to His right and to His left. He capped their ultimate heights with snow, though they stood on the equator.

'After the highlands he created a deep gorge and named it Rift Valley and dotted it with a string of freshwater lakes. He ordered a huge stock of fish and birds in the lakes. Looking around at the beauty He had just created, He was most satisfied with the care and degree of perfection with which His majesty had performed. He named the land Kuzania. It is picturesque and magnificent. The garden of Eden was created in the centre of this wonderful land. It had a proliferation of fruits, flowers, vegetables, cereals and herbs. The seeds of these plants would find their way to the rest of the earth.

'The journey from heaven to earth is a long one as the distance is light years. Calculating that His visits to the garden would be infrequent and far between, He saw the need to leave behind someone to manage the enterprise. It was for this reason that Adam was created. The Good Lord promised to return every now and then to relax, enjoy the yields and to review the progress Adam was making. Adam's pay was not discussed.

'Adam was created big, strong, tall and handsome in the image of the Lord Himself. With his strength, the job of weeding, watering and scattering the seeds would be chicken feed.

'However it was not the pay or the work that bothered Adam, but the fact that he would be left alone, a solitary creature on the vast earth.

'"Lord," he called. 'This place will be very lonely when you are gone. I beg you, please give me someone to talk to."

27

'The request was passionately and humbly made and it sounded reasonable. The Good Lord caused Adam to sleep and He cut a piece of his flesh from which He cloned Eve. The Good Lord must have cloned Eve with His mind preoccupied with the rumblings in heaven. As a result, there were excesses and deletions in comparison between her anatomy and Adam's. Standing side by side the glaring difference between them was pronounced. For this reason Adam was given the code-name man and Eve woman.

'Eve, unlike Adam, was fleshy and beautiful. Her eyes were soft, watery and sexy. Her chest had two large glands to be known as breasts. Her hips were rounded and tantalising and she walked with a captivating sway.

'Adam was most fascinated with his partner. He thought he had got more than he had bargained for. Perhaps this was his reward for not asking for pay. If it was the case, he thought it was well worth it. To Adam, Eve's body resembled the topography of Kuzania with its mountains and valleys, beauty and mystery. The valley between her thighs, he thought, resembled the source of the Nile. The area housed an apple-shaped organ that looked like a well, though partly hidden with soft hairs. It was magnetic. After a number of weeks, the apple-like organ would issue forth a red discharge, which came to be known as a monthly period. The difference was that though the flow of the Nile was endless, the flow of Eve would only last for days. Adam promised to explore the mysterious organ when the Good Lord departed.

'The Good Lord read Adam's mind and sensed trouble. He had to dent Adam's curiosity. He called them both and warned,

'"You must respect one another and never mess around with the gifts in the centre of your bodies. Adam, you must never touch the apple I gave Eve and, likewise, Eve, you must not touch Adam's snake. If you disobey me, Eve will become pregnant and I am afraid we do not have a maternity hospital around here. These parts contain seeds of wisdom and they should be handled with utmost care. Have I made myself understood?"

'"Yes, Lord," they both replied, though they had no idea what seeds, pregnancy and maternity meant. They spoke more out of fear and courtesy than out of knowledge.

'Innocence, pure sweet innocence, the great mother of misery... With this warning and promise the Good Lord boarded his UFO and disappeared in a cloud of smoke. He was going to relax a little bit more before heading to heaven to put the house in order.

'A couple of seasons passed and the Good Lord had not returned to the garden. Adam, however hard he tried, could not get over his fascination with the magnetic attraction of Eve's apple. His curiosity was close to inviting defiance. Eve, on her part, kept wondering what the seeds, pregnancy and maternity stood for. She thought that in sum total they stood for wisdom. The more she thought about it the more she wanted to know.

'In the season of hailstorm, thunder and lightning when many things happen, Adam and Eve lay next to each other on the bed in the cave that was their house.

' "Adam, are you asleep?" Eve asked.

' "Not yet. The thunderstorm keeps waking me up," he said.

' "About the apple..." she did not even finish what she was about to say before Adam intervened.

' "What about it?" he asked.

'"The Lord said if we mess around with it we shall be wise, like Him," she said.

'"So He said."

'"Adam, why shouldn't we be wise too? I do not find ignorance a bliss."

'Adam's pulse increased and his heartbeat became a throb. This was an invitation to explore the apple! Deep down inside he felt fear. This strange thing called wisdom, he thought, could turn out to be dangerous.

'"Let's remain the way we are," he cautioned.

'"Why?" Eve asked.

'"Because He said so."

'"But we cannot make sound judgement on the matter," Eve insisted.

'"Why not?" Adam asked.

'"Because we are not wise," replied Eve.

'Adam felt at a loss, growing weaker in the head by the second as his blood rushed to his loins.

'"Adam," called Eve softly.

'"Now what?" He responded weakly.

'"May I touch your snake?"

'Adam did not reply. He lay on his back as Eve caressed his snake. Involuntarily, Adam found himself exploring Eve's apple with his fingers. Like two magnets the two prohibited parts found each other. There were sparks of passion as they made love in the night of hailstorm, thunder and lightning. They had obeyed signals more powerful than obedience and self-restraint could control. When their passion was satisfied Adam kissed Eve.

'"Wisdom is a wonderful thing!"

'"The best on earth!" responded Eve.

'Holding each other, they drifted off to sleep a whole lot wiser, they thought.

'Nature in its wisdom delivers its gifts bountifully. A couple of weeks later Eve was vomiting each morning and her stomach began to swell. Still they kept eating the forbidden fruit.

'One morning after making love Adam asked Eve, "How do you feel?"

'"Wet, wonderful and heavier," she responded.

'"You don't feel wiser?" he asked.

'"It is too soon to tell," she replied.

'"We shall see," said Adam, aware that something had gone very wrong.

'"Seeds, pregnancy, maternity, wisdom." He kept wondering which of them made Eve vomit and which of them made her stomach swell. Since he had no answer, he concluded that he had not grown any wiser. He waited for Eve to provide the answers to these questions. Nine months later the twins Cain and Abel were born.

'After a long working holiday, that took Him to many galaxies, the Good Lord returned to review the progress in the garden before ascending to sort out the brewing mess in heaven. He was shocked by the state in which he found His once beautiful garden. Its size and shape had been altered to accommodate the booming population. It had become a big slum with shacks everywhere. In the yards there were dogs, cows, sheep, goats, pigs, cats, chicken and donkeys. The sight was most horrifying and oppressive to His eyes. He turned to Adam in anger.

'"I warned you not to eat the apple, didn't I?"

'"Blame it on Eve," was all Adam could say.

'"And what do you have to say, madam?" He asked Eve. Eve kept mum, her eyes fixed on the ground. She was visibly pregnant for the umpteenth time.

31

'The Lord looked at the garden and contemplated wiping it from the face of the earth. He took another look at Eve, the clone accused of having caused the mess, and He decided to leave the garden alone. He knew He should have changed her when He noticed the anomalies in her anatomy on the day she was created. He shared in the blame of what had come to pass because of His indecision.

'"I bequeath this stinking confusion to you and your offspring," He said in anger. He made up His mind to create another garden in a place far away, where Adam, Eve and their offspring would be prohibited immigrants. With this new plan in mind He majestically marched towards the UFO. Before boarding He called Adam. "This mess shall no longer be called the garden of Eden. Like the rest of the land it shall be called Kuzania. To keep the population in check I now introduce death."

'This said, He was lifted in a cloud of smoke in the chariot of fire. Kuzania had fallen from grace. He never returned.

'That night there was a quarrel and in the ensuing fight Cain killed his brother Abel. At first, what had happened to Abel was incomprehensible but as the body began to rot and stink, Adam pronounced, "This is death, the most terrible curse." They buried Abel.

'Adam died soon thereafter of a heart attack but Eve lived to be an old lonely, unhappy, remorseful and crestfallen woman. In inviting disobedience they had not found wisdom but chosen pain and death.

'The Lord scanned the earth for a patch on which to plant a new garden. It was in the search that He discovered major structural weakness, resulting in landslides, earthquakes and volcanic eruptions in the foundation of the earth. He shelved the idea of a new garden to first deal with these unexpected problems.

'As he stabilised the western hemisphere there was a massive volcanic eruption in the Far East. Dashing there in the UFO, He was amazed by the fire and fury of the eruption. When it died down new islands in the ocean appeared where He had planned none! This was soon followed by an eruption that made Mount Etna, followed by the Himalayan range. What surprised Him most was that the mountains were higher than planned. Mount Everest was bigger than the two snow-capped mountains He had created in Kuzania! How accidents overshadowed his careful plans He could not explain.

'"What is this?" He asked himself. "First I create man and he defies me, then nature rebels!" He took out His calculator and started working out fresh calculations of mass and density. Just then His most able general, Gabriel, chief-of-staff of the Royal Celestial Forces, relayed to Him an urgent e-mail message. It read, "Satan is plotting your downfall."

'The Lord's return to heaven boosted the morale of His loyal forces under Archangel Gabriel, the chief-of-staff. When the urgent meeting of the Celestial Security Council convened, Satan, the deputy-head, was not invited. Heaven was so tense that you could hear from a distance the swish of feathers as angels flew urgent errands.

'Jittery and unsure of himself, Satan launched a pre-emptive attack on key installations. He had under-estimated the morale and preparedness of the loyal forces and he met stiff resistance. His second wave of attack was dealt with most ruthlessly. Then Gabriel and the Royal Celestial Forces launched a counter-attack with air and ground forces. The relentless fire was intense and heaven became a simmering inferno of smoke, chemical gasses and heavy explosions. Sensing imminent defeat Satan made a clever and deceptive manoeuvre to the control room of doomsday missiles. He keyed the lifting codes and the missiles emerged from their deep silos. He had in mind blackmailing the Lord into sharing power and if his demands were not met then he would annihilate heaven.

'As a warning he decided to fire a low-yield tactical missile against the advancing royal forces. To his chagrin he found the firing codes had been changed. In anger and fury he fired intergalaxy doomsday missiles towards the faraway void in which the Lord had recently created the earth.

'The descendants of Adam and Eve saw five missiles descending like bright suns. They thought it was the legendary Good Lord returning to save them from the misery that had become their lot with death, hunger, diseases and pestilence. Others argued that it was the Good Lord returning to execute vengeance and to uproot evil. In next to no time the earth was shaken with deafening sounds, flashes of bright light and the sun was obscured by dust and debris.

'One missile hit the Sahara region turning it instantly into a desert. Two missiles hit Siberia and killed all dinosaurs and mammoths. The fourth missile fell in the western hemisphere, giving the Americas their current shape. The last missile landed in the ocean off the coast of the southern seaboard of Africa. Its impact detached huge chunks of lands and sent them floating thousands of miles away.

'When the mayhem died down the once-rounded earth

was in ruins. Clans of earthlings found themselves detached from the motherland by miles of hostile waters. Thus the descendants of Adam were separated, incommunicado for centuries to come. A look at the distance between Africa and the islands of Malagasy and Australia gives an idea of the force of the blasts. Earth as it sits today is the mangled remains. It took many years for earthlings to recover from the shock and fallout. Satan achieved no more than to disorganise the earth.

'Fortunately Kuzania as a country was not greatly affected because it was far away from the epicentre of the blasts. This was the reason elephants, rhinoceros and giraffes also survived. Today tourists flock to Kuzania to see these wonders. The only other time the earth was attacked with missiles was when Sodom and Gomorrah were destroyed with low-yield tactical missiles when the people exceeded the limits of evil. The next target will undoubtedly be Kuzania, which has exceeded the limit by far! Unless...

'Back to heaven... Satan and his band of devils surrendered and were court-martialled. For punishment they were banished to a hot and hostile galaxy called hell. The galaxy is not shielded from the rays of the sun by an ozone layer and that is why they call it hell.

'Agu, you might wonder what these events have to do with the present plight of your people but, if you are patient, it will be revealed to you,' the celestial voice assured him.

Agu turned heavily in his bed and was half-awake. Suddenly the celestial presence was gone. He opened the door and went outside to urinate. It was when he was returning to his hut that he noticed a bright star in heaven whose light pointed directly to his hut. Awed, he got back into bed and fell into deep sleep once more. The celestial voice returned and continued to recount the story:

'Satan and the rebels were loaded in a fleet of UFOs for the journey to hell. The journey was to take several seasons, as hell is light years away. Celebrating their victory, pilots of the Celestial Air Force staged mock intergalaxy wars on the journey.

'Innocence, sweet innocence, the big mother of misery... Taking advantage of the relaxation and diverse manoeuvres, some crafty prisoners hijacked a UFO and quietly slipped away. The loss was not noticed until the crafts fell into formation again. Two fighters, a refuelling and repair ship were dispatched to look for the missing craft. They searched and searched but could not lock on to the craft's radar. All they registered out of the ordinary was a weak bleep coming from the depths of the ocean near Bermuda. The signal was distorted by the heaves of the rough ocean and it did not make intelligible reading. Rejoining the fleet they reported that the craft was lost without trace. They also reported the strange signals near Bermuda. From then on there were no more mock dogfights. They accomplished their mission without further hitches.

'What really happened was that once detached, the hijackers landed the UFO near Bermuda. The landing was bumpy and the craft badly punctured. It began to sink. Using lifeboats and other crafts on board, everybody took to the ocean, uncoordinated save for a band of rebels and their leader in the biggest craft. Satan was not in the hijacked UFO.

'The survivors mastered the ocean heading in different directions. The main rebel vessel with the leader on board rounded the Cape of Good Hope and headed northward until it sighted the white sands of the coast of Kuzania. It was a place like no other on earth and it was like an extension of heaven.

'"We shall go no further," said the leader. "On this beautiful land, we shall build our heaven." That said, the devils and their leader disembarked and settled in Kuzania among the descendants of Adam and Eve. They found the daughters of men both beautiful and wonderful. They took them for wives and planted their seeds in them. A higher breed of men emerged in their siblings. It was they who introduced a central system of government, commerce, industry and polygamy. They were demigods and their harems reproduced like colonies of rats. The emerging communities were named after their founders and given the name 'tribes'. With prosperity and conquest, some became kingdoms.

'A strange vocabulary emerged with words such as corruption, intrigue, subjugation, domination, war, assassinations, genocide, slavery and colonisation. The words were given practical meaning as tribes and kingdoms sought to expand at the expense of others. Since then, bloodshed has been a permanent feature of the life in Kuzania and so have other ills. From wars of conquest the vanquished trekked many miles in search of peaceful settlements. No sooner did they begin to flourish than feuds and wars would follow, and the vanquished would be enslaved, displaced, or would run away to become refugees.

'Different dialects were born with immigration. Soon they became distinct languages. In Kuzania different languages emerged at the coast, in the plains, in the highlands, in the Rift Valley and in the lakes beyond. It became the house of Babel. Different climatic regions also gave rise to different physical features and pigmentation. The world's races emerged. The rebel devils' achievements had surpassed their wildest imagination. They had stumbled upon a mighty weapon, which they named "divide and rule" and it served them perfectly.

'The demigods and founders of tribes and kingdoms have long gone. Their legacy lives in the names of the tribes, nations and kingdoms they founded. It lives also in the myths surrounding the origins of tribes, nations and kingdoms. Each tries to outdo the other in the tales of its origin but none comes anywhere close to that of the children of Israel. It is the most complete account going back to the garden of Eden. It is found in a bestseller called the Bible. How the Bible does not mention Kuzania can only be explained by the rivalry between kingdoms and tribes and the policy of divide and rule.

'An attempt to return to Kuzania from Israel was made by a group called Falashas. Their efforts fizzled out in the Abyssinian Mountains. They never got to the Promised Land. The Israelites, Eskimos, Japanese, Aborigines, Red Indians, Zulus, Luos, Kikuyus and the Tutsi were once one people before the great trek from Kuzania and the continental drift. They are of the stock of Adam and Eve, though they now look different and cannot communicate with each other except in English. Even in Kuzania people speak English. I wonder why English? It is also the language of world dominance, colonialism, slavery, Christianity and commerce. In all these, Kuzania fits only as an appendage, a staging post and its main export is vice. Kuzania has sunk so low in the league of states that it permanently occupies the bottom position. It has statistics on GDP, income per capita, infant mortality, life expectancy and unemployment, which prove that the continued existence of Kuzania is a burden to mankind, yet the world will not leave Kuzania alone because of its strategic location, minerals and history.

'Were you to make a serious review of the events in Kuzania, I doubt that you could ever fathom the gravity of the present situation. It takes one who has been in the thick and thin of it to understand the nature of its disorganisation. As you cannot swear on the colour of a chameleon, it goes without saying that you cannot fully fathom the mysteries of Kuzania. Few have the desire, patience, stamina and heart to look at Kuzania in the face. Just pictures of police brutality, tribal clashes and massacres send chills all over the world. Newspaper and television pictures cannot capture complete reality. They are only the tip of the iceberg of the horrors in Kuzania. A full dossier on Kuzania could render you impotent if you are soft hearted, mad if you are compassionate and dead if you are humane. Tourists and investors come to Kuzania with blinkers. They look at animals or make quick deals and leave as fast as their jets can fly.

'The people of Kuzania have borne the weight of this burden for far too long. They need help in the struggle between good and evil. If there are no changes in Kuzania, worse vice will find its way to all the four corners of the earth. The madness in Kuzania is not isolated, it is the first step towards infesting the world with the virus. In the mythology of the Israelites, they say that Satan and his legions shall rule the earth for a thousand years. It is obvious that the way things are going in Kuzania, that period is not too far off.

'The Good Lord looks at the scheming of the devil and his legions and finds the experiment fascinating.

This struggle between good and evil was not in His original master plan. It is an accident, just like islands forming in the sea, or earthquakes and volcanic eruptions. He is amusing Himself with it. You see, He has never forgiven Adam and his descendants for messing up the garden. The situation was exacerbated when the rebel survivors married earthlings, which was, in God's eyes, "a double betrayal". When He later sent His most obedient Son to reverse the situation, He was arrested and crucified in one of the kingdoms! He is not in a hurry to send another son and certainly not to Kuzania, not just yet. He fears that he might be assassinated, executed by a firing squad, arraigned in a court of law on trumped-up charges, detained without trial, or that he might suffer many of the inhuman ills, enshrined in the policy documents of Kuzania under the title, "State protection". Neither will He send His favourite Son twice, though the Son is willing to give it a second shot. The Good Lord vividly recalls how His favourite Son Jesus returned with spear wounds in His ribcage and a pricked skull from wounds inflicted by a crown of cactus thorns, which had been squashed into His head. He was indeed very lucky to get away with His life after resurrection. Had it been in Kuzania, the state security organs would have assured Him of a second death, this time more brutal and absolutely total. Had it been in Kuzania, a commission of enquiry would have been instituted to investigate how He had risen from the grave in the first place, and heads would have rolled, beginning with the executioners, those who conducted the autopsy, mortuary attendants, the grave diggers and the undertaker. Kuzania is thorough, very thorough in these matters, as the state protects itself from its enemies. You know these things.

'For the time being the Good Lord has nothing to do with the chaos in Kuzania, the land He made as a living symbol of His majesty and perfection.

'On the other hand, Satan exiled in hell is overjoyed with the events in Kuzania. The introduction of devil worship and its embrace at the highest level has greatly pleased him. His influence is strongly entrenched and protected in the land. He is glad that those who escaped in the hijacked UFO pioneered the conquest of the earth. He compares them with explorers and missionaries who invaded Africa to soften African hearts for civilisation, commerce and colonisation. These pioneers will be given the highest honours, as the missionaries received OBEs and MBEs! In his estimation the battle for the minds, hearts and souls of the earthlings is the mother of all battles. For him, the coming Armageddon will be the final one. He plans to settle old scores with heaven and avenge his defeat in the first Armageddon. By coaxing the earthlings to his side he will have a huge reservoir from which to recruit his army. He will swell his ranks so much so that he could win the war by sheer numbers. This he views as a big tactical advantage.

'Secondly, he has won many key earthlings involved in space programmes. Sooner or later, they will be manufacturing intergalaxy UFOs, putting heaven within range. The other breakthroughs expected are in the tactical and strategic doomsday missiles, both in yield and range. The only snag is that the earthlings in their excitement are threatening one another with the missiles. So far he has managed to avert a major conflagration between them, and hopes to do so until the day of the final Armageddon, the day of judgement. However, he allows for the relaxation of muscles among the earthlings in selected zones such as Vietnam, Yugoslavia and the Middle East. He will not allow this relaxation to touch Kuzania and that is why not even one coup d'état has succeeded. They are all quelled in the planning stages.

'As the strategy takes shape the people of Kuzania have become guinea pigs in the devil's workshop.

'The descendants of the Royal Celestial Forces are seething inwardly for action. They believe they can turn the tide. To them a single good leader is all it takes to start a revolution. However, those who have tried to bring about sanity and morality in Kuzania have met with most horrifying deaths. There are not many willing to stick out their necks any more.

'The bishops, deacons, reverends, kadhis and traditional healers have cried themselves hoarse cursing the influence of the devil, but their prayers have not been answered, either. Every Sunday the congregations are swelling, pleading with the Good Lord to intervene. Probably He will when they start the struggle in earnest, or when the battle enters a decisive stage. He only helps those courageous enough to help themselves.

'If the people of Kuzania are not courageous enough to rise up and fight, there will be dire consequences. If the devil has to be stopped then the fight must begin in Kuzania. Evil must not triumph over good, or do you want to bequeath to prosperity an empty, shimmering, uninhabitable shell of a lifeless earth? Do you?'

Agu turned restlessly in his bed. By the time he was still again, only the song of the morning bird could be heard. His celestial communicator had gone.

'We must fight to bequeath to posterity a better earth. Good must triumph over evil and the fight must begin in Kuzania,' Agu heard these words coming from his mouth and was surprised at how clear his mind had become. It was as though he had not slept the whole night, as if he had had a long conversation with a friend. It was now time to sleep.

To the rhythm of the morning songbird, Agu drifted into deep sleep. He dreamed of long queues of people registering for war on the side of good. Others were standing by and he was urging them to join the ranks.

'As we don the armour, you must choose your side. The choice is yours, the pleasure is mine,' he was shouting in his dream. A column of soldiers came by. They were heading for the battlefront. At the head of the column was a youthful and stately general. His face radiated light, brighter than that of the morning sun. He walked with long, strong strides, as though he were not just going to battle, but was already assured of victory. As the column drew closer Agu could see the face clearly. He recognised it at once and shouted in joy. 'Shaka! Shaka! Wait for me!' Shaka was his friend, the son of the late leader of the Kuzania Liberation Army, who was betrayed to the colonialists and hanged. In the background Agu could hear his people singing a new song, a song of hope. From that day on the links with the celestial voice were lost.

The message had been delivered in full.

He kept asking himself, 'If Satan and the rebels could mount an assault on the throne of the omnipotent, omnipresent and omniscient Good Lord, what chance has man on earth against evil?' He also knew that evil has the uncanny resilience of self-rejuvenation like the tail of a lizard. The story of the hijacked UFO proved it. He resolved to fight to the end.

3

Season of Thunder

The fury of the rains was to set many records. Nothing like it had ever been recorded in Kuzania. It rained day and night ceaselessly with short spells in between. It was blamed on a strange phenomenon called El Niño. Rivers came into being where none had been before. Huge dams appeared where there had been farms and playing fields. Houses, plantations, roads and bridges were swept away. In subsequent news bulletins the numbers of those drowned were rising. Rains are always welcome as they signal bounties. This time, they spelt disaster.

In the night, thunderstorms shook the foundation of the land as they pounded the earth relentlessly in staccato stereo fashion. They were followed by streaks of lightning that illuminated every corner of the land and took many victims and split open giant trees. That night the heaven's wrath was intense, like that of an angry monster tearing its prey. The wind howled like an evil demon. You could hear the eerie whistling of trees and the sound of iron sheets clattering desperately on roofs.

On a night like this when the demons are loose,

many things happen. Old people die and pregnant women give birth prematurely. On a night like this many women are made pregnant and young girls lose their virginity. On a night like this nobody sleeps deeply and those who do, never wake up. There are many stories of a night like this.

Shaka's father, General Jongwe Mkombozi's heroic campaign against the colonial forces was known all over the world. The unique attribute that endeared him to friend and foe alike was the clinical manner in which he executed the war. His targets were well chosen and civilians never came in harm's way. In the few instances when colonial administration massacred civilians and tried to heap the blame on the Kuzania Liberation Army, they were immediately exposed. He thought no evil and did no evil.

When the colonialists tried to cajole Mkombozi into an agreement leading to a cease-fire and sham independence, he refused. They were infuriated. It was the landowning settlers who offered the ultimate solution. The plan was to split the Kuzania Liberation Movement into 'hawks' and 'doves', with the doves to take over with independence. The hawks were to be eliminated. The settlers found a number of bootlickers from the nationalist political ranks very eager to have the plan executed. The Kuzania governor legalised the KLM and challenged it to engage in an open campaign for independence. The KLA was meantime branded an outlawed bandit army. This move split the liberation army. Some from within its ranks sold out and became collaborators. The other faction under Mkombozi vowed not to be hoodwinked into accepting remotely controlled independence. To them, the struggle would go on unabated.

Nevertheless, there was the semblance of freedom in the making. This new 'freedom' confused the masses. They were divided between supporting the politicians or the guerrilla army. It was in this confusion that Shaka's father was betrayed, shot, wounded, given a sham secret trial and hanged. On the night of the day he was hanged, the heavens opened, pounding the earth with rain, thunderstorms and lightning. After that it did not rain in Kuzania for two years. Independence was given to the newly emerged politicians and former members of the colonial administration. With the death of Shaka's father, the KLA was splintered and weakened. With independence the last group surrendered, leaving the land in the hands of half-baked politicians, traitors all.

Out of the drought that followed General Jongwe Mkombozi's death and independence, the nation was sent reeling and begging. In this desperate state many agreements were signed with foreign companies and governments, virtually mortgaging Kuzania for food. People did not know what went on behind closed doors but they were happy the new government had imported enough sugar, maize, beans and milk and that nobody starved to death. Little did they know of the high price they paid for this generosity. In the importation, transportation, storage and distribution of relief food, indigenous companies mushroomed overnight and they became bigger and bigger with the prolongation of the drought. Their owners and managers were seen in the city of Glitta eating in hotels, formerly exclusively for whites, and being driven in limousines. Truly, independence had come to Kuzania. Soon the drought would be over and the population could look forward to a life of prosperity.

Somehow Shaka and his mother were erased from the history of the struggle in a flash. The politicians began to sing the song of, 'When we were fighting for independence!' True, they had signed agreements and hoisted the new flag, but when did they fight for independence? They had another catchy phrase, 'Forget the past'. So as the days went by the past was forgotten and nobody cared about Shaka's mother or even tried to find out where his father was buried. The wind of change had come to Kuzania, riding on the crest of black devils known as politicians, who had enriched themselves overnight out of a natural disaster.

The end of the drought did not bring any cheer to the people. The masses discovered that politicians are a special breed of people, very powerful, arrogant, mean, and only available during political campaigns. This, the people learnt, is the modern way of state management, otherwise known as democracy. Whatever it was, the mismanagement of the state and its wealth did not need an angel from heaven to shout about it. It was visible everywhere. Here and there poor families were settled on former settlers' land, but this did not improve their lot. A single white settler used to own one thousand acres. Now the one thousand acres were divided between a thousand families. They were told they were no longer landless and they would soon be producing like settlers.

Some people started to mumble and grumble that this was not the kind of independence they had fought for. They said that had Shaka's father and others like him succeeded, Kuzania would have been a radically different country and the people's needs would have been addressed in a humane and organised way. Those advocating this line of thought were put in detention. Many laws were enacted: the 'State Protection Act', the 'Public Protection Act' and so forth, all of which curbed the freedom of expression and assembly. Kuzania slowly drifted into dictatorship. The organs of the state, especially the police, had power of life and death. It was as if a strange breed of people had invaded Kuzania and made its people prisoners en masse.

For two years Shaka had been in search of a job befitting his level of education. He knew the pains of living in a country in which the government existed only for the rich and the powerful. The rest did not matter and they served as pleasure and labour reservoirs in the service of the demigods. The national cake was too small to share, it appeared, but it was big enough for leaders to eat, waste and give away to their lackeys. It was big enough for foreigners to steal huge slices and still leave some. It was big enough for all to have a piece, he knew, if only those who dished it out had a heart. On his bed he pondered on what to do next.

He recalled the image of his sickly mother. Had his father lived, things could have turned out better for the family. He would have been here to give the family the support it now so badly needed. The nation needed him now more than in the days of the struggle. More than the nation, Shaka himself needed his guidance. If it were not for Agu, he wondered how he would have understood the world and all its complications.

His mind drifted back to his mother. When he was young he did not see any difference between himself and other boys. These were the harsh days of the liberation

48

struggle and all the able-bodied men were either in the forest as freedom fighters, in detention camps, in exile or in the service of the colonialists. Everybody's father was away and so there was no difference between the boys. Then independence came and a lot of men came back home, all except a few, including his father. The few families whose fathers never came back suffered the most with independence; they were bullied and cheated when it came to land demarcation and distribution. Their homesteads were leaderless and the children became wild as mothers tried to eke out a living. Some single mothers became harlots, soon to be followed by their daughters. His mother, however, though cheated out of their land, did not lose her dignity. She tightened her belt and worked hard to give Shaka the best she could.

Recently his mother had suffered a severe bout of malaria that had almost killed her. With rains, mosquitos breed day and night and malaria afflicts many. With the long El Niño rains, malaria had become an epidemic and many people had died. It was in the course of her diagnosis and treatment that it was discovered she also had tuberculosis. This explained the endless bouts of coughing and wheezing, which she had attributed to the early-morning cold and the chemicals sprayed on the crops in the farms where she worked. She was wasting away, far too fast for Shaka's comfort. Fatherless, he feared he would soon be motherless, too.

Shaka had passed his last examinations very well. He had always been an A student. He was admitted for a degree in law at the University of Glitta. His mother was happy and so was Agu. Armed with a law degree he would be a powerful and rich man. Shaka took a second look at his ailing mother and decided it was time for her to take a rest. It meant declining the university placing and looking for a job.

When he broke the news to his mother, she broke down in tears.

'All these year I have laboured to give you the best, as your father would have done. You cannot let go when you are so near to graduating to an important man. Don't worry about me. I will manage as I have always done. I... I...' Her breathing was arrested and she had another terrible bout of coughing.

That did it. When it was over, Shaka said, 'Mother, I understand you very well. This will not be the end of my education. With a job I will register with the University of London as an external student and I can still get a degree in law.' He said this with the certainty and finality of a resolute man much older than his age. The two had never fought over any issue. 'All right, so be it,' she said, believing in the wisdom of her son.

Two years had passed since and he had not found a job. The dreams he had of making his mother a comfortable woman with a nice, warm bed to keep away the cold and a good meal each day to restore her ailing health had become nightmares. His mother had not stopped working and her health was at its lowest ebb. Frustrated, he had been forced to seek all sorts of manual jobs, such as digging and mixing concrete on construction sites. The jobs were very demanding physically and the pay was a pittance. He was not the only educated man doing odd jobs. Many university graduates were on the tarmac in a country that employed expatriates and technical advisers in all arms of government and the private sector. Shaka was bitter, very bitter with the state and with the society that allowed the existence of such an insensitive regime.

He had also promised Agu a heavy woollen blanket

and an overcoat with his first proper salary. Agu was still waiting. He had admired Shaka's reasoning on the need to support his mother at the expense of a university degree. He had comforted him that sacrifices are always rewarded with time. What Shaka had become resembled more of a curse than a blessing. His hands were rough from working with soil and cement and he had several scars as a result of mishaps, which are quite frequent on construction sites. He was wearing secondhand clothes and living in a rented one-roomed shack in a slum area called Kawempe. Were these the blessings Agu had in mind? He highly doubted it.

'God, life is hard. Hard on me and hard on my people. There must be a way!' Shaka was searching for an answer in the small holes in the old corrugated-iron sheets that made his roof. The rain had eased and there was calmness in the air. Outside he could hear voices of people as they plodded the thick red mud, each going to their calling of the day. He wondered what to do with himself, this being Sunday. He remembered the pounding of the rain, the thunderstorm, hailstorm and lightning the night before and recalled the words of Agu: 'In a night like this, many things happen...' He resolved at once to visit his sick mother and Agu, who lived across the valley. He had moved away from his mother's house on Agu's advice that 'a man who is circumcised should not share the same roof with his mother!' Agu wanted him to be a man, independent and in control of his life. He did not regret the advice. His shack was very close to the bus stop. After a quick wash in the communal bathroom, he put on his Sunday best and left. First he would visit his mother, and then go to see Agu.

'They told me that education was the key to success. I passed my sixth-form exams with straight As and society

51

has slammed the door to success on my face! All I get are manual jobs! No, I deserve better'. He plodded the red gummy mud, deep in thought, as he went to see his ailing mother. He prayed that neither she nor Agu had been targeted in the night. If anything had happened, somebody would have informed me by now, he consoled himself. Soon he came to his mother's house. He saw the padlock hanging on the door and was happy. His mother had gone to church. She was still strong enough to walk to the church a mile away. He thanked God for little mercies. He promised himself he would call on her later, then went on his way to Agu's house.

Agu was sitting in his hut, dimly lit but very warm from the wood burning in the fireplace in the middle of the room. One of his great-grandchildren had woken him up that morning. He had brought him porridge and tea in a flask, made the fire and gone to Sunday school. Agu was well looked after, and God had been good to him. As he pushed the firewood to the centre of the fire, he felt the special warmth that engulfed him when the celestial voice spoke to him. This time its intensity was less, far less, but he had no doubt it was the same. He imagined that he was once again establishing the broken links, but was surprised it was daytime. These things only happen at night in dreams.

His chain of thought was broken by a knock on the door.

'Come in.' There was another knock on the door. 'Come in, I said,' this time more loudly.

The half-ajar door was gently pushed and in came Shaka. 'It is me, Great-grandpa. I bring you greetings.'

Agu could not find his voice immediately. His mind

was locked on Shaka leading his people in the battle against evil, as had been revealed in the vision.

'Great one, it's me – are you all right?'

'Yes, I am, my child. Please, do come in and take a seat.' Agu regained his composure. 'You've done well to come, my boy. It has been quite some while since we last saw each other. How are things with you?'

'Just the usual, Great-grandpa, nothing has changed,' Shaka replied.

'Things will change, Shaka, they have to change for the better.' He spoke emphatically and with such a high degree of certainty that Shaka felt consoled.

'How is your mother?' Agu asked.

'She is well, I think. I have just passed by her house but she was not there. I think she has gone to church,' Shaka replied.

'She is a strong woman, the strongest and the best we ever had,' Agu's words rang true in Shaka's mind. His mother was the very best woman on earth but, as for strength, well, maybe Agu's failing eyesight had not seen how far she had withered.

'Yes, she is a great woman,' Shaka responded. 'And how have you been?'

Agu hesitated for a while. 'Ah, my boy, I am as strong as a lion and as fit as a veteran soldier marching to another war! I have eaten a lot of salt in my lifetime and I tell you as long as Lake Munyu continues to produce salt, I will be around to eat some more.'

Yes, Agu had cheated death for many seasons, long past the oldest of his age mates. Indeed, he was an extraordinary human being. Women do not produce the likes of him any more.

But Agu knew his strength was waning. The frailty and stiffness of his old limbs was beginning to announce the beginning of the end. These days as he stood up he needed to hold on to something for support. It was not so last season. It was obvious to him that he would be gone long before Lake Munyu ran dry.

'I am not immortal though,' he told Shaka in amusement. 'No man is immortal, not even these powerful demigods of politicians who think they can buy anything.' There was a tone of anger and defiance in Agu's voice that Shaka had never heard before.

'They cannot bribe God to live for ever and enjoy their ill-gotten wealth! I tell you, Great-grandpa, you should see them riding in their sleek Mercedes. They behave as though they were a special breed of men. But look at how we are suffering because of their blindness. They are evil devils, and their day will come. Evil cannot prevail over good, never!' Shaka did not know where he found these words. They came out of his mouth effortlessly like a speech well rehearsed.

Agu was astonished. These were the same words the celestial voice had spoken. He remembered the warmth he had felt enveloping him before Shaka knocked on his door. He recalled his dream of Shaka leading a long column of liberators in the war against evil, and he wondered... He locked these things also in his granite-hard heart that had become a safe deposit for celestial revelations.

'So it is true,' Agu said.

'So you believe me, Great-grandpa?' Shaka asked.

'Shaka, there are many weighty things I could tell you. But let's talk of something else, young one. These days even walls and roofs have ears and I do not want trouble for anybody, not just yet. Where is my blanket?' Agu asked Shaka in a jocular tone.

'You know, Great-grandpa, I have not forgotten the

promise to buy you a brand-new, heavy blanket. But the money they pay us...'

'I understand. They call it living from hand to mouth, but even this is a gross exaggeration. Most times, the hand has nothing to give to the mouth. I recall how in the last political campaign the politicians made such promises. But you give them your vote and that's the last you see of them. I remember how Hon. Tumbo humbly came to my hut and sat on a three-legged stool. He made it a huge thing in the rallies that he had my blessing. It made a difference in the votes. He owes me one. They say this is not the era of education, qualifications and experience. This is the era of who knows who; the era of tribalism and nepotism. Well, Tumbo is of my tribe, he knows me well and he is an honourable minister. If he so wished he could get you a good job merely by making a phone call.

'Check in that drawer and bring out a pad, a pen and an envelope. Through your own hand I will ask him to give you a job. I can not wait for my blanket for ever!'

But Shaka felt a rebellion within him. He turned to Agu. 'Great-grandpa, let us not beg anybody for anything. Let us hold on. Things will change...'

'No, no, no, my young one. I have known people holding on to dreams, hopes and wishes to their graves. If I can, I want to use my blanket before I am gone. Write the following...' The letter was done and Agu signed it. 'Fine, fine,' said Agu. 'The rain has stopped and I want you to go to Tumbo's house and give him the letter.' Agu dug into his pocket and gave Shaka some money. 'Use this for the bus fare. You can refund me when you get a job.' It was more of a command than a request. He took his snuff bottles and helped himself to a good sniff. He sneezed twice, wiping his nose with the back of his hand. He felt good as his head became lighter.

Shaka went past his mother's house, which was still locked. He was glad because his mother would have protested very strongly about the whole affair. She was too proud to beg and would have scolded her son. Shaka made a promise to return to see her after visiting Hon. Tumbo.

Shaka knew the general area where the hon. minister lived, though he had never been in that area before. It was an estate for the exclusively rich. Unlike his slum area of Kawempe, here roads were tarmacked and there were paths and a drainage system. There were flowers and shrubs and hedges were neat and trim. Beyond the hedges were huge mansions, each of which resembled an institution. He wondered how many people lived in each house and how big the families were. It was such a glaring display of wealth, like he had never seen. Each house had a large metallic gate and the compounds were guarded by watchmen and alsatians, bulldogs and German shepherds. The dogs were a different breed from the scruffy mongrels they called dogs in his village and three times as big.

He came to an intersection that had a flower garden and a fountain. He reckoned that one of the roads must surely lead to Hon. Tumbo's residence. He approached two watchmen. To his surprise they eyed him with suspicion and hostility.

'Could you please direct me to Hon. Tumbo's house?' he asked politely.

'You want to go to Hon. Tumbo's house, do you? What business do you have with the hon. minister?' one of them asked him rudely.

'I've a message for him,' he replied.

'Message? Here messages come by telephone, by fax, by e-mail or in the mouths of those riding big cars. Messages are not brought by messengers!' That said, they turned away from him and continued their conversation.

A young man in a jogging suit came running by. Shaka hailed him and asked him the way to Hon. Tumbo's house. Politely, the boy directed him. It was about five blocks away. Still uncertain of his mission, Shaka arrived at Tumbo's gate. A fierce-looking policeman immediately confronted him. He had an automatic rifle in his hands.

'I have come to deliver a message to Hon. Tumbo,' he said.

'To deliver a message? What kind of message?' The policeman asked coldly.

'I've a letter for him,' Shaka replied.

'Letters are posted and not delivered to people's houses! Where do you come from? Have you never been to school?'

'This letter is from an old man. I've been asked to deliver it to Hon. Tumbo by hand,' Shaka retorted.

'OK, give it to me. I'll hand it over to him,' said the policeman.

'You don't understand, I need a reply to take back to the old man,' Shaka insisted.

'Young man, no one pushes us around here. When I say hand over the letter, I expect to be understood. Hand over the letter or take it back with you.'

'Let me tell you, neither Hon. Tumbo nor the old man will be happy with you, and you will be very sorry if you don't let me hand over the message,' he said.

'Who are you to threaten me, young man? I could

beat you senseless and nothing will happen to me. Hand over the letter or be gone from here at once!' The policeman menacingly moved a step towards Shaka. Seeing contempt and defiance written on the young man's face, he halted.

Just then a young woman came walking down the driveway towards the gate. She was followed by an alsatian bitch and six fat puppies.

'Go away at once!' the policeman shouted at Shaka.

Shaka stood there looking at the angry policeman, at the gun, the beautiful young woman and the dogs.

'What does he want?' the young woman asked the policeman.

'He says he has a letter for the hon. minister but he will not give it to me,' the policeman reported.

Shaka seized the opportunity, 'Lady, I was sent by an old man who is a friend of the hon. minister to bring this letter and to take back a reply. I will have failed in my duty if I do not carry out the instructions. I beg you, help me if you can.'

Just then the rain began to fall.

'Who is the old man?' The young woman asked.

'His name is Agu, we call him Great-grandpa in the village.'

'Oh! I've heard my father talk about him. He is the oldest man alive! Can he see? Can he write?' she asked excitedly.

'I wrote the letter for him,' Shaka said, feeling as if the ground under him was about to give way.

'So what is it all about?' the policeman asked.

'That's rude of you, you've no business asking him such a question. Letters are confidential, not articles in newspapers!' the young woman scolded. 'Open the gate.'

The policeman opened the gate.

'Come with me,' she told Shaka.

Shaka was wary about how the dog would treat him. On a command from the young lady, however, the big dog ran towards the house, followed by the fat puppies, running like ducks, their backsides swaying from side to side.

'My name is Nzinga. I am Mr Tumbo's daughter,' the young woman said, offering Shaka her hand.

'Glad to meet you.'

'What is your name?' she asked.

'My name is Shaka,' he replied simply. Well, he did not have a father to mention and in his community children do not identify themselves with their mothers. So he was Shaka, full stop.

The drizzle was mild and the sun was shining. A huge rainbow stretched over the hill. It originated in one river, curved itself towards the heavens and then dipped into another river on the other side of the hill. The clouds were laboriously drifting in the gentle wind. It was the kind of weather in which friendship is planted, warm and calm, watered by a gentle drizzle.

'Come in.' Nzinga welcomed Shaka into the house. 'Take off your shoes.'

Shaka did as he was told. He was aware that his worn-out shoes had let in dirty water and he took off his socks, too. Barefooted he stepped into the lobby.

'Sit there while I call my father.'

Hon. Tumbo, the honourable minister, was in the bathroom. He always woke up rather late on Sundays.

'You will have to wait for a while,' Nzinga said. She offered him a glass of orange juice and biscuits.

Shaka's heart was beating like a bongo drum as he surveyed the display of items in the lobby. There was a television, the biggest he had ever seen and a huge music system. There were stuffed animals and beautiful paintings everywhere and the furniture was a mixture of golden metallic, ebony and oak.

Nzinga came back to the room with a glass of orange juice for herself. 'You speak very good English. What do you do with yourself?' she asked.

'Well, I ... I ... work,' Shaka stammered.

'Where do you work? What do you do?' There was something about the young man from the village that intrigued Nzinga. He seemed educated and yet he was wearing torn shoes. She wanted to find out more.

'I work on construction sites as a labourer,' Shaka said with dignity.

'A labourer? But you sound educated!'

'Yes, I was called to study law in the University of Glitta but my mother is very sick and I opted out. I want to help her as she is very weak.'

'But that's awful! You should have taken the degree first. That would give you a better job and you could have looked after her better.'

'In life one has to make sacrifices. I had hoped to get a good job but, unfortunately, I did not have connections,' Shaka said forcefully.

'Connections? Does one need connections to get a job?' Nzinga asked.

'Yes, lady, these days one needs connections to get a good job. As a matter of fact, that is why I am here. Old man Agu thinks that your father can help me get a better -paying job.'

'I see,' said Nzinga. 'I guess he should be able to. He always gets me a well-paying holiday job wherever I ask –'

'Nzinga, whom are you talking to?' came the booming voice of Tumbo from upstairs.

60

'I am talking to Shaka, Dad,' she said. 'He is a man from the village. He has a message for you.'

'A message from the village? What do they want this time? They always seem to have endless problems in the village. I will be down soon.'

'Tell me, Shaka, how is the village? You know, I've never been there, though Dad says that's where we came from and we have a lot of relatives living there,' continued Nzinga.

'The village does not change. The people are very poor but we manage somehow.'

'What do you eat?'

'Food,' he said, wondering what else to say.

'Like what?' she asked.

'Like maize, beans, pumpkins, cassava, yams, millet and bananas,' he replied.

'That is all?'

'Yes, that is all.' He wondered what else there was to eat.

'What about spaghetti, macaroni, rice, cake and custard?'

'Those are for the rich. We only read about them in books. At Christmas we eat rice and meat,' he added.

'People must be very poor, then!'

'Yes, very, very poor.'

'I am so sorry,' she said, as her father's footsteps descended the stairs.

'You said your name is what?' The hon. minister asked Shaka.

'My name is Shaka,' he responded.

The people's representative did not extend a hand of greeting to him. 'You are the son of whom?' he asked in his deep voice.

'My father is dead. I am a friend of Agu,' he said, almost in self-defence.

'Ah! How is the old man? Still alive and kicking, eh!' He laughed, but Shaka did not see the joke. 'What does he want?'

Shaka gave him the letter.

'What is wrong with these people? Does he think I am the ministry of labour? He wants me to get you a job from where? The economy is not doing well and people want jobs. I cannot work miracles! I am not Jesus Christ, do you hear, I do not work miracles. Go and tell him there are no jobs. We – the government has frozen employment!'

Shaka was to be ashamed of his next action for years to come. He went down on his knees begging Mr Tumbo.

'Please, hon. minister, sir, please help me. I have a very sick mother and if I do not help her, she will soon die. Please help me,' he pleaded.

'Stand up, young man! This is not a church for you to kneel in prayers. What do you think I am, God Almighty? I've told you there are no jobs and that is final. Now go!'

Shaka stood up without a further word and began to put on his socks.

Nzinga had left the two together but had heard the whole conversation from an adjacent room. She came bursting in. 'Father, you can't treat him like that! He is begging you! You can help him if you really want to!'

He looked at his daughter and turned to Shaka. 'All right, come to my office Monday morning at nine o'clock and we will see.' Turning to Nzinga he added, 'I've a fund-raising meeting this afternoon. I will not be back until late at night. You can go to the movies if you so wish. Do you have money?'

'Yes, I've some money but I want to stay at home today.'

Shaka heard the conversation as he tied his shoelaces. He marvelled at the kind heart of this young woman who moved the heart of her cruel father.

Tumbo went upstairs to pick a jacket, without looking at Shaka.

'I am sure he will get you a job. Here, take this.' Nzinga gave Shaka some money.

He did not look at it as he put it in his pocket. 'Thank you very much for all you have done for me today. Some day, I hope to return your kindness.'

'It is a small matter; I want to visit the village one day and that's the way you will pay me back!' Nzinga had a very warm smile on her face.

'Any time, I will take you there any time. You must meet Agu, the old man. He has wonderful stories to tell,' he added.

'Take this telephone number. Once you get a job, call me and we shall arrange something.'

Nzinga escorted Shaka to the gate and they shook hands as they parted. It was then that Shaka realised how astonishingly beautiful she was. He turned to look at her one more time and found her eyes fixed on him. They both smiled.

With her father gone, Nzinga was alone in the house. She went into her room and put an album on the turntable, plugged in the headphones and lay on her bed. It was an old record by the Four Tops. The second track was her favourite. 'If I were a carpenter and you were a lady, would you marry me anyway, would you have my baby?' It brought back memories of Shaka; tall, handsome and well built. She wondered if he had a girlfriend in the village and whether he ever sang to her such sweet songs.

Music had become her most faithful companion. With

no one to talk to, save the cook, the gardener and the policeman, it killed loneliness and boredom. She regarded the vocals as voices of storytellers. There was Sam Cooke, Wilson Pickett, Aretha Franklin; all good storytellers in her collection. The rest of her house she regarded as a museum or an art gallery, exhibiting her father's eccentricities. One day she would no longer be in this museum. She would have a warm house to herself. She longed for the day, which she knew was not too far off.

Her father hated visitors and did not seem to have friends. All he had were political hangabouts and business partners. They were like demons, chasing money, money and more money all the time. She had nothing to do with the lot, including her father. Worse still, he did not let her entertain friends in the house. Neither was she allowed to visit just any home she fancied. She was told of the 'good homes' from where to make friends; homes of inhuman tycoons who were very much like her father. She neither had the time nor the heart for them. In her own way, she felt very different. She had grown up without the guidance of a mother. Her mother had died of childbirth complications as soon as Nzinga was born and she had been brought up by a succession of nannies.

As she grew older Nzinga increasingly blamed wealth and power for her father's insensitivity to the feelings of others, including her own. Such a life, she argued, 'is rotten, ungodly and cursed.' She longed for real life, in a real world, with real people who were warm, full of laughter and genuine love. A people with feelings for each other in times of joy and in times of pain. A world in which the best and the worst could be shared. Such a world, she argued, must exist in the village they had left behind, because it was certainly not in the world of power and money, in the so-called Happy Valley. Here, there was no hunger, no want, no tears! There was just joy, parties and good living. Maybe if her father had remarried her life would have changed, but she was not sure any more. The kind of women she had seen visiting were a breed of vultures and hyenas. They came painted in all colours and their only calling was to siphon money from him in the name of love.

Nzinga got up an hour later and showered. As she reached for the towel on the rail, the sun's rays streaking through the half-parted curtains played games with the water drops on her body. Moving her body from side to side she watched in the mirror as drops twinkled like tiny diamonds, dancing all over her. The picture she saw was that of an African queen, Cleopatra, or the Queen of Sheba, with garlands of diamonds on a beautiful, smooth, naked body. It was magic. 'Someday, I will be an African queen,' she said, as she took the towel and wiped herself dry.

Lately, she had become increasingly conscious of her maturity as a woman. At twenty Nzinga was still a virgin and not in a hurry to get involved carelessly with men. It was not that she was shy or scared, but she believed things must be done in a very orderly manner. She had seen many of her friends drop out of school with pregnancy. It was not the proper way to handle one's dignity. A top student at the University of Glitta, she was studying political science, economics and anthropology. Nzinga was very level headed and she believed in achieving things the right way.

Still, at night, she dreamt of wonderful things with handsome men. In the morning she would muse about it and at times it lingered on, refusing to die. The tension in her body remained like a throbbing boil. She was a strong woman and she knew she was not going to let it burst carelessly like a balloon. She would wait.

Agu was seated on his three-legged stool outside his hut. People came and went and he had a word for each. He was revered almost to the point of worship. You could see from his frame that he was once a big and strong man. That was long ago but the sinews and veins that seemed to come out of his skin told a story of a man that was once a giant in his own right. All his peers had died a long time ago but, for him, old age and senility had come as though in slow motion. He had even buried some of his own children. It was as though nature and the gods favoured him with special gifts for rejuvenation. 'When a snake feels old, it sheds its skin and its youthfulness is restored. When a leopard begins to lose the spring in its legs, it eats a dog and it can jump high again. For Agu, however, the secret to long life was locked in his heart.

He sat and pondered why, since the last general elections Hon. Tumbo, the people's representative, had not returned to the village. Tumbo is from my village but he doesn't behave like us, Agu thought to himself. It is as though he were fathered by a stranger from other lands. He will come to no good; he is evil through and through. Where shall we get men of conscience to head this nation? Men like Shaka's father? Ah! But he gave birth to a bright boy and, if the stars are right, the likes of Tumbo will soon pay a heavy price for betraying the cause.

As he sat there he began to feel guilty that he had sent Shaka to Tumbo. But hunger cannot be dignified, he defended himself. He had seen hunger coming. His people once owned huge tracks of land. First came the railway line, which split Kawempe into two like a knife through butter. On one side of the railway line land was given to white settlers to grow coffee. The owners of the land were not compensated. Then came the Veterinary Research Station to deal with a disease called East Coast Fever, which was killing cows imported from Europe. When the fever was dealt with, more land was taken for European cattle. Then came the church, and more land was taken to build churches and schools. Kawempe shrank to a village and the people were squeezed like sardines in a can. Now it was a slum, like the garden of Eden in the vision. The land was gone, forests were no more and people become labourers on settlers' farms. They worked like donkeys and they were paid peanuts. Further, the peanuts were taxed. Life became more unbearable by the day, and you could touch the tension in the air. It burst into open confrontation with the war for independence. People sacrificed their sons and daughters and gave food to the freedom fighters. The war went well and many settlers left the country. Soon the people thought all the land would return to its rightful owners. Then came betrayal by the collaborators and all was lost. Sham independence was quickly proclaimed and the new leaders urged the people to forget the bitter past and forgive the colonialists. All the sacrifices and dreams were washed away in a sea of greed.

True, some of the white farms were bought by the government and given to the people, but families got small parcels that could not sustain them, while the best went to politicians and their friends. Each family had something called a title deed, for which rates had to be paid. Can you imagine: for the grace of a piece of land that had always been yours, you had to pay rates to the government. Kawempe being so close to the city, a quarter of an acre was deemed adequate for further development. And so it was that the people built shacks, which were rented by the growing urban population from the countryside. The village became a huge slum, a den of harlots, criminals, drug pedlars and illicit brews. In Kawempe, there are no roads, only paths with deep potholes, no streetlights, and nobody is safe – not even a policeman armed with an automatic rifle.

This is the new Kuzania that has emerged with independence; a Kuzania that has become the garden of Eden after the apple was eaten. Old man Agu did not understand what the crime the common man had committed to deserve this punishment from his own government. Kawempe was a perfect microcosm of Kuzania. Its people were poorer and more desperate than anywhere else in the world, Agu thought. He was too poor and too old to think of migrating to a saner place, if any existed. He remembered how the Good Lord had thought of creating another garden of Eden after the first one became a slum. He abandoned the idea of ever moving out.

Agu knew sooner or later something would give. Tension was mounting as desperation and disillusionment ate souls. There was no sense of purpose in life, no sense of direction, no sense of leadership. It made him angry. No! no! no! In the young generations and in the wombs of mothers lies many a saviour. One day they will clean this mess and Kuzania shall shine like a pearl. He remembered the revelation with Shaka leading a column of liberation soldiers and felt calmness within himself. He looked upwards towards the heavens, whispered Shaka's name and spat on his chest in the traditional way of blessing the person mentioned.

The wind was chilly and Agu's lips began to quiver. The words which had hung on them like a parasite, were no longer there. Now he had the answers. Supporting himself with the wall he retreated to the warmth of his hut and the glowing fire.

On leaving Tumbo's house, Shaka felt both elated and deflated. He knew his mother would surely scold him and he did not even know whether he was going to get a job or not. But these negative feelings were compensated by the fact that he had had the courage to carry out Agu's instructions to the letter. And he was happy that with the help of Nzinga he had confronted a policeman and made him look stupid. Ah! Nzinga, so kind, so beautiful! He had nothing good to say about Tumbo, the people's representative.

Life might change and life might not, he argued with himself, but what does it matter? One way or the other I will continue to live and somehow, with or without Tumbo, there will be a better tomorrow for the people. This he believed very deeply.

The first minibus he took was to the city centre from where he would connect to Kawempe. The bus station was opposite the imposing Milton Hotel, which was owned by an international chain of hotels. Before independence the whole area housed the Kuzania Bus Service fleet. Later the station was relocated, paving the way for modern skyscrapers such as the Milton Hotel and Kuzania Commercial Bank. He promised himself that if he got a well-paying job, he would give Nzinga a treat in the Milton Hotel.

Touts were shouting at the top of their voices, announcing

the arrival of minibuses to the endless stream of commuters. The revving of the engines, the hooting and the shouts of the touts were a spectacle worth an instant headache. Shaka squeezed on to the over-crowded minibus which took off like a cruise missile. It weaved its way at high speed through the traffic and sharp corners, narrowly missing pedestrians. The driver, a young man hardly twenty years old, was chewing gum and singing along to the music blaring from the loudspeakers as he overtook anything in sight: people, buildings, buses, trucks and cars. Each trip made meant more money, as he was paid a percentage from the day's takings. His concern was not the safety of the passengers but the number of trips he made per day. The drivers were permanently high on cannabis Sativa, or bhang, as they called it. It helped to steel their nerves through the daily ordeals.

On the roundabout near the University of Glitta, the driver jumped a red light and missed a petrol truck by a whisker. Shaka saw the university buildings as they sped past. He looked at them with controlled anger. By now, he would have been in his third and final year of a law degree! But poverty has no mercy and the sooner you come into terms with it the better, or you will ruin yourself, he said to himself.

The minibus was literally flying along the dual carriageway, Freedom Highway. The driver was doing fine and in minutes, he would be on the return journey with another cargo. Often, things went wrong with a burst tyre or when overtaking. There would be the sound of crashing metal and flying glass. As the minibus disintegrated there would be pieces of metal, glass and human flesh strewn on the road and beyond. Hardly anybody survived. It was accepted as one of the hazards of the trade. Of course there were policemen on foot, on motorbikes and in patrol cars all over the place. They were the vultures, getting bribes from the drivers, while the minibuses were carcases. Freedom to do the illegal was bought cheap in Kuzania; bribery was deeply enshrined in the values of society.

The minibus came to a stop with a jolt at Kawempe shopping centre. The tout was proclaiming at the top of his voice 'Glitta, Glitta.' The driver was revving the engine, ready to fly again, oblivious of the beauty and joys of life. Shaka thanked his maker that he had survived the hell run. He decided never, ever to be a minibus driver.

He went to brief Agu and his mother on the events of the day and the likely possibility of a better-paying job, which would guarantee Agu a brand-new blanket and an easier life for his mother. A new life would begin. Innocence, sweet pure innocence, the great mother of misery...

Hon. Tumbo was seated at the back of his Mercedes-Benz, his legs astride on account of the discomfort from the heavy lunch he had just had, resembling a woman very heavy with pregnancy. This afternoon he was the guest of honour at a fund-raising event for St Agnes Church, located in the more affluent areas of his constituency. He was late but that did not bother him. The congregation had the obligation and duty to patiently wait for the guest of honour, the honourable minister for Commerce and Industry.

On arrival he was received by Reverend Mwago, the deacon of the church, amid clapping and music from the church choir. In times of trouble or calamity many seem to turn to the church for solace and they were extending the church to accommodate the growing numbers in the congregation.

Rev. Mwago praised Hon. Tumbo as a good man of God who always answered the call of the needy. He called him a good neighbour and an exemplary leader. Trained in Scotland Rev. Mwago had a way with words and he spoke with a captivating Scottish accent. He talked of the youth who all must fully embrace Jesus as their personal saviour. He admonished them for the growing immorality, prostitution, the smoking of Indian hemp (which he blamed on rising crime rate) and the carnage on the roads at the hands of youthful drivers. He reminded the young men they were the leaders of tomorrow and should emulate the great qualities of their leaders such as Hon. Tumbo, the people's representative.

Rev. Mwago cut a rather saintly figure in his white robes. In the front pew sat his exceedingly beautiful wife, Jennie WaMwago. They had been married close to twenty years now and they had three children. Looking at her you would have thought she was hardly thirty years old. She had a dark and shining complexion and her eyes were big, soft and sexy. Even men of God like Rev. Mwago knew how to choose beautiful women for life companionship. Rev. Mwago had done well for himself, indeed very well. She was forty, mature and vivacious. Hon. Tumbo looked at her and their eyes met. He saw a smile on her face. Evil and sinful thoughts crossed his mind. He quickly brushed them aside. He was on holy grounds, in the public limelight and seated right next to a man of God. He had to concentrate on the matters at hand. He asked God for forgiveness.

The sermon by Rev. Mwago over, the guest of honour,

Hon. Tumbo, took centre stage. As usual he underlined what the government had done for the people even in the very difficult times facing the nation. He blamed short-comings on the IMF, the World Bank, falling crude-oil prices and the weather – especially the El Niño phenomenon. He implored the people to work very hard for the nation to recover. The congregation nodded in agreement and said 'Amen'.

The fund-raising was a great success. Hon. Tumbo had brought a whole bag of money donated by himself, his friends and even the president of the republic. The mention of the president received deafening cheers and another huge 'Amen'. The congregation chipped in and the day was recorded as a memorable blessing. Rev. Mwago moved a vote of thanks for Hon. Tumbo and promised him that the congregation would re-elect him time after time as their member of parliament.

With the function over everybody was invited to refreshments. Hon. Tumbo declined on account of a very busy schedule that afternoon.

He turned to Rev. Mwago. 'Those were very kind words, Reverend! You know, the church and the politicians need to get together more often to shape the destiny of our nation. With cooperation we can bring about great changes in the hard hearts of our people.'

Rev. Mwago could not agree more. 'You deserved every word I said and even more!'

'Your sermon touched people's hearts,' Hon. Tumbo continued. The church has a special role to play in giving our society a new sense of direction. We politicians talk a lot but we do not seem to be carrying the message across. People seem to think we have created hell instead of heaven in this country ... I mean ... on earth,' he quickly corrected himself.

'We will do the very best we can. To me, preaching is a job like any other. I am myself scared stiff by the entire list of dos and don'ts in the scriptures, just like everyone else. My calling is to scare people from doing wrong. I believe heaven and hell are here on earth, in the daily lives of people. I want people to enjoy their heaven on earth while I am at it. When we die, well, that's another story,' said Rev. Mwago.

'What do you mean while you are at it? I thought the calling is for life?' the hon. minister said.

'Well, you see, I joined the seminary by accident. I've been preaching for too long, saying the same things over and over again. It gets boring, tiring and monotonous. I feel time is coming soon for me to call it quits. I want to plunge into the world of business and become a real man. I am tired of driving an old Volkswagen and living from hand to mouth,' Rev. Mwago spoke with the seriousness of a man who has had enough.

'I see,' said Hon. Tumbo. He could see the potential in Rev. Mwago as his new campaign manager in the forth-coming general elections. A preacher on your side can work wonders in political campaigns. 'You come and see me sometime. There are a few openings here and there in business.'

Just then Jennie WaMwago joined them.

'Hon. Minister, this is my wife,' said the reverend.

'It is my great pleasure meeting you, madam,' said Hon. Tumbo, his eyes feasting freely on the angelic face of the most beautiful woman he had ever seen. She was even more beautiful at close range and her hand was soft and warm as he took it in greeting. The rest of her body must be equally as wonderful, he thought. The whole encounter resembled the meeting between King Solomon and the Queen of Sheba, when the king abandoned his

74

350 wives and 700 concubines the moment he laid his eyes on Sheba. Hon. Tumbo was transfixed.

'It is my pleasure and honour to meet you, hon. minister, and thank you very much for coming to our assistance. I am so glad I voted for you in the last elections!' the woman said in all innocence.

'Rev. Mwago, you have a very charming wife, if I may say so. You are a blessed man in many ways! Life has been kind to you! If I were you I would hold on to what you've got and not change a thing! I am glad and grateful you voted for me, Mrs WaMwago. In my next campaign you are invited to be the campaign manager in charge of women's affairs,' Hon. Tumbo offered with a smile.

He had killed two birds with one stone. This afternoon had been a roaring success. Soon, Tumbo thought, he would be enjoying the fruits of his labour and generosity. Power and money are twin gods that work wonders in Kuzania.

Innocence, pure sweet innocence, the great mother of misery, and the road to hell is littered with wandering souls who sold their lives for a farthing.

Jennie WaMwago was not just another woman from the village. Far from it. She had been born with a silver spoon in her mouth and had an impressive record of personal achievements. At the age of six she could play the piano in her father's house and the church organ. In school she always won the music prize, year after year, and had won awards in the national music festival.

The daughter of the first African bishop in Kuzania, she had been educated in the best multiracial schools in the country. As a teenager she began to cultivate a liking for pop music and often sounded better than the original singer. She read about the lives of pop stars, the most fascinating being that of Aretha Franklin. Like her, Aretha was the daughter of a preacher and she developed her voice singing in the church. Jennie knew by heart every record by Aretha Franklin. In school they nicknamed her 'Queen of Soul', like her idol. Soon she had dreams of singing professionally and gaining fame. This led her to join the school band known as the 'Honey Girls'. She became the group's vocalist and the fortunes of the group began to change instantly. Invitations for performance arrived from other schools and soon the band was on national television.

When the bishop learnt of the exploits of his daughter, he was most cross. He asked her to immediately 'stop that rubbish'. She pleaded with her father that she wanted to make a career in music but he would not hear of it. She talked to her teachers about it and they urged her to obey the wishes of her father. She talked to the members of the band and they would not hear of her quitting. They called her father outdated and out-of-touch with reality. 'You are a big girl now and you can do what you want!' This to her was the very sound of reason. Who was her father to dictate her life, anyway?

Jennie had an aunt who lived in the suburbs of the city. She had five children from different fathers. One day Jennie packed her bags, left school and went to live with her. When the bishop was informed that his daughter had run away from school, he was infuriated. Afraid to inform the police on account of his high standing in society, he asked his wife to search quietly for her.

Soon he found out that she was living in her aunt's house, the woman the bishop always referred to as 'that harlot' due to her drinking and string of men. He went raving mad, but all attempts to persuade Jennie to return home were futile.

Tall, black and exceptionally beautiful, Jennie stood heads above other women. Her eyes were big, black and seductive. When she smiled she was electrifying, with her strong white teeth and the deep dimples in her cheeks. Her breasts were fully developed and her waist was slim, which exaggerated the size and roundness of her sexy buttocks. Jennie became a big hit in night-clubs. People came to hear her sweet voice as well as to look at her charms. They gave her money, drinks and loaded her with praise. It all went to her tender head. She started wearing heavy make-up and had developed a taste for brandy and coke 'to ease the tension of the long hours of performing'. Her aunt was delighted about her new career, since she could go to her performances free of charge as her manager.

It was after performing in front of an international audience at the Milton Hotel that an overseas promoter approached her. The following day, a contract was signed. Soon Jennie had her passport, visa and air ticket and was performing in London in nightclubs from night to night, weeks without end. She had also become the lover of the producer. When not performing they were in the pub drinking or in the house making love. At first she enjoyed it very much but soon it became boring. Jennie had been given very little in terms of money by the producer as she was told her salary was safely banked for her dressing and jewellery once she broke into big time. She was to learn that the man was not a producer at all but a pimp who had exploited many African artists from Southern and West Africa. There was a huge row and Jennie was thrown out. Left to fend for herself Jennie found it very difficult to get singing contracts. It was as though there was a cartel that controlled black performers and, if you were not in it, you didn't get a contract. Jennie began frequenting bars, broke and hungry. Soon she was prey to many lusty men and, finally, she found herself in Soho, the red-light district of London.

Her father was worried. He had had no news of his daughter for over two years. He only knew that she was in London pursuing a music career. One of the young men from the seminary was going to the United Kingdom to pursue a degree in divinity. His name was Reverend Mwago. The bishop asked the reverend to check on the whereabouts of his daughter. Six months passed. One day while visiting London from his college in Scotland, he visited fellow Kuzania students and enquiring about the bishop's daughter, one of them told him where to find her.

Reverend Mwago had made a promise to the bishop and he was determined to keep it. That evening he went to Soho to look for her. He learnt that there were many women from Kuzania operating in Soho. Soon he was directed to the pub from where Jennie carried her trade. He found her at the counter looking like a creature from a horror film. Her hair was painted gold, she was wearing thick red lipstick and she was clad in next to nothing. It was just as well that he was not wearing his white collar, otherwise it would have been a terribly embarrassing evening for a man of God.

Reverend Mwago told her about his mission. She was receptive and looked sorry for herself. She, however, told him point-blank that she was not ready to go back home. So he gave her his telephone number and address in Scotland. At least he had something to tell to the bishop – not the whole truth, though, oh no; sometimes the truth is too heartbreaking.

Jennie felt relieved when Mwago left. Somebody cared about her well being! She thought Rev. Mwago was the kindest man on earth. She remembered the good times she had had in Kuzania before she was overpowered by madness in her dream of stardom. Having lost her voice through drinking, she knew it was all over.

'Waiter, give me a double brandy and coke,' she ordered.

'Hello, babe,' came a booming voice of one of her regular customers. 'I'll pay for that, waiter. Put that on my bill and give me a double scotch on the rocks.'

It was business as usual.

Months passed by and Rev. Mwago did not receive a reply to his letter to the bishop. He wondered whether the bishop had read between the lines and didn't want to hear any more about his daughter. To his utter surprise he then received a letter from Jennie. Since their encounter she had found the light and embraced Jesus Christ. She had begun to think about home and all those who cared for her. Ashamed of herself, she was seriously contemplating returning home 'for good or bad'. However, she wanted a place to recuperate before returning home and wondered if the good reverend could put her up for a few days. Without giving it a second thought he wrote back, requesting her to come as soon as she was able.

And so it was that a week later Jennie arrived in Rev. Mwago's flat. She had no make-up on and her hair was no longer golden; it was jet black in Afro style. At first the reverend could not even recognise her. Her former beauty was beginning to show.

Jennie was very useful in the flat, washing and cooking. A week passed, a month passed and she did not announce her intended date of departure. Neither did he ask. He had found a companion and a house help, just like Adam had Eve in the garden of Eden. They became good friends. As in the garden of Eden they began to enjoy the apple. Six months later they were married. Jennie WaMwago, as she was known from the day of their wedding, became a member of the local church choir and won praise from the congregation for her sweet and melodious voice, which seemed to get better by the week. Their first child was born in Scotland.

When the bishop received news of the wedding, he was delighted. 'The lost sheep has at last come to safety,' he told his wife.

Jennie WaMwago was not just another village woman.

After the fund-raising event, Hon. Tumbo was to proceed to another function, this time as the guest speaker in a dinner hosted by the United Africa Club at the Milton Hotel for various international investors. As the car cruised towards the city, the thoughts that had germinated in the church began to sprout in his mind. He had seen a lot of women in his lifetime but none quite like Jennie WaMwago. She seemed to have special qualities of beauty and warmth and a wild look about her that indicated she was not necessarily a devoted Christian. He knew many such women who went to the church in the morning and were in the bars in the afternoon. Such women, he thought, were true reflections of Eve in the garden of Eden. They were the aggressive type, who said a lot with their eyes and their bodies. Many men of God had been exposed in sexual scandals involving other people's wives of this character.

If Jennie WaMwago turns out to be as sweet, why, the reverend is expendable, Tumbo thought. Come tomorrow! he said to himself.

Reverend Mwago, meanwhile, had never reconciled himself with his stupid and rash action all those years ago. He had married a common backstreet whore! He knew it, his friends knew it. He was increasingly embarrassed whenever he met them. They told him, 'Once a whore, always a whore and, sooner or later, the call of the wild will win her back.' One can forgive, pretend or overlook but one can never forget or mask reality. But he had been lonely in Scotland and, being a man of God, he had not been exposed to the callousness of women; she had come into his life when he was seriously thinking of marriage. As well as being extremely beautiful, she had shown him wonders of the flesh that had made his body tremble with desire. He was a captive. He had not married out of love, no, no, no; love was not given a chance to show its face. By the time he recovered his senses he had a wedding ring on his finger. Like Adam, there was nowhere to hide. He had sworn that he would not live the rest of his life in shame. He would disengage first from the church and thereafter from her. Sometimes he cried quietly at night, wondering what curse it was that had led to this shame. He took consolation in his plans to leave the church and get into business. After all, Hon. Tumbo, the minister for Commerce and Industry, had guaranteed him success. As soon as he freed himself from the church, he would kick her out of his life. She would be left lonely and desperate once more, paying for past sins. Heaven and hell are on earth as part of everyday life and the sins committed on earth will be punished on earth. He was going to plant a new garden for himself and his children in which the likes of Jennie would be prohibited immigrants. He was a man recharged, rearing to make a new and wonderful start.

I tell you, the road to hell is crowded with 'believers' who live and die like moles out of their burrows, marching to eternal damnation in a hot planet.

From the bus stop in Kawempe Shaka plodded through the mud and crossed a seasonal stream, which with El Niño had become a wide, shallow river. He went to his mother's house. He could hear her voice as she sang:

> This world is not my home,
> I am just passing through
> My treasures are laid up
> Somewhere beyond the blue
> The angels beckon me...

He knocked on the door before the angels could take her away.

'Come in,' came the happy but frail voice.

'Mother, how are you?' he asked.

'Very much better than before. The medicine I am taking is very effective and my coughing is almost gone. I am feeling much stronger,' she said joyfully.

'I am happy for you, very happy indeed,' Shaka told his mother. But he had been told that when a very sick person shows signs of abnormal recuperation, it is a bad sign. Death has a habit of giving the victim a few days of false joy before it strikes. 'I called on grandpa and we had a good chat,' he continued.

'I know all about it. Well, what can I say? Hunger knows no shame. You have my blessings. You've already sacrificed too much without grumbling. There will be no fight between us,' she said.

'I must go home to wash my clothes for tomorrow,' said Shaka, getting ready to leave.

'Sit down, son, what's the hurry? Whatever shirt or trousers you wear tomorrow will not matter. The word of Hon. Tumbo will suffice to give you a job even if you dress in rags. These men have become gods. Let's share a cup of tea and pray.'

Soon Shaka left for Agu's house. He found him in his house, warming himself by the fire.

'What took you so long?' Agu asked.

'You know it takes two bus rides from here to Hon. Tumbo's house. When I got there the policeman would not let me in!'

'Young man, there is a lot you've got to learn. The dog of a rich man knows it is guarding a big man. It, too, is big. Look at the mongrels we have in this village! Anyway, did you give him the letter?'

'Yes, I did and tomorrow morning I will be reporting to his office. If all goes well you will have your new blanket very soon!' There was excitement in Shaka's voice.

'Very well, my boy, I am happy for you. You know, devils never shave their heads, that's why they have long dreadlocks but, let me tell you, no devil lives to the grave before someone has cut its hair. Today I cut the hair of the devil Tumbo. He will give you that job or I will destroy him come the next elections.'

That night there was drizzle, no thunder and no

lightning. The skies seemed to have declared a cease-fire with the earth. For once in a very long time Shaka slept very soundly.

4

Sowing Wild Oats

If the Good Lord returned to Kuzania and asked the people what they wished for as a special gift, there would be two categories of answers. The general population or the masses, the people who live in Kawempe, would ask for work. To them, well-paid employment is the foundation of a noble life, one in which you can provide with dignity the basic needs of your family, such as food, clothing, shelter, education, medicine and an occasional drink with friends. It would satisfy the conditions of heaven on earth.

The second group of Kuzanians would ask for money (preferably in convertible currency), eternal perpetuation of the status quo, inheritance of power by their children and more comforts. Believe you me, this group would ask for manna from heaven, for slaves to pick the manna for them and for the protection of the manna from unruly and hungry masses.

Kuzania is split, so split that society cannot see eye to eye on any single subject or speak with one voice on any issue. Even the ruling class, which was once seemingly united, is breaking up into factions, divided by region, tribe, academic level, wealth, age and religion.

These divisions are not so pronounced among the poor, the disinherited and the dehumanised masses. They speak the language of poverty and hunger and their ranks are solid.

The two worlds are on a collision course. They operate on different frequencies, like people from different planets. The world of the rich and the powerful in Kuzania seems to operate on long-range wavelengths. They have communication gadgets such as telephones, faxes, e-mails and mobile phones. They are so powerful that their network is worldwide and it works twenty-four hours a day. Kuzania has developed a name for itself in the world as the regional centre for communications, business and finance, thanks to its strategic location, natural endowment and the ingenuity of its leaders – people such as Mr Tumbo, the hon. minister for Commerce and Industry, the people's representative. These are great strides by any standards – or they are artificial trappings in a country where people do not have sufficient water, shelter, health facilities, schools, roads, employment and food to eat. But that's another world. That world is a marginal world, one that does not feature in the world market. Its very existence is a nuisance. The people in that world make demands that the government can never hope to cope with.

Hon. Tumbo arrived at the Milton Hotel to deliver the address on 'The Economic Future of Kuzania' to the United Africa Club. Seated on the high table was Mr Nelson from the American State Department, in charge of third world development – or was it fourth world? Nelson had cropped hair that stood straight on his skull, like golden needles. His eyes were bright and sharp. They seemed to penetrate the minds of others like an X-ray.

Most seriously, they were X-raying Hon. Tumbo, evaluating him in the face of the predicted forthcoming crisis of succession in Kuzania.

'We want more foreign investment in Kuzania. Our privatisation programme as agreed with the IMF and the World Bank is already ahead of schedule.' There were nods of agreement from the representatives of two major institutions, amid wild cheers and stomping of feet. Hon. Tumbo was grinning so much that you could count all thirty-two teeth. Nelson also had a grin of approval and was nodding his massive head up and down.

'The government is disengaging from all commercial ventures and we will not dream of nationalising a single venture for the next hundred years or until kingdom come. Our natural resources and our industries are at your disposal! We have also liberalised the foreign-exchange regime and you can take out as much money as you want. The Bill outlawing strikes and trade unions has passed through the third reading in parliament and we expect it to become law before the end of the month. In this manner we hope to protect investors from unreasonable demands for higher wages. If these measures are not sufficient, the government is receptive to proposals to improve the investment climate.'

Mr Nelson's local contact was William Stans. In recent years Stans had overshadowed the American ambassador in his dealings with the government of Kuzania. He had become the key link between Glitta and Washington, between White House and State House. He took the floor and narrated how he had come to trust the hon. minister's vision of a better tomorrow for Kuzania, which had resulted in their very close working relationship. It had 'deepened and strengthened the ties between Kuzania and the United States of America, for the mutual benefit of the two peoples.' He termed Hon. Tumbo as 'a brilliant economist, a bright son of Africa, an honest man with a mission, a clear vision and wonderful to work with.'

Nelson then took to the floor. He praised the political stability in Kuzania and its able and mature leadership. He called the country a model of democracy, an oasis of peace in a sea of trouble, endowed prodigiously by nature and with an educated and hard-working pool of labour. These, he said, were the necessary and sufficient conditions for foreign investment and for the economic take-off of Kuzania.

So Kuzania became an IFO, or Identified Flying Object, ready for take-off in a test flight with aliens at the controls. If all went well this IFO would not be hijacked by devil rebels and would not suffer an irreparable crash landing in the sea of troubles near Bermuda. To Nelson, all systems were perfect and the final countdown had begun for the blast. The only hitch to be rectified was a minor one; an ailing president. This could be easily fixed by remote control with an amiable successor.

The United Africa Club remained a mystery to many people, like a well-guarded cult. The centrepiece was Hon. Tumbo, whose bank accounts were fat enough to run the country for many financial years without the help of the IMF and the World Bank. However, on behalf of the nation, he was the leading international beggar. His speech would hit the press with a big splash, headlined 'Africa Awakens at Last'. So big and powerful had Hon. Tumbo become that he was above the law. How far Tumbo would go remains to be seen. He was gunning for vice-presidency first and he had been assured of international support from very powerful world centres.

William Stans, the American link, was a truly remarkable man, whose main qualities were cunning intelligence and brute force, which he deployed interchangeably as the situation demanded. He could hypnotise, cajole, seduce, love and murder with utmost ease; a truly intriguing man. He was very satisfied with the results of the gathering of the United Africa Club and especially the congratulations heaped on him by Nelson.

He had read somewhere that 'the African is a child', and he remains so until death. Africans never grow up, whatever position they hold, regardless of their level of education. He was their godfather and he would teach them how to grow up, especially the rebellious ones threatening to rock the boat. William Stans marvelled at the fast changes in his status and fortune. He was thoroughly enjoying it all.

Hon. Tumbo, the minister for Commerce and Industry and the people's representative, had that evening demonstrated the benevolence of the African child in his speech. Kuzania was there for grabs. Kuzania was ready for takeover, not take-off, he smiled to himself. In this takeover, Hon. Tumbo was the key man and he must be protected and promoted. Stans would personally guarantee that Tumbo became the next president of Kuzania. To him, the crisis of succession was no more than a figment of imagination in the heads of those who did not understand the mighty quality of money, power and guns. William Stans was shaping the future of Kuzania for the benefit of himself and others, in the name of peace, stability, development and democracy.

Kuzania, he said to himself, the oasis of peace in a turbulent region, the garden of Eden in hell. He was the manager in the garden but Eve had not been cloned, not just yet. Kuzania, the IFO with an uncertain trajectory, in the orbit of chaos.

Some days are very critical in the calendar of one's life. Such days include the day you were born, the day you were circumcised, the day you married and the day you died. Shaka was going to add another important day to this list; the day he went to get a job from Hon. Tumbo.

That Monday morning Shaka dressed himself the best he could from his assortment of secondhand clothes. He plodded through the mud and joined the throng of commuters. If all went well, there was going to be a new beginning for himself and his mother.

As usual the minibus sped down the road towards the city in characteristic reckless fashion. It was upon getting off the minibus that Shaka saw the state of his shoes, plastered with red mud. He could not report to Mr Tumbo's office like that. He sat on a stool at a street corner and a shoeshine boy polished his shoes. That cost him his return fare; he would have to walk home.

Gaining entry into the office of the president building was a nightmare, as policemen demanded something small in the way of a bribe. He had nothing to give. The entrance into the building was equally well guarded. It took a telephone call to the office of the hon. minister before he was allowed in. Had he not had the luck to polish his shoes, he certainly would not have got that far. Hon. Tumbo's secretary, a well-dressed woman, told him to sit down and wait. He was given a newspaper to read. He read the story of a new beginning in Kuzania, to be spearheaded by international capital with Hon. Tumbo as the pilot of the scheme.

Shaka was finally instructed to enter the minister's office. His conversation with the minister was short, cold and unnatural. He was asked about his background. Hon. Tumbo had known Shaka's father and mother as they had grown up together in the village of Kawempe. He was then asked about his level of education. Hon. Tumbo called him stupid for turning down the offer from the university, adding, however, that education was not everything as he himself had done very well without a university degree.

The phone rang and Hon. Tumbo stood up. As Tumbo answered the call, Shaka heard him say, 'Let her wait for a minute. Could you get me Mr Valaris?' Hon. Tumbo sat rocking in his chair, tapping his fat fingers on the table. There was a smile on his face. In next to no time Valaris was on the line. 'I am sending you a young man for employment. He will bring a letter with him.'

Hon. Tumbo then dictated a short letter to his secretary over the telephone. 'Make it snappy,' he commanded. He jumped to his feet and Shaka wondered whether he had the intention of escorting him to the door or shaking his hand. Instead Hon. Tumbo went to the window and gazed outside. Confused, Shaka heard his own voice: 'Thank you very much, sir, thank you ever so much.'

'Go!' came the single command. Shaka opened the door and did as commanded. In came Mrs Jennie WaMwago.

'Welcome, welcome,' Hon. Tumbo was heard to say as the door was closed.

The secretary typing on her machine seemed angry

at something. She was not the same jolly woman Shaka had seen a couple of minutes earlier. She mumbled something like, 'Another one!'

Armed with the letter, Shaka left for Kuzania Insurance Company, as was marked on the envelope. He walked fast to get there for a reason he could not explain and was out of breath when he arrived.

'My name is Shaka ... I ... want to see Mr Valaris, the general manager,' he announced.

'He is expecting you,' came the reply.

There was not much of an interview. All he was asked was his relationship to Hon. Tumbo and, for once, he lied. He told Valaris that Hon. Tumbo was his uncle.

'Lucky man,' came the response.

The hon. minister sat in the rocking chair face to face with Jennie WaMwago, the most beautiful woman he had ever seen. This morning she seemed more beautiful than the last time he had seen her after the fund-raising meeting.

'I am glad you could find the time to come,' said the hon. minister.

'On the contrary, I am glad you could find the time to receive me,' she responded.

The charms of Mrs WaMwago all came crashing like a storm. The hon. minister sat there like a zombie, transfixed, trying to clear his throat.

'It must be extremely exciting working as a minister! I was reading your fantastic speech before the investors, in the local daily, as I came here. Is it true that money will be poured here from all corners of the world?' she asked.

Hon. Tumbo took a handkerchief to wipe beads of

sweat from his forehead. 'Yes and no. Yes, because investors will be investing here in large numbers and no, because money will not be there to be picked like manna from heaven. Some people will certainly be employed but it will take a long time for the rest to feel the effect.'

'But surely there must be some immediate benefits,' she wondered.

'Yes, there will be for those politically correct and well connected – and you are one of them!' he declared with a smile.

'Me? Why me ... I mean, how?'

'That's the reason you are here, isn't it? To do business. Believe you me; it is not all that easy and you have to sweat quite a bit,' he said.

'I would do anything to get into the world of the rich and famous,' she responded.

'Anything?' he asked with a cheeky smile.

'I mean, work hard, you know,' she said guardedly. 'You know, in all my life I have dreamt of big things, fame, money and comfort. Somehow, they have eluded me.'

'Yes, I saw it in your eyes the very first time I looked at you in the church. I said to myself, there is a beautiful woman who could do with some polishing to bring out the sparkle in the jewel. What happened to your dreams?'

'It is a long story, one I would rather not tell.' She suddenly looked pale and a shadow of herself. Tumbo had touched a raw nerve.

'Look, look, cheer up! Don't worry, very soon, all that will be forgotten,' he reassured her. 'Take these tender documents with you. I want you to tender supplies for the national hospital. The items and the prices are listed on a separate sheet.'

'But I have no budget and no experience in these things,' she protested.

'Just put the figures in as indicated. I will take care of the rest. By the way, I would rather you use your maiden name instead of that of your husband. Sign Ms not Mrs. Return them here on Wednesday morning without fail.'

Something in Jennie WaMwago gave way. With Hon. Tumbo's guarantee she knew this was going to be a huge financial windfall. Her day of greatness was knocking on the door. She was going to sign the documents Ms Jennie and her husband would never know the extent of the fortune. She was going to reshape her life. Of late, her husband had started acting strangely, talking in his sleep, crying, calling her all sorts of names. She needed to guarantee her future. Her soft eyes, fixed on the hon. minister, were like two shining marbles. Her face was radiant with warmth. Softly and sexily she leant towards the minister and, with a naughty tongue sticking out of her curled mouth, she said, 'Thank you very much. One day I will repay you for your kindness.'

The hand that the hon minister stretched out in farewell was wet with sweat.

'I ... I ... I will see you on Wednesday.'

Shaka did not follow the main road on his way back home. There was a path along Glitta River that led to Kawempe and beyond. Both sides of the river are inhabited by the well-to-do for the first five kilometres. A section is set aside to preserve indigenous trees, called Arboretum Forest. Seven kilometres upstream, there is a steep break in topography, marking the separation of the plains from the highlands. While Glitta city centre is in the plains,

Kawempe and the western suburbs of the city are in the highlands. Kahindo Falls marks this break between the rich side of the city and the slums. Its drop is no less than forty metres. The water as it hits the pond at the bottom looks like dripping flour, which becomes foam and then water as the river meanders downstream towards Glitta city centre. Its organised grace is a contrast to the disorganisation on the Great Northern Highway running parallel a few kilometres away.

The drop is also marked by massive black rocks of granite, which look like giant monuments. Shaka decided to rest here for a while. There were two boulders that formed a cave big enough to house four people. In this temporary comfort generously offered by nature, he was shielded from the sun and forgot the pangs of hunger and the fatigue that had tormented his body, as he walked from the city centre. Behind him was Kawempe, the slums. In front of him were the dwellings of the rich on both sides of the valley. This juxtaposition awakened in him thoughts on the differences between the haves and the have nots in Kuzania. Nowhere was this contrast more pronounced than between his life and that of Nzinga.

Nzinga must be the luckiest girl in the world, he thought. She did not know the meaning of poverty. She did not know the meaning of hunger or patched secondhand clothes. Her world was one of flowers, music, good food, pocket money, servants, bodyguards, fat dogs, cars and theatres. She lived in heaven on earth! His world defied meaning. It was the world of the deprived, disinherited, dehumanised, the world of the scum of the earth.

He was one of those sliding towards an early death,

or so it was until this morning. 'In these days, it is a question of who knows who.' Agu was right; the days of tribalism and nepotism had arrived to replace merit, qualifications and knowledge. In other countries jobs are advertised and interviews held and the most competent are employed. In Kuzania goons and semi-illiterates had been placed in high positions of responsibility beyond their competence.

For now, Nzinga's world and his own were divided by a big chasm, wider than Glitta River and deeper than the Kahindo Falls. So he was going to take her to Kawempe or buy her a card to say thank you and that would be all. He felt angry with himself and with society, that two young people could not be good friends because of the values imposed by power and money. What if his father had lived to become a big man in government, the head of the armed forces of Kuzania? He would have met Nzinga as an equal and probably they would have fallen in love and he would have married her! Those were ifs. Now he was a beggar and beggars cannot be choosers. He should be grateful for small mercies, he rationalised. It was time to wake up from his dreams and proceed to the village to break the good news to Agu and his mother that, at last, he had found a job and the world around them was to change for the better. He was hungry and he prayed that either at his mother's or Agu's place he would find something to eat.

The world is full of bastards, street urchins and parking-meter boys sniffing glue and smoking Indian hemp. They grow up to become adults if they are not shot dead by Indians or the police reserves, run over by minibuses, frozen to death in the cold gutters at night or killed in fights over garbage.

I would like you to meet my friend Musa. Musa is a very light-skinned man, they call him a half-caste as he is neither black nor white. He is a tailor by profession, specialising in making clothes for the poor and especially in patch-ups. He is a master of secondhand motleys. For a hobby, of which I gather everyone has one, he is a drunkard. His background has remained a mystery to this day and each day he tells a different story about his past. Maybe he has something to hide although he swears by the Tusker bottle that it is not so. By his accent I'd say he comes from the coastal region of Kuzania but he swears he is from the plains and only lived on the coast for a short spell.

If Musa could find time to wash himself regularly and generally tidy himself up, I am sure he could land himself a job as a comedian in the theatres of Glitta or on TV. He has the looks, the disposition and the language of those who make megabucks by just acting silly. But Musa has no time for such trash. He is happy being a simple tailor in Majengo's old town, with a bottle of beer after a hard day's work. At forty-five, he has no wife or even a regular girlfriend, no bank account! Yet he is always happy. One can safely conclude that my friend Musa has mastered the art of simple life.

Listening to his stories – and they are many – one gains the impression of a man who is very self-confident, who can find solutions to any problem except his own. They call him a 'doctor in rags'. He can offer you a cure to your social, political and economic problems. If you are suffering from such common and silly ailments as a headache or any of the diseases of the rich such as gout, his prescription is always the same: 'drink, man, drink and forget these things ever existed.'

'Look,' he says, 'while you live as a man on earth, get your full share of what this hell has to offer and don't be shackled by little things such as body aches, a wife, a preacher or a politician. Live a life of total freedom, a life without worries, each and every day for the rest of your miserable life.' It is a simple philosophy, one that has endeared him to many whose lives have ceased to have meaning. Simplicity in life, he believes most strongly, is the foundation of true happiness.

There is a story he tells of a sailor who visited him while he was a tailor in Mimosa, making Kaunda suits. The sailor asked Musa to make him a suit in less than twelve hours as his ship was about to set sail. He offered to pay twice the going price. Musa declined and told the sailor that it took at least three working days to make such a suit. The sailor told Musa that if he worked very hard, he could do it in twelve hours. 'After all, God made heaven and earth in only six days,' the sailor had insisted. Musa smiled and said to him, 'Look, man, take a good look at the earth and see the mess it has turned out to be. Do you want a suit like that?' The sailor left Mimosa without his Kaunda suit. Musa moved to Glitta soon afterwards. If the sailor ever locates Musa in the old town and has three days to spare, Musa swears he owes him a Kaunda suit, the best he ever made.

I want Musa to be your good friend. But now you complain that you don't even know *me*! Christ, how long do I have to be with you? My name is Everywhere, I am the wind that sneaks through the cracks in the walls to hidden places. I am the soul without a human body. I am the spirit that helps the struggling masses in Kuzania. I am of the stock of the good in the fight against evil. At times I enter into a human body and try to help. But the world is very cruel and many in whose bodies I lived have been killed or jailed or maimed in the name of state security or such other trash.

I remember once I entered the body of a peasant farmer in the highlands to test the chance of a good man surviving in Kuzania. I found the poor man working hard on his land, growing cabbages, carrots, potatoes and tomatoes and many other good things. The labour he was expending was truly superhuman, and his yields were exceptionally good due to tender care. The middlemen from Glitta would come and buy his produce at throwaway prices. He was none the better for his labour, though his limbs ached with his efforts. He had made himself their slave. You'd better believe me, slavery still exists to this very day.

I entered his body and made him sell his land with the promise that, armed with money and his energetic body, he could make a fortune in the city of Glitta. He got on to a train and we were coming to the city, filled with wonderful ideas. But before we hit the city I realised the folly of the scheme and departed him, leaving him to his own sagacity. I followed him closely. The man thought of business and kept a kiosk. He was doing very well until he discovered bars and the women of Glitta. There he was, broke and looking for a job, any kind of a job. Had he met Musa quite early, he would have been all right, but it is still not too late.

I sometimes wish I had not led the poor soul from his farm. He had been happy working on his land and had enough to eat and somewhere to sleep. Now he lives in the slums, doing any kind of odd job that comes his way. The drift to the city was not the solution. Perhaps I should have made him a leader of peasant farmers, founder of a cooperative movement that sold produce directly to Glitta. I have only established the innocence and the gullibility of the poor but I've not helped the situation; if anything, I've made it worse for him. The city is not for the poor, I tell you. He is a ruined man, but then who isn't? We are all ruined. I cannot help one individual, I need a whole battalion to bring about change. What we need is a new sense of direction. I was only trying to help. Let's leave him to Musa and all will be well in the end. Musa's eyes, like mine, can see what is hidden. His sense can smell things the eyes would rather not see nor the ear hear. Sometimes I like dwelling in him. I believe it is mutually beneficial but, this time, I will be more careful with my experiment. I like him just the way he is.

His mother was a harlot in Mimosa, and his father must have been a sailor from some distant land where skins are light. He is a half-caste bastard, no less and no more. Before he could walk he was abandoned into the tender and caring arms of his old grandmother, who lived on the plains. As he grew up he spoke the language of these people, though he did not look like them. They teased him everywhere he went: 'bastard, child of a harlot, conceived on a quid.' He left school and his caring grandmother and went to Mimosa to look for his mother. He did not find her and became a parking-meter boy, sniffing glue and smoking Indian hemp. They were many in that street family, both boys and girls, in a wonderful world without any worries. They begged, ate from dustbins and slept in gutters. But he wanted to be a somebody and found work helping an old tailor who taught him how to make Kaunda suits and repair old clothes. By and by, the old tailor died and Musa inherited the business.

Musa loves and hates harlots. He loves them because many of them are ex-parking-meter girls and, to him, they are his real sisters. He hates them because he knows, sooner or later, they will be mothers of bastards whom they will abandon to suffer, just like him. They fascinate him and he thinks by understanding them maybe he can understand the despicable behaviour of his mother and, in the end, forgive her.

Near his shack in Majengo is a big brothel. It is a modern building owned by a tycoon, the permanent secretary, ministry of health. It is filthy. It is the only house with electricity, water and telephone in the old town. It has a bar that sells beer, whisky and brandy and a restaurant specialising in roast goat meat, fried chicken, fish and chips. Its rooms are self-contained. They have a bathroom inside and each has a telephone extension. They are available for short periods or all night, for a fee. Most times they are booked in advance. Some high-class twilight women rent the rooms on a monthly basis. These are the girlfriends of big shots who frequent the place after a hard day steering the affairs of the state. Come twelve o'clock midnight and you will find parked in the yard sleek new vehicles. Musa knows them all, both the big shots and the women in the brothel. Once in a while, he drinks there.

In the bar the language one hears is obscene. It makes Musa think it is impossible to forgive his mother. When the jukebox starts blaring, the favourite song is 'The Milk Song'. It has a catchy chorus, which goes, 'Keep swinging your body up and down, up and down, side to side and up then down, then shake the bastard and milk him dry.' I have never heard the song on the radio, but there you are. There are many worlds on this earth we call our home.

The harlots are not stupid. With the proceeds of their labour they have become landlords in the slums. They own minibuses, some of them own cars. They are victims of the social order – or disorder – in Kuzania and they contribute a great deal in perfecting its image as the undisputed Sodom and Gomorrah on earth. Musa's mother is one of them, but he does not know which one. There is a rich one who really likes Musa. When business is quiet, she invites him for a 'quickie' in her room. She drives a Toyota, which was imported duty-free by her boyfriend, the managing director of the department of Inland Revenue. The man swims in money and she loves him very much.

With Aids around Musa has decided to be less available as a plaything. Maybe he should wear condoms, but he cannot abstain from sex, however hard he tries. 'Eat your hay in silence if you can find any,' a small voice keeps ringing in his ear.

But, tell me frankly, you know my friend Musa well now, don't you? Thank you. Pray, hold him dear to your heart. He is a very good man. If only Musa was more conscious of the wonderful opportunities Kuzania has to offer, he could become a megabuck comedian! But he won't! He is not like Hon. Tumbo, the honourable minister for Commerce and Industry, the people's representative, who will leave no stone unturned in his quest for money and power, then lift every skirt to release the tension of his national responsibilities. Both Musa and Tumbo are honourable citizens of Kuzania, with a common destiny in this land.

When Shaka arrived in the offices of Kuzania Insurance Company, he was shown his desk. It was in a big hall, seating clerks and section heads or managers. He was a claims clerk. He was trained by a young man called Apunda, who taught him what insurance was all about and how to use a dictaphone. Apunda was a very patient and kind teacher. Shaka knew he was in safe hands. On the first day Apunda took him for lunch. As they were eating Apunda advised Shaka to do something about his appearance. He talked to him about making sure his clothes matched. Shaka responded that all he had were a couple of old shirts and trousers and a single coat. Apunda informed him of a good tailor in Majengo, the old town, who could make him a couple of suits on credit. Apunda bought fabric for two suits and after work they went to seek out Musa. Apunda paid the deposit and Shaka promised to settle the bill in full at the end of the month. Musa invited them for a drink and they stepped into the bar-cum-brothel in Majengo. That was how Shaka met Musa and became the proud owner of two brand-new suits.

On Wednesday Jennie WaMwago reported to Hon. Tumbo's office with the tender application forms duly filled and signed, 'Ms Jennie'. Hon. Tumbo was not in but he had left a message, asking her to meet him at noon for lunch.

At twelve noon Jennie WaMwago met Hon. Tumbo in the revolving restaurant of Glitta's conference centre. She was treated to a sumptuous four-course meal, the best she had ever had. With the meal came wine and, after the food, came brandy. She was feeling very good. She had arrived. She observed that Hon. Tumbo's eating manners were primitive. He talked with his mouth full and stuffed in too much food. You can take a man out of the village but you cannot take the village out of the man! she mused in silence.

After the meal Hon. Tumbo suggested they change venue to his private suite at the Milton Hotel, where he would go over the documents. WaMwago was given money to take a taxi and Hon. Tumbo rode separately in his official vehicle.

Soon Hon. Tumbo was seated on the sofa with a glass of brandy in his hand and a grin across his face. WaMwago was invited to sit next to him, a glass of brandy in her hand.

'We have plenty of time to scrutinise the documents. I guess we should get to know each other better as we are going to be working very closely,' he said. 'I am going to make you very rich, the richest woman in Glitta!' he declared. 'Come and sit here.'

Like a somnambulist WaMwago found herself seated on the bed. Her body begin to tremble, her will breaking in the face of Tumbo's might.

After they made love, Tumbo lay on his side stroking her body. 'I'm going to make you rich, the richest woman in Glitta,' he kept repeating.

At first WaMwago felt guilty about what she had done but she rationalised that otherwise she would get nowhere with Tumbo. In view of her past experience, it was a small sacrifice but she was now a married woman – or was she? Had she not signed the forms Ms Jennie? This was her new status, with a promise of success. Soho had been different, she had done it for survival. This was special, it promised heaven.

Soon, Hon. Tumbo was on her again and, this time, she showed him what she was made of. It left him mesmerised, weak and confused.

Finally, WaMwago left the suite but not before Hon.

Tumbo had given her an amount of money 'for the taxi home'. She did not count it but she knew it was substantial. She would open a bank account with it, a business account.

5

Across the Divide

Shaka first collected one suit from Musa. The fact that he now had a brand-new suit to call his own felt wonderful. It signified the dawning of good things to come. Employment is the biggest blessing a man can have. Deny him employment and you reduce him to a worthless soul, ready to turn to anything just to feed himself. Shaka owed his new manhood to many people but most of all to Nzinga. Tumbo had fulfilled his side of the bargain, not out of courtesy or humanity, but simply to please his daughter. Whatever the case was, Shaka felt a new man.

He settled down in his work easily with the help of Apunda. As promised he bought a couple of things for himself and for his mother. Agu was all smiles with his new blanket and a warm overcoat. But by the end of his third month at work, he still had no savings. One evening Apunda told him there was easy money to be made in claiming broken windscreens and writing off cars that didn't have a scratch. He promised to bring him into the 'operations', which Musa had initiated him into. This new scheme was all Shaka needed to move his mother out of Kawempe. Apunda told him,

'Our leaders are eating left, right and centre without shame. We, too, are justified in eating something small. Do you think with your salary you can ever hope to move out of Kawempe or buy a car like me? Grow up, man, grow up.' The children of a spitting cobra are not taught by the mother how to spit. It comes naturally!

To Shaka, Kuzania and Glitta were more complicated than anyone could imagine. Security of employment was illusionary and one needed to augment one's salary in order to be a man. What a world, he said to himself. He still had a lot to learn. In all the confusion he had not called Nzinga. He had nothing to offer her.

It was morning and Shaka had a pile of files and a dictaphone.

'Excuse me, sir,' said a customer. 'May I have a claim form? I've just had an accident.'

Shaka gave the customer a claim form but the man had a problem filling it out, as his hand was injured. 'Let me fill it out for you,' Shaka offered.

As Shaka filled out the form, Apunda came to say hello to the customer, an old acquaintance.

'How bad was the accident?' Apunda enquired.

'It is not much, but I think it is slightly higher than the excess.'

'In that case I advise you to repair the vehicle yourself because, together with the excess, you are going to lose your no-claims bonus, which is fifty per cent,' Apunda advised.

'Apunda,' the man said, 'life out there has become very difficult for us. There is a slump in business with banks charging forty per cent interest on loans. I am, to tell you the truth, broke right now. I would rather lose the fifty per cent no-claims bonus than borrow from the bank to repair my vehicle.' The man looked desperate.

'Which police station is handling the case?'

'I have not reported the accident yet. There was no third party involved. I skidded off the road and hit a tree. You know the state of our roads, and it has not been made any better by the rains.'

Apunda called the man aside. Within no time, the man was gone, leaving Shaka with the accident claim form. Shaka did not understand why the insured had changed his mind so fast about borrowing money to repair his vehicle.

'Forget about the form,' Apunda told him. 'We'll meet him at lunch-time and I will tell you more about it. There is bread here.'

Over lunch a fresh claim form was filled in. In the afternoon Apunda made a call to a policeman and an assessor who were insiders in the operation. The following day the file contained reports of the vehicle declared a write-off by the company assessor. In a day the cheque for settlement was out. Shaka got his share of the loot. The insured had been paid the full value of his vehicle and used some of the money to repair it. The same vehicle was insured with a different registration number, by the same company, a month later. Shaka was slowly learning that employment opens the way to great opportunities. He did not feel like a criminal. He was now a pawn in the great money game in Kuzania. It was a good game, or so he thought. His bank account was swelling and he began looking for a piece of land on which to settle his mother. Under the tutelage of Apunda and Musa, he began frequenting bars, which was giving him an ailment known as a hangover. Each morning after a drinking spree, an attack of acidity would accost him; he was suffering from ailments of the affluent.

It was Saturday morning and he woke up with a terrible hangover. He could not remember how he had got home the night before. He went to the communal toilet and vomited. It eased his stomach and lessened the headache. He took a headache remedy and drank a pint of milk. Within an hour, he was feeling a lot better. He walked to the bus stop and bought a newspaper. He could afford small luxuries like newspapers, now.

The lead story in the paper discussed the possibility of snap general elections, both presidential and parliamentary. This was serious business. He went back home and read the story very carefully. There was speculation to the effect that the president would resign immediately after the elections, leaving the State House to his heir, yet to be chosen. In Shaka's mind this either meant the incumbent vice-president, Hon. Fikira or Hon. Tumbo. Hon. Tumbo! He shuddered. We shall wait and see, he said to himself. The thought of Hon. Tumbo brought Nzinga to his mind. Nzinga could soon be the daughter of the president of Kuzania, with her every move watched by hordes of bodyguards. How then could she visit the slums? He remembered that the university was on holiday and he decided to call her to apologise for not getting in touch after he got the job. He was much better dressed now and he had money. He could face her without shame. She would be pleased to see the transformation her kindness had brought to his life. A burning desire to speak to her gripped him.

At the public telephone booth, Shaka's heart was throbbing. He did not know exactly what to say or what to expect from Nzinga. On a neatly folded piece of paper was the telephone number Nzinga had given him. The phone rang twice, with Shaka praying that

Hon. Tumbo would not pick it up. A mellow and sweet voice on the other end answered.

'Hello, is that Nzinga?' Shaka asked, trembling.

'Nzinga speaking,' came the terse, no-nonsense response.

'This is Shaka. How are you?'

'Oh Shaka, I am fine! Where have you been all this time? I thought you promised to call me sooner! Did you get a job?'

Nzinga's voice had mellowed and sounded friendly. It gave Shaka courage.

'I got a job, thanks to your kindness! I've been planning to call you...'

'Don't let it bother you; I am happy you called at last!'

They discussed Nzinga's visit to the village, which could not take place for at least two weeks as the rains were flooding the roads. In the meantime Nzinga suggested Shaka call in and tell her how he was getting on.

Shaka left the telephone booth with a big smile spread across his face. Momentarily the discomfort in his stomach disappeared. He spent the afternoon with his mother and Agu, but not a word of his intended visit to Nzinga was spoken. He locked it in his young heart, not knowing why.

That evening Shaka went through the rest of the newspaper, reading every article on any subject. He knew his life was changing but in which direction, he could not tell. His first meeting with Nzinga had yielded big dividends and who knew what the second might bring. He was no longer desperate, scared and scruffy. He felt self-assured, with a bright future. Who knows? Soon he could be registering with the University of

London for an external degree in law to become a top lawyer in Glitta and then he would mix with the cream of society. In such a position, he could marry anybody's daughter, including Tumbo's. Nzinga would be within his grasp! These thoughts continued criss-crossing his mind late in to the night.

The sudden loud clatter of a thunderstorm and streaks of lighting jolted him back to reality. As the raindrops pounded his iron roof, Shaka found the rhythm lulling him to sleep. He slept without dreaming until the next morning.

Shaka alighted the bus and walked to the gate of Hon. Tumbo's house. The policeman at the gate – the same policeman he had met before – greeted him with a smile.

'She is expecting you.'

Nzinga had changed quite a bit. She looked very grown up and much more womanly. On her face was the most radiant smile Shaka had ever seen, brighter than a thousand stars. Shaka walked into the house, fear and happiness playing like naughty twins in his heart. He was led to the sitting-room, a big room full of wonders of furniture, electronics and game trophies. He felt completely lost. The items he saw were of a different kind and quality from those he had seen in the best shops in Glitta. No doubt, he concluded, save for the game trophies, everything was imported, duty-free of course.

As Nzinga fetched some drinks, Shaka listened to the beautiful music filtering from the wall speakers. The words of the song were crooning: 'If I were a carpenter and you were a lady, would you marry me anyway, would you have my baby?'

They chatted politely about Shaka's job for a while, until the conversation came round to Agu.

'I am dying to see him and the other folk in the village,' said Nzinga. 'For us who went to the mixed schools, we missed a lot in life. We lived a very artificial life in which one was supposed to forget one's background and skin colour. During the holidays, my father did not take me to visit my relatives. Instead, he took me to the homes of his friends, Greeks, Italians and Americans! I did not know how lost I was until I joined the university. Other students would laugh at me because I could not speak my mother tongue. Shaka, I suffered such a humiliating experience because I was like an alien in my own country! A lot has changed since then. My friends have been helping me to a point where I now feel comfortable. That is why I asked you to take me to the village so that I can learn more and fully identify myself with my people...' She paused. 'Going to the university has taught me a lot. I've learnt about our past and our customs. I feel like a fish out of water because these things seem so far removed from my life. We learn about our culture and yet I cannot sing a single traditional song. Do you know any?'

'Very many!' Shaka replied, beaming. 'Agu has taught me many songs and stories.'

'Will you teach me some?' she asked excitedly.

'Of course I will.'

There they sat, quietly singing, like two innocent children totally captivated by a new game.

Their game was interrupted by the sound of vehicles driving in to the compound. Hon. Tumbo had returned. Shaka's heart started pounding. Shaka could hear him angrily shouting: 'I am going to teach them a lesson! Those damn journalists, and their paymasters! And those university lecturers, if they want trouble, they are going to have tons of it!'

Nzinga opened the door. Her father stormed into the house. He walked heavily to the sitting-room.

'And who the hell is this?'

'Hon. Minister, sir, I am Shaka. We met —'

'And what the hell are you doing in my house?'

'Dad, I invited him over,' said Nzinga.

'You invited him? What is the meaning of this? You are bringing strangers into my house? Young man, who is your father?' he yelled at Shaka.

'Sir, as I told you before, my father is dead,' Shaka answered, irritated.

'Told me before? Have we met before?' Hon. Tumbo shouted.

'Yes, sir, I am the boy from the village you assisted to get a job with Kuzania Insurance Company —'

'Oh, my God! You are from the slums! How dare you enter my house! Nzinga, I've told you never to fraternise with the scum from the village, haven't I? What shame is this? What disgrace is this? Young man, get out of here before I beat the hell out of you!'

'Father, he is my friend, I invited him —'

'Shut up, woman, or I'll throw you out of my house, too!'

Shaka was out of the house when he heard footsteps following him.

'Shaka, please wait, I am so sorry...' Nzinga was in tears.

'Nzinga, come back straight away,' Hon. Tumbo shouted from the doorway.

Shaka continued, with Nzinga still behind him. The policeman opened the gate for them and locked it behind them without a word. Nzinga caught up with Shaka down the road.

'Nzinga, please go back before your father gets really mad,' he pleaded.

'This is the worst day of my life!' she cried. 'If this is what wealth and power are all about, I will have none of it! It is inhuman, it dehumanises, it destroys, it kills!'

'Nzinga, please...' he pleaded again.

'I want to go far away from here, far away from him! He is a devil!'

'Please stop crying.' Shaka took his handkerchief and wiped tears from Nzinga's cheeks. He felt as if an electric wave had gone through his body the moment he touched her.

'I am sorry,' she said. 'I will walk with you. Which is the way to your bus stop?' Nzinga never caught a bus. She was either chauffeur-driven or she drove her own BMW to wherever she wanted to go.

'I had intended to walk home, Nzinga. My home is only a couple of kilometres from here, over the ridge, down the valley and across the river.'

'I will escort you,' she said. As if it had been a long-agreed plan, they marched in step down the road to the intersection and turned, heading in the direction Shaka had pointed.

'Nzinga, I am very sorry to have caused you all this trouble. Believe you me, in all my life, I have never wanted to cause anybody any trouble.' Shaka spoke as if all the troubles in the world had been caused by some carelessness on his part.

'Don't be silly, Shaka, you are not to blame for a single damn thing and neither am I! Is one not supposed to have friends? Must my father choose for me who my friends should be? I am a grown-up person and it is time he woke up to the fact that I am old enough to run my life.'

'But your father is very tough, very uncompromising,' Shaka commented.

'My father is nothing but a brute, a fool with a bloated ego. He is a bully. You know, people are talking about him running for presidency but, let me tell you, they don't know what they are asking for. I fear for this country should he win the elections. Life will be absolute hell. I know it!'

'Don't talk like that about your father, Nzinga, it is not nice,' Shaka cautioned.

'Shaka, I am no longer a little girl, and I can judge things for myself. Some of those things you read in the newspapers about my father are true; he is aggressive, a womaniser, a drunkard. There is a lot also that the world does not know. At the university, I have read many books about politics. Have you ever read Frantz Fanon's *The Wretched of the Earth*?'

'No,' Shaka replied simply, fearing that the world of knowledge that Nzinga was about to open would be out of his depth.

'What about *Black Skins, White Masks*?'

'No.'

'There is a chapter in *The Wretched of the Earth* that talks about "pitfalls of national consciousness". As I read the papers and see my father's actions, I think we should pay a lot of attention to what Fanon has to say. First, the likes of my father think and act as if they are white men and, secondly, they don't give a damn about national consciousness. This is why their best friends are foreigners and their major preoccupation is personal aggrandisement. Power is a tool to guarantee the flow of money into their accounts and protect their wealth, that's all. I will give you both books to read, you have to!'

The afternoon was wearing on. They had walked a while and were approaching the valley that separated the slums from the wealthy area, known as 'Happy Valley' in the language of the rich who lived there.

'What's that?' Nzinga asked, pointing at the waterfalls that marked the beginning of the highlands.

'We call them Kahindo Falls.'

'Wow! It is a beautiful sight! Just imagine I live only a few kilometres from here and I've never heard about it! How many other beautiful things around me have I been missing?' The last question was addressed more to herself than to Shaka. 'Let us sit here for a while,' she suggested.

'This is not all!' said Shaka. 'Over there, beside those rocks, there are lovely spots for one to sit.'

Shaka led Nzinga over big black rocks until they came to the spot where one huge boulder jutted out over another, forming an open cave. It was where he had sat the day he got his job.

'Wow! Look at this!' exclaimed Nzinga.

They sat under the rock, shielded from the sun and from the world. Down the valley, the Glitta River meandered to the city and beyond. Before them they faced the most ostentatious display of extravagance and wealth in the form of architecture, caressing Happy Valley. It was the world in which Nzinga lived. Behind them lived the slum dwellers, the scum of the earth. It was the dark world that Shaka belonged to. This day, the two worlds met in a cave like the one that had housed Adam and Eve in the garden of Eden.

Nature in its mercy has a habit of mixing things in order to bring out the best in each. Shaka was looking at Nzinga's hands, which were clutching her raised knees. The hands looked clean and very soft, almost artificial. He could not resist the temptation to feel them. He took one hand and looked intently at the fingers without saying a word. They were very real and warm.

'Do you like my fingers?' Nzinga asked with the innocence of a child.

'They are very beautiful and unsoiled,' he said softly.

'What do you mean, unsoiled?' she asked coyly.

'Like they have never touched a hoe or any digging implement.'

'As a matter of fact, I have never dug in my life.'

'Yeah, some people are born lucky,' Shaka said.

'Your hands are beautiful, too.'

'Only in recent times, Nzinga, only in recent times. Before you helped me get a job, they were as rough as sandpaper!'

They both laughed. They relaxed and chatted in the cave, lost to the world surrounding them. They were like two friendly children from the neighbourhood, playing hide and seek. In between the conversations, they stole glances at each other; each in some way fascinated by the other.

'I like you very much, Nzinga,' Shaka heard himself say. He immediately regretted it. His place in society had been underlined in red by Hon. Tumbo. Was he deaf or was he blind?

'I like you, too, Shaka,' came the reply from Nzinga, looking at him straight in the eye.

Shaka's heart leapt. He had thrown his peasant voice across the valley and its echo had come back like a boomerang, magnified, reverberating again and again, shaking Happy Valley. Nzinga, the lonely and lovely daughter of the billionaire minister, the people's representative, sat there in a cave touching the soiled hands of a peasant boy whose self-assuredness and comportment reminded her of Hannibal the Black Prince! The two worlds were intertwined in the confusion of innocent friendship, and the simple instinct of love; the foundation of all human society.

'How far is the village from here?' Nzinga asked.

'We are almost there. It is over the hill behind.'

'Take me to the village.'

Shaka was shocked. 'Today?'

'What is wrong with today?' she asked, looking at him defiantly.

'With all the mud? And how will you go back home? It is getting rather late! I would rather escort you back and plan the visit to the village when the rains are gone,' he pleaded.

'Take me to the village now.' Her tone was firm and urgent. He felt he had no choice but to grant her wish.

'All right, let's go.' Shaka helped Nzinga to her feet.

As they crossed the river and started to climb the hill, Shaka was in doubt as to whether the whole thing was real. It was like a dream. Soon, they were on the paths winding through small plantations of all sorts of crops. Hovels of houses were thickening as they moved deeper into the village. Crowds of people were increasing and some would greet them as they passed by. Soon, they came to the hub of the village.

'Where are all these people coming from? Was there a rally here today?' Nzinga asked. The village was like a beehive with people in hordes moving in all directions, seemingly aimlessly.

'No, Nzinga, these are the village dwellers going about their normal business,' Shaka replied.

'What do they do for a living?'

'Anything goes! A lot of them are unemployed. Others are lowly paid workers in the city and others are touts, pickpockets, harlots and brewers of illicit brews.'

'This is not the Kuzania I know,' she said with concern.

'Yours is a different world,' said Shaka.

'No, no, no, this is my world, too, these are my people, my cousins, my uncles, my aunts! We came from here!'

'It is different now,' Shaka said. 'I want to move my mother from here. It is getting too overcrowded. A lot of people are tenants and they have brought with them very different values and behaviours from ours. One cannot bring up children in a place like this. Before you know it, young girls hardly out puberty are harlots and young boys are criminals.'

'It is a crying shame!' Nzinga said.

The rows of houses were squeezed together and there were kiosks and temporary shacks on each available space. Soon, they came to another row of wooden houses with old corrugated iron sheets. There were forty rooms on a quarter acre of land. In the corner were communal toilets and bathrooms. Water from the clothes hanging on lines between the houses dripped on you as you walked under them to the door. To the outsider, it looked very disorderly but to the tenants, this was their home, the very best they had and Kawempe slums were not the worst in the city. Nzinga followed Shaka in silence as they weaved their way under the clothes on the lines. Luckily, the linen was not dripping.

Shaka opened the door to his two-roomed dwelling and invited Nzinga in. One room served as the sitting-room-cum-kitchen while the other was the bedroom. A two-burner gas cooker, cooking pots, cups and a frying pan sat on a wooden table. There were no electrical appliances in the house and no electricity either. A sofa, two easy chairs and a coffee-table made for all the comforts in the sitting end of the room.

'Would you like to have some tea? I am afraid I do not have anything else to offer,' Shaka asked Nzinga, with the dignity of a man in full command of a situation.

'Yes, I will have some tea,' Nzinga answered. 'Where does your mother live?' she enquired.

'She lives in a different part of Kawempe, and so does the old man Agu. I moved here because it is near the bus stop.'

'Can we go and say hello to them after tea?' she asked.

Wait a minute! Shaka said to himself. There are things you do not do in a hurry and one of them is to take a girl to your mother without prior warning. It is an unwritten law in the community. You only introduce to your mother the girl you want to marry.

'Nzinga, I promise I will take you there next time but today it is rather late to cross the river as it is swollen with the rains and there is no bridge,' he said most convincingly.

'There is no bridge? How do vehicles get there in the rainy season?' she asked.

'Vehicles don't go there in the rainy season'

'What about in the case of an emergency, like when someone is very sick and an ambulance is needed or a woman needs to be rushed to the maternity?' she asked.

'The sick are carried on home-made stretchers to this side,' he said.

'This is awful, dreadful.'

After tea, Nzinga needed to use the communal toilets. It was dark outside and Shaka gave her a torch. The stench that hit her with each step towards the toilets was awful, acrid and oppressive. She suppressed a cough. Better judgement led her to a space behind the shed where she eased herself. It was not just a release of the bladder; she felt a relief of her soul, too. Something very wonderful had happened, as if a big load had been lifted from her back. Her blinkers had been removed and she could see Kuzania in a different light. Kuzania was not the artificial world she had been confined to. It was bigger, complicated and very real. All she had read about different classes in societies was dancing in front of her eyes as she went back to Shaka's simple dwelling. She found Shaka waiting for her outside by the door.

'Did you think I was going to get lost?' she asked, laughing.

'Nzinga, I bet if you had found the door closed, you would have wondered which house you came from. This place is not as simple as it looks,' he said.

Nzinga looked at the doors and agreed with him. They had no numbers and they were all identical, differing only in degrees of cleanliness.

'You count the doors to know which one to enter. Next time you come around, remember my door is the third from the road and the fourth from the toilets, in the last row,' he advised.

'I will remember that: third from the road, fourth from the toilets, last row – easy.'

As they sat in the sitting-room-cum-kitchen, they could hear the conversations of the neighbours next door. The walls were very thin.

'In this place, there is no privacy!' observed Nzinga.

'That is the way we live. We have no secrets to keep or anything to hide. We love and reproduce freely,' Shaka commented with a laugh.

The rooms had no ceiling and if gaps in the partition walls were too large, you fixed them by hanging newspapers over them. Nzinga looked at the whole scenario and shuddered. There was a hurricane lamp burning on the coffee table in the middle of the room. She looked at the flame and remembered numerous cases she had read of gutted houses in the slums. Now she understood. It was a miracle there were no fires in the slums everyday!

'Nzinga, it is getting late. You really should be going,' Shaka suggested.

'Yep. Thanks a lot for everything.'

'I will take you to your place by bus as we cannot walk back at this hour.'

So the two went to the bus stop and boarded a minibus. The music was blaring so loudly that conversation was impossible. Nzinga kept trying to tell Shaka, 'This is fun! I've never ridden in one before.' He couldn't hear her so he kept on shouting, asking her to repeat herself. She couldn't hear him either. They sat there, close to each other, stealing glances with smiles. As the minibus sped past the university, Shaka felt a pain in his heart. If only his mother had not been so poor, by now he would be completing his law degree and talking to Nzinga as an intellectual equal. He would be quoting Frantz Fanon and all the other names in the big books. Surely, all children have a right to proper education so that they can build the nation together and engage the rest of the world from a point of knowledge. He thought he had found the answer to the economic and financial malaise facing Kuzania. Too many white elephants had been introduced into Kuzania because semi-illiterate leaders had signed documents they did not understand. The answer to the problems of Kuzania lay in educated leadership!

The minibus came to a halt and they boarded another to Nzinga's home area. Still, it was too noisy to talk. When they got off, Nzinga asked him how much the journey had cost him.

'Not much,' he replied. He had paid for the fare and he would be returning the same way. Nzinga felt guilty about taxing Shaka's pocket.

'I left the house without a penny. I will repay you...' she promised.

'Don't think about it! You deserve more,' he countered.

As they approached Hon. Tumbo's gate, Shaka felt uneasy; joy, fear and pain intermingled. He did not want to face Hon. Tumbo again, ever.

'Nzinga, you are safe here. I really must go back. Tomorrow is a working day, you know.'

'I understand. Promise you will call.'

'I will. Don't forget to give me the books next time.'

'I will give you the books and, in turn, you've to take me to see your mother and Agu before the university re-opens.'

'I will call you. Goodnight.'

'Goodnight, Shaka, and thank you ever so much. You don't know what this day means to me.'

They shook hands and parted company, the best new friends in the world. It seemed the valley was not wide enough to keep them apart.

Innocence, sweet and pure innocence, the great mother of misery! Be warned.

That night Nzinga dreamt that the two cities were

locked in a furious battle. She saw the people of Kawempe attacking Happy Valley in waves. She saw Shaka dressed as a general, leading the forces of good against the army of evil. She was shouting in her sleep, 'Shaka, I want to join your army.' Next, she was in full army gear, fighting side by side with Shaka.

Nzinga woke up the next morning extremely exhausted but very clear headed. She knew her life had changed, but she could not measure the extent of the transformation. There was no doubt in her mind about the direction. Never again would she be blinded by the twin demons power and money.

6

Castles on Sand

Do you think anybody in his right mind would build castles on sand if they had solid ground on which to build them?

Musa's physical build tells you nothing more than that he is a lean and healthy man. However, those who work with dangerous and sharp instruments develop a morbid fear of pain. Imagine a tailor working with scissors, razor-blades and needles. If he did not take great care, his fingers would be perforated and lacerated beyond repair. Too much fear, though, makes one a coward. Musa is meek but I cannot attest to his cowardice. There is an old prophecy that the meek will inherit the earth. If it is so, Musa will be allocated a huge chunk of land; an island or whatever will remain of the earth after the nuclear Armageddon. With his care and patience, he will rehabilitate his inheritance in record time, regardless of the degree of its devastation.

A sewing-machine needle is a miniature devil. Once the cloth has been lined, it moves into high gear as Musa peddles the machine and you can hear the fury of the little devil as it ties the cloth together with thread and another Kaunda suit is made. If you moved your fingers a fraction beyond the safety margin, you would certainly end up with your fingers stitched together. Musa is not a fool. Not once has he stitched his fingers. Lucky man. He walks with a springy rhythm. He is meek and careful while working but the moment he leaves the machine behind, all care is abandoned as he ruthlessly deals with beer and women, to release tension.

Vuruta Bar in Glitta city centre carries the nickname of the Church. This is where sinners congregate to partake their daily 'communion'. The spirit is uplifted with liquor. No hard-core boozer, prostitute, intellectual, journalist, wayward tourist or university student worth his salt has had his fill until he steps into Vuruta Bar. It operates twenty-four hours a day. When Musa gracefully steps into the organised chaos of the bar, he is as sober as judges were in days of old. These days, judges are drunkards like everybody else. That is why they are setting free criminals who can pay their way out of courts and those connected to political godfathers. Either way, the pockets of the judges are made heavier with each case and, to hide their shame, they have developed the veil of whisky and brandy. But life marches on and for those good citizens not in jail, they can sing their songs of freedom in Vuruta Bar as long as they don't offend the state. They come here for 'one for the road' and end up taking one too many for the grave.

'Hello, Musa,' 'Hello, Musa,' voices greet him from every corner in the bar. He pulls up a stool by the counter and orders two beers. The first he drinks straight from the bottle in quick gulps until all that is left is bubbling foam. This is before he 'starts' drinking as he says, 'It is not wise to drink on an empty stomach.' He settles down to drink. He has a duty to catch up with the pickpockets and harlots who have had the good fortune of the whole afternoon with nothing else to do. He is going to drink like he is paid to do so, until his body is limp. Tomorrow, he will suffer a massive hangover. So what.

A lot like him ends up in gutters each night. Some are knocked down by speeding vehicles as they zigzag to their hovels in the slums. Many are just killing themselves, with the liver rotting slowly. Excessive drinking very soon releases one from the miseries of life, with death.

Apunda, Shaka's colleague, arrived and sat next to Musa.

'Where have you left Shaka?' Musa asked Apunda. 'Or is he still suffering from his acid thing? I tell you, that young man has no stomach for booze! He makes it sound as if a bar is a chemical factory manufacturing poisonous acid and a virus called hangover!'

They laughed. Musa, the 'doctor' in rags with solutions for all social problems; all except his own.

'Musa, have you read today's daily?' Apunda asked.

'No, I did not have the time,' Musa replied. 'What's so special about it?'

'The paper has statistics on Aids. Do you know Kuzania has the highest incidence of Aids in the world?'

'Apunda, the next thing you will tell me is to be careful and cease visiting my friends next door! Apunda, a man cannot control an erection and once you have one, it drives away caution and reasoning. Read about Adam and Eve, read about King David and Bathsheba, read about Solomon and the Queen of Sheba, read about presidents making love to interns! Tell me, which man can control an erection?'

127

'My dear friend, Musa,' a journalist sitting next to Apunda said. 'People are dying like flies in this country. Aids is a serious scourge and it has reached epidemic proportions in Kuzania.' He appeared knowledgeable.

'Young man,' Musa said, 'the voice of the Good Lord warned Adam and Eve not to eat the apple. Did they listen? Doctors, priests, ministers and presidents cannot control themselves! An erection is a mighty force. It is like a rebellion and it gains momentum with each throb until it is uncontrollable! But tell me, why are people still dying of malaria, cholera, tuberculosis, typhoid and other curable diseases? These diseases have reached epidemic proportions, too. The government has a huge campaign against Aids just to protect the tourist industry. Why is there no campaign against hunger? I've argued this case of Aids until my jaws have ached. Let us get our priorities right,' he concluded.

'I think Musa has a point,' said Apunda. 'If we cannot control Aids, let us at least save those who can be saved from other curable ailments. Aids is not the worst scourge in this country; poverty is! This talk of the dangers of immorality is only a diversion from real issues.'

'If making love is immorality,' Musa continued, 'then this is one commandment that was made to be broken. Adam and Eve made love against God's wish and there will be lovemaking until the end of time. I am going to live in this world as I found it and not waste my sleep on ways to make it different. Sex has always been a magnet between man and woman. It is the highest expression of love, a sacrifice, which creates strong bonds. Unfortunately, it has been turned into a money-spinner, a commercial thing, and a means to livelihood.

128

Do you know that in western societies, prostitutes have trade unions? Why are they telling us to stop making love in Kuzania? I'll tell you, they want less hungry mouths to feed, that is all.' Musa was visibly getting drunk. He continued, 'Little girls hardly out of puberty are taking pills and young boys of the same age carry condoms in their pockets, so what are we talking about? Their bigger sisters, their mothers and their aunts are having free sex. The beggar, the poor man, the rich man are all having sex and it is not only in Kuzania, it is all over the world. What the paper was telling you is that the poor have no right to an erection but the rich have the right to a permanent one! I am broke, who is buying the next round?'

This is Vuruta Bar, the Church where important issues touching on life and death are seriously discussed by doctors in rags, drunk. We live in a world of dreams, building castles in the air. If we had solid ground, we would build the castles there but the nation has no sense of direction. There are dreams with labels such as 'confidential', 'top secret' and 'classified materials'. Other dreams are openly shared. Ours is an artificial world without shared goals, without common sense. It is cruel and unjust. Still, in the confusion we exist, we do not live. Everybody with his dreams, some extremely wild, as we justify our meaningless existence.

A woman clad in next to nothing entered the bar. Her face was gaudily made-up and she resembled a miniature rainbow. She sat and crossed her legs, exposing pure white panties, a mark of cleanliness. She was a prostitute on the prowl. Black or white, to her any colour goes, as long as you pay. She had not read that day's paper and, even if she had, it would not make a difference in her daily routine. She must eat.

Different epochs, seasons and experiences give rise to ever-sophisticated ideas and dreams. Dreams are products of minds half-conscious of objective reality. They are soon shattered. Nowhere are these dreams in greater abundance than in the realm of the poor, the wretched of the earth, whose lives are nasty, brutish and short. Dreaming fills in the void of an empty life. Perchance, like in a lottery, a single soul should realise his dream, one out of a million. The prostitute seated there has her dream of some day becoming somebody. She is forty years old and has been frequenting bars each day year in, year out hoping to achieve her dream. She has been tightly holding on to her dream, since she was fifteen. She is dreaming still. Very soon, the folly of her reasoning will dawn on her. I guess through cracks in her broken heart, Lord Jesus will enter and she will proclaim salvation and the fulfilment of her dreams. Then she will be swallowed by a grave that will have no name or epitaph. Another child of Kuzania, after completing her labour on earth, will have gone to eternal bliss – or would it be just another dream, another castle in the air? Ask Musa, he should know.

Don't forget that the Good Lord had a dream of a beautiful Garden and it turned out to be another castle in the air. It took a weakling called Adam with an apple he got from a woman called Eve to shatter the dream, while a huge serpent looked at them in amazement. After the débâcle, the Good Lord intended to create another Garden, which He hasn't done to this day. It remains an idea, just a dream, another castle in the air. Let's keep Him company. We render him moral support by dreaming, because actualising a dream is truly elusive; but who knows who will win the lottery next?

A tourist walked in. He had a long yellow beard like one I saw in the picture of a man they call the Saviour. He sat next to a prostitute. They kissed and hugged, dreaming still before fate judges them in time, I hope not too harshly. And again they will write another alarming story of the wide-spreading Aids in Kuzania.

The journalist looked at them. 'Women are a bigger tourist attraction than the animals in national parks! We should invest more in brothels!'

'Yeah, yeah, I will drink to that,' said Apunda, also getting drunk. Musa, who was very quiet, was watching everybody in the bar as though he pitied them all.

'I will write an article on this, and it will be a scoop!' continued the journalist. 'I will reveal the potential of this untapped, lucrative market. I will use statistics to show how brothels full of whores can transform the economy of Kuzania. The shareholders in this new venture will be Hon. Tumbo, controlling 51 per cent and the whores, 49 per cent. The economy of Kuzania will take off like the Tupolev 144.'

'Shut up,' Musa said. He was thinking about his mother and did not want anybody to talk ill of these victims of a directionless society, from whom he owed his life.

'What is a Tupolev 144?' Apunda asked.

'It was a Russian dream of a Concorde jet, which crashed in an airshow in Farnborough in 1975,' said the journalist.

'Our women are too hungry for money,' said Apunda.

'Who isn't?' retorted Musa.

'And then I will conclude,' continued the journalist, 'there will be big subcontracts for mortuary attendants, coffin makers, gravediggers and undertakers as Kuzania buries her best in the thousands!'

'Shut up,' said Musa. 'If you cannot stomach beer like your friend Shaka, it is time you went home. It is clear to me you are suffering from verbal acidity!'

They had had enough. Apunda and the journalist drifted away. Tomorrow they will meet Musa in Vuruta Bar, all the faithful members of the congregation of drunkards. They will review another topic in the long catalogue of the never-ending vices in Kuzania.

Musa sat there, looking at those around him, to the best his eyes could focus. Unknown to them all, Shaka had bought some books and had read until he fell asleep. At that moment, he was dreaming of a great future, bigger than Vuruta Bar could ever hold.

Hon. Tumbo, the aspiring presidential candidate, never became what was expected of one aiming for such a high office: civilised. If anything, he was no more than a juggler, a political magician. His box of tricks had wonders that involved a legerdemain of money and power. Power was the key to success and its foundation was money. Hon. Tumbo had money and power but he wanted absolute powers. He wanted the highest office in the land, the presidency, and Kuzania would be his to manipulate. He had an array of local and international supporters. While the locals benefited directly from his power, influence and wallet, the foreigners were excellent business partners who designed strategies on how to rape the country. It was a mutually beneficial relationship although the riffraff in Kuzania condemned it as corruption. It didn't bother Tumbo. He had grown so powerful that he could make major policy decisions without referring to the

Cabinet. The president was no more than his rubber stamp.

He had a thorn in the flesh, though; a preacher by the name of Rev. Mwago, who had become very outspoken on the misuse of power. He had preached a stinger on immorality and how leaders were breaking homes by luring wives with corrupt business. They were also impregnating schoolgirls! He had called them immoral and unfit to hold public offices. The sermon had received wide media coverage. Tumbo smelt a rat. He called the archbishop and broke the good news that the government in its moral duty had offered Rev. Mwago a national award to pursue further studies overseas, so that he could lead the flock even better. The archbishop was delighted. Details of the lucrative scholarship were sent directly to the archbishop's office with a caution that no substitution was allowed. The archbishop called it a generous government offer, he did not mention the name of Hon. Tumbo, who had acted 'on behalf of the president'. Rev. Mwago looked at the offer and his heart was filled with gratitude. He knew it was time to change his career. He would seize the opportunity to read economics, commerce or banking. Upon return, he would be a somebody, armed with a Master's degree! And so it was that, as blind as a mole, Rev. Mwago boarded a plane and headed for the United States of America to a university in Vermont, which William Stans had contacted.

After the departure of her husband, Mrs Jennie WaMwago became a true business woman. Tenders increased by leaps and on Tumbo's orders she was armed with a diplomatic passport. From then on whenever Hon. Tumbo went abroad, whether on official or personal business, Mrs WaMwago went a day ahead or followed thereafter. This was common practice with others in the leadership. It was during these trips that she learnt that shortages of sugar, maize meal and rice were artificially induced and they resulted in huge spin-offs. She learnt that government boards were staffed with operatives whose mandate was to create wealth for the political leadership, hence the glaring nepotism in appointments. If there was a bumper harvest, it was the duty of the managing directors to off-load the harvest in the world market immediately in order to create a shortage, as the stocks would fall below the national strategic reserves level, necessitating imports. As the shortage began to bite, prices would rise. It was at this point that those in power ordered the commodities in the world market. With the situation desperate and the goods in the high seas, the government would issue a statement to the effect that such and such a commodity could now be imported duty-free within a limited period. Sugar, previously unavailable, would suddenly arrive from Brazil within ten days of the announcement. In this way, the leaders were making millions while ignorant citizens were simply happy that they had this or that item on the shelves again, albeit at a higher price.

The same went for the national currency. It was hiked or lowered against other currencies depending on whether those in power wanted to take out money or bring in money. To them, it was just a game. Meanwhile they wrecked the economy. Jennie WaMwago intended to play these high-stake games with the limited resources that Hon. Tumbo availed to her. He provided her with a car. He also gave her keys to a flat in a wealthy area and her children were placed in expensive boarding schools. She had not yet received the transfer

documents for either the car or the flat. There was
no hurry; the transfers would be effected all in good
time. What mattered to her were the yields of the
friendship and trust between her and Tumbo. They
were there in abundance. WaMwago had never dreamt
of such easy fun. At last, she was a star. Her dream had
come true. She had not become famous like Aretha
Franklin but she saw herself in the same league as
Jacqueline Onassis. Life was worth living! She was a
queen, the queen of an unknown, underground
kingdom.

With her mobility and newly acquired wealth, she
sought the circles of successful women in the city. She
found them in the private elite clubs, which offered
leisure pursuits such as swimming, bowling, tennis,
snooker and golf. She opted to play the game of the rich
and lazy, golf.

After one such game, WaMwago headed straight for the
bar in the clubhouse. She found Kimondo, Hon. Tumbo's
campaign manager, seated in the company of others.

'Come and join us for a drink,' Kimondo invited. 'Did
you shoot a hole in one?' he asked jokingly.

'Golf is not for me, it is too childish. May I have a screwdriver, please?' she asked him.

'I love women who like a screw!' said Kimondo, causing
laughter all round.

'I asked for a screwdriver, Kimondo, not a screw!'
WaMwago was visibly annoyed. Kimondo was ugly,
ungainly and uncouth. Tumbo only kept him as his campaign manager because of his ruthlessness. He was an ex-
member of a gang of armed robbers. He had escaped
hanging a couple of years earlier by a whisker and
remained very faithful to Hon. Tumbo, to whom he owed

his life. However, there was no love lost between WaMwago and Kimondo.

'One of these days...' Kimondo was silenced by the arrival of Hon. Tumbo, who came in the company of William Stans and a Greek man called Scudulis.

'Let's leave it as such,' Tumbo was saying, 'we will pick it from there next time.'

Stans and Scudulis left without having a drink.

'My dear, how was the golf?' Tumbo asked WaMwago.

'It is not as easy as it seems from a distance,' she said with a smile.

'Try bowling or tennis,' he suggested.

'I will,' she said with a smile and a wink.

After a single drink, Hon. Tumbo turned to WaMwago. 'Let's go.' The single command was executed like one addressing a dog.

WaMwago jumped to attention and they left. They would ride in separate vehicles and meet in Hon. Tumbo's suite at the Milton Hotel, for the usual. She would be richer but misused and cheapened. It did not matter any more. WaMwago took solace in the fact that she was not the only wife ensnared in this trap. With Aids spreading like bush fire, the rich and powerful had turned to other people's wives and schoolgirls. It was a national plague that grew in magnitude in direct proportion with the spreading of poverty and the moral decay of society. She had a chilly feeling that, as had happened to others, she too might one day be very lonely but, for now, she was scaling the mountain of affluence and fun in style.

'Today,' she promised herself, 'I am going to screw this bastard so hard, he will slip a disc!' She did not understand where the anger and need to hurt emanated from but she felt a need to hit back. The suite had become a slaughterhouse and it was Hon. Tumbo's turn today. 'I am going to skin the beast!'

She hissed silently as she took off her clothes. When they started making love, she wilfully overcarried herself. She gripped the honourable minister hard; her arms around his neck and her legs around his fat waist were like vices. She was like a python strangulating its prey. She cried all sorts of sweet things – 'My dear, you are killing me, – as she executed her plan. She had overestimated her strength. Hon. Tumbo enjoyed every moment of it and was in ecstasy. The harder she tried to punish him the more he enjoyed it. It left both of them sore, exhausted, sweating profusely and out of breath.

'That was wonderful,' Tumbo said.

WaMwago did not reply, she was nursing aches and pains all over. They showered and parted company. WaMwago went home to nurse her self-inflicted injuries, consoling herself that the pain was worth it.

Hon. Tumbo arrived at the appointed house in Happy Valley, where a meeting to map out his campaign strategy was being held. As he stepped out of his limousine, he realised with agony the truism about mixing business with pleasure. There was a slowness, almost painful, in the way he walked.

The meeting was under the guise of a goat-eating party. His faithful bunch of cronies was waiting for him. Goats had been slaughtered as one could tell from the smell of roasting meat in the backyard. In reality, it was an illegal political meeting. His faithful supporters read like a list of who is who in government and the private sector. The deference they conferred to him was both a mark of gratitude for his assistance in acquiring unsecured loans, government contracts, duty-free importation of commodities, allocation of state property, plots and lands; and an indication of the faith they had in his future political fortunes, and the windfall to accompany it. This was the season of change, as they called it.

The meeting was in the house of Kimondo, Tumbo's campaign manager, security strategist and close confidant. Kimondo was so feared that no stranger ever dared enter his house. In his heyday as a gangster he was said to have been a sharp shooter in whose hands many policemen had come to their early deaths. That was the past. He had since become a respectable and feared member of those who mattered in Kuzania. In his hands the future of Kuzania was entrusted, as the campaign manager of the future president.

'A round of applause for the honourable minister, one, two, three. Welcome, Your Excellency!'

Hon. Tumbo, his big stomach leading him, slowly and painfully took a seat. 'She must have fucked the marrow out of your bones!' Kimondo whispered. They both broke into loud laughter. Others joined in the laughter, though they had not heard a word. If Tumbo laughed, they laughed; if he ever cried, I guess they would cry, too. It was a strong solidarity dictated by money and power.

Next to shake the hand of the hon. minister was Mr Twisted Mamba, the chairman of the Kuzania Workers' Union. He was a double-edged man who promised the workers higher salaries and better working conditions that somehow never came. Workers contributed generously to the union to keep Mamba in a healthy position to fight for them. Unknown to them, the chairman had a secret deal with the government and

Hon. Tumbo to keep the demands of labour in check. It was a delicate balance that so far he had managed well. Someday, he would be minister for Labour, he hoped. Next came Mr Fissi, chairman of the Kuzania Teachers' Union. He addressed Hon. Tumbo as 'Your Excellency'. His role and that of Mr Mamba were similar and so was his dream of a Cabinet post. Mr Kata Nyama owned the biggest abattoir in Kuzania, in which Hon. Tumbo was a major shareholder. He supplied Kuzania Armed Forces and all key government institutions with meat. He was one of the wealthiest men in the land, though he could neither read nor write. There was Hon. Pesa, the member of parliament for the largest slum area in Glitta, half of which he owned. Recently, he had diversified by opening a savings and deposit bank in which Hon. Tumbo was a shareholder. Teachers and workers were encouraged to put their money in the new venture, whose future was highly doubtful due to its unprofessional nature of operating. People in power were getting huge unsecured loans. Predictably, the bank would collapse with depositors of workers and teachers the main losers.

The list was long but one should not overemphasise the presence of Hon. Nyoka Mrefu, the minister for Internal Security. He was the former head of the Criminal Investigation Department, whose main speciality was the protection of those with money and power from the greedy and illegal adventurism of 'the riff-raff', and of the intellectuals. His loyalty to Hon. Tumbo extended to the use of all means at his disposal, including physical elimination, detention and torture.

It was a meeting of critical national figures, of friends with a common purpose touching on the future leadership of the country in the season of change. Although the issue of snap general elections was significant, the main focus was events beyond that. Political succession was the key issue. It was known that the president was suffering from a terminal disease, cancer of the colon, in addition to his advanced age. He had also become visibly senile. How soon he was going to lose his senses or what remained of them was anybody's conjecture. Sooner, rather than later, he would be gone and the vice-president would take over. Tumbo had to be named vice-president after the snap elections.

Hon. Nyoka, the minister for Internal Security, had accompanied the president on a recent trip to Europe for a medical check-up. He had classified information on the health and the remaining length of life of the president. He had planted his boys in all key areas, including the State House, to monitor the expected collapse of the head of state. An alliance between himself and Hon. Tumbo was unassailable. They came from different tribes and regions in Kuzania, which gave their coalition a national outlook, as opposed to a tribal alliance. The strategy adopted by the meeting called for the continuation of praise singing to the president, while at the same time fermenting trouble between ethnic groups, teachers, workers and students. The minister for Internal Security and the union leaders would make sure that the troubles went only as far as tarnishing the image of the president and the incumbent vice-president but should be monitored and controlled. In the meantime, the unrest would give the minister for State Security an excuse to eliminate opponents of Hon. Tumbo, in the name of maintaining law and order. Journalists, university lecturers, members of the opposition, fellow Cabinet ministers, student leaders and others would be arrested, detained without trial, tortured and eliminated to ensure smooth transition to power for Hon. Tumbo. These measures were aimed at alienating the president from the people as well as speeding up his physical collapse. He would be kept awake day and night trying to solve the insoluble. It would also lead to schism with Hon. Fikira, the vice-president, western governments, human rights groups and the large Institutions which would result in the isolation of Kuzania. These conditions would be ideal for the manipulation of currency and importation of commodities, which would yield fortunes for Hon. Tumbo and his stooges. Armed with bags of money, they would put the final nail in the coffin. Everything was neat and sound and there was much merriment among them. The gathering resembled the house of Babel. It was like the final act of the coup Lucifer and his rebel devils had plotted in heaven. Tumbo rose to the occasion with his self-perfected wisdom.

'Gentlemen, it took men like us to build Rome and it was not built in a day! It was through the patience and foresightedness of men like us that the foundation of that great empire, which ruled the world, was laid.'

He was greatly applauded. Kimondo interjected, 'We must save Rome from the current sick leadership!' He was applauded. In their own eyes, they were not selfish and corrupt leaders, they were the saviours of Kuzania.

Shaka's life was changing within and around him. He had not come into terms with the fact that it had taken Agu's intervention for him to get decent clothes, a square meal, to buy his mother some basic necessities of life and to buy Agu a new blanket. The early contentment with getting a job had given way to a negative introspection that was eating his heart. How on earth had he agreed to Agu's plan of begging Hon. Tumbo for a job? Would it not have been more dignified if he had struggled on in the hope that, by pulling himself up by his own bootstraps, maybe someday he would stumble upon a well-paying job without opening himself to ridicule? And ridicule it was, because it had taken Nzinga's intervention to save him from a ruinous disgrace in the hands of Tumbo. But then, he argued further, maybe destiny had conspired with Agu, because from a single letter he had found a job and a friend in Nzinga, which had led to his rediscovering the world of books. With each chapter read, he had a better view of the world around him. Not only had he read those books but he had continued to read others. He was maturing in a very schooled manner, something that would never have happened had he continued as a manual worker.

He was angry and happy with himself at the same time. He had had little time to mix with Musa and Apunda in the bars. At the same time, he wanted to read a few more books before his next meeting with Nzinga, though he felt guilty for not calling her sooner. He argued that their meetings would be more meaningful if they discussed things as equals, or almost as equals in knowledge. It was only knowledge that could elevate him to a new status. He started asking Agu probing questions about nationalism, past history and how the present chaotic situation came to be. The knowledge he was gaining from Agu was an eye-opener, more valuable than books could be, although he felt Agu was holding back on certain aspects, as if he were not yet fully mature to bear the full weight of it all. He filled the gaps with knowledge from his books. The picture emerging was one of an incomplete victory for his people. It was the incompleteness, which the likes of Tumbo were exploiting, that stifled manhood, happiness and humanity. His two encounters with Hon. Tumbo, both in which he had been reduced to subhuman level, reinforced his evaluation. He felt trapped like an animal in a cage. Restlessly, he was looking for any weak link from where to burst free. Agu had promised to tell him a lot more. Shaka waited impatiently; Agu was not in a hurry.

After a weekend in which Shaka did not appear in Vuruta Bar, Apunda had asked him what was bothering him. He was as sober as a judge and not suffering from any physical ailment either and yet he had become very changed indeed. Shaka would sit all day by his desk and work on files, talking on the dictaphone. Even more alarming to Apunda was Shaka's lack of interest in writing off vehicles that were still on the road or parked in garages without a scratch. What kind of an African is this, not interested in a quick buck? Apunda asked himself.

Nzinga and her father were no longer on talking terms. In their last quarrel, Hon. Tumbo had called her 'a fool with no sense of direction'. Nzinga's only crime was to have reasoned that she was now old enough to choose her own friends and that she did not cherish the tailor-made and artificial relations to which her father had confined her for years. 'Friends? Friends? You call those animals from the gutters friends? You are a bloody fool and very soon you will come to grievous harm,' he had warned her in anger.

Nzinga's world had begun to change and she was happy with its new direction. As her father was out most of the time, she had a lot of time to herself. Her reasoning was taking a definite line of commitment. It was not that she did not know on which side the bread was buttered, but that she knew only too well. Her constitution agreed neither with bread nor with butter, as provided, with conditions, by her father. Power and money were not a panacea to her pangs of hunger for knowledge, for true friendship, for the realisation of herself in the real world. The way her father saw her and the way she was were poles apart. They lived in different worlds. She had seen both worlds and understood her true existence, the meaning of life. She felt like a balloon disengaged from the string, free to soar to the skies, unfettered and, unknown to her father, happier than he would ever be with all the money and power in the world.

It was early Sunday afternoon and Nzinga was in a rebellious mood. From her bedroom window, she could smell fresh air and the sweet scented breeze over Kahindo Falls on Glitta River. Beyond, she could see the muddy paths winding through patches of peasant plantations growing maize, beans, cabbages and other crops, after which were throngs of people, walking in all directions. This was the world of Shaka, the world of real people not confined to stone walls, kei-apple hedges with thorns and big alsatians with armed guards by the gate; a prison called home.

Nzinga dressed in jeans, put on her make-up, a leather jacket and went to the servant quarters. She told the housekeeper to inform her father she had gone to town. She drove towards Kawempe shopping centre. Shaka's house was near the main road and she drove on to a spot as near to the compound as possible. Children gathered around the BMW, feeling its metallic blue paint and watching their reflections in the wing

144

mirrors. Everyone was surprised to see the driver, a young, beautiful girl. In Kawempe, if you saw a clean, expensive car, it was a stolen one. Elder people watched the young woman as she walked into Shaka's compound. Nzinga counted the doors, and knocked. Shaka opened the door.

'Nzinga!'

Some primordial instinct that first manifested itself in the garden of Eden took hold as they reached out and embraced.

'Please come in,' he said breathlessly.

Having found out Nzinga had driven to the compound, Shaka quickly went outside to find the flashy BMW surrounded by a crowd, both young and old.

'Is she your friend?' one of the children asked.

'Yes, she is. Please take good care of the car,' he requested.

'We will, Shaka, we will. Will she give us money for sweets if we take good care of the car?'

'Yes, she will.'

People on the road were discussing the strange occurrence.

'And you saw the way she held and kissed Shaka! Like a professional!' The hug had been modest, most friendly and very innocent but, in the world of small things, events must be given their disproportionate prominence.

'Poor Shaka, he was employed only the other day and now he is giving his whole salary to prostitutes!' another said.

'Ah, but the young man is doing well! Look at his mother now, she has changed, and old man Agu sings his praise! Surely, Shaka is not stupid. If anything, he is the brightest boy we have ever had in this area.'

There was general agreement that Shaka was a good example to be emulated by the youth, both in his personal conduct and in the way he cared for others.

'Shaka is not like other boys from the slums, he is brilliant and carries himself like a prince. Women regardless of their social background and status will fall for him,' another offered.

'That young lady did not look like a prostitute to me. She looked well mannered and dignified,' an elderly woman said.

'I agree with you,' a neighbour said.

The final verdict was that Shaka, the darling of the slums, had found a rich girlfriend. This was a good omen.

Shaka and Nzinga, oblivious of the commotion Nzinga's arrival had caused, were enjoying a cup of tea and discussing life in general. Nzinga was astounded by the depth with which Shaka was analysing Kuzania and the world, past, present and future. He talked of an inevitable rebellion if things did not change. On each and every topic, they spoke with one mind, with one voice.

'I want to visit your mother and Agu,' she said, finally.

'OK, but we'll have to walk because there is no bridge,' Shaka said.

'That's all right with me.'

They locked the house and walked to the car.

'Will she buy us sweets?' the children asked again.

'Yes, she will, when we come back,' Shaka promised.

'Here,' Nzinga took out some money and was about to give it to the children.

'Don't!' Shaka stopped her. 'They will fight over it!' Shaka called one of the elderly ladies over. 'Give the money to this woman and ask her to buy herself a drink and sweets and biscuits for the children.'

The woman took the money and spat on her chest, blessing Nzinga's kindness. An orderly procession of children followed her to the nearest kiosk.

Shaka and Nzinga arrived at the house of Shaka's mother. She welcomed them in great surprise.

'Shaka, why do you bring a visitor to my house without prior notice?'

'It is OK, Mother, I am to blame. I dragged him here!' said Nzinga.

Shaka's mother looked at Nzinga. She was not from their world and yet she spoke like a humble and well-brought up girl.

'Shaka, go and get some milk and bread,' his mother commanded, giving Shaka some money. Shaka's mother and Nzinga were left alone.

'How is your health, Mother?' Nzinga asked.

'I am much better. Shaka has taken good care of me. How did you know I was sick?'

'He told me.'

'So you are old and good friends?'

'Yes, we are.'

'You said your name is Nzinga. Where do you come from?'

'Dad says we came from here. We live in the ridge behind Happy Valley.'

'Who is your father?' Shaka's mother asked.

'Mr Tumbo,' Nzinga said.

'Oh! Sorry, excuse me. I am glad to meet you.'

'Me, too,' Nzinga said.

A chill came into the house. Nzinga felt it, and Shaka's mother did not know how to blow it away. Soon, Shaka was back.

'Mother,' he said clearing his throat, 'Nzinga is the daughter of Hon. Tumbo.'

'She has already told me,' Shaka's mother said quietly, almost in a whisper.

Shaka sensed trouble.

'We are very good friends,' he continued.

'She has already told me,' his mother said tersely.

'It was on her insistence that I got the job from her father,' Shaka continued.

'You had known each other before then?' Shaka's mother asked in surprise.

'No!' Nzinga said. 'Shaka came to see my father with a letter but my father did not treat him well. I insisted that he be given a job.'

Shaka's mother looked at her son. 'Is that so?'

Shaka nodded. He sensed his mother's attitude changing.

'You are a very kind woman. Welcome to my house and make it your home,' she said, offering them tea.

Shaka's mother watched them later as they walked happily away. Back in the house, Shaka's mother said a quick prayer, asking God to protect her son, and continued her chores, deep in thought.

Shaka and Nzinga found old man Agu seated outside his hut. He had two elderly people with him, deeply engrossed in serious discussion. They greeted the elders, who left their seats to Shaka and Nzinga.

Sunset in the tropics is quite a spectacle. As the fireball slowly falls off the cliff of the earth, shadows lengthen. When the ball is gone, its rays in a kaleidoscope of colours hang in the air, disappearing with a slow, calculated reluctance. The sunset is a sweet ballad sung by the wind, which once made Agu's lips quiver. They don't quiver any more.

'Sit down my children,' he said with a steady and

commanding voice. 'I see you've brought a friend with you!' Agu addressed Shaka.

'Yes, Great-grandpa, this is Nzinga, a very special friend. We've been to see Mother.'

'Welcome, young one. Shaka, there are many things you are keeping from me! You never told me you had found a woman!' Agu said jokingly.

'She is not exactly my woman, she is a good friend,' he defended himself.

'Shaka, don't be a fool! A beautiful girl like this one should be taken into the house without wasting time. In my days of youth, that is what we did. These days, we do not have men, we have boys who never grow up! There is a saying: "A beautiful woman will go past the homestead of the poor without anyone asking her to enter because they have nothing to offer." Shaka, you are a man now, don't be a boy – you have a lot to offer!'

Shaka and Nzinga were getting more than they had bargained for.

'Great-grandpa, Nzinga is a university student and she is studying our culture, songs, dance and history. I told her you could help,' Shaka said.

'My daughter, whatever you want to know, I've already taught him. Maybe he is too shy to let it out of his mouth but it is all in his head! Am I telling a lie, Shaka?' He continued, 'What do you wish to know, my daughter?'

As the evening wore on, they learnt a lot from Agu. Nzinga was absolutely mesmerised by what she heard. She gave Agu some money to buy snuff and he blessed her by spitting on his chest. Agu was impressed with the depth of Nzinga's probing questions. He felt a deep liking and admiration for her, and was impressed by her help towards Shaka.

149

'Nzinga, you are a blessed woman! If it were not for your kind action, I would have died of cold by now! You see this warm coat I am wearing? It was bought by Shaka. On my bed there is a warm blanket, which he also bought me. Your kind act has given a new lease of life to many. My child, shake my hand again.'

They shook hands and this time, it was a long and warm handshake. Agu once again spat on his chest.

'Both of you, whichever land you will cultivate, may its yields be multiplied a hundred fold.'

They both had received the highest blessing in the land from the sage, the prophet, and the seer.

Agu's eyes dimly focused on them as the two happy souls disappeared into the night. As he moved into the house, he felt a warmth engulf him and momentarily his mind locked on the procession of liberation forces marching to the war against evil. He saw Shaka as their commander, with Nzinga marching by his side. What does this mean? he asked himself. These two are not ordinary people, they are friends of the gods who guard good in the fight against evil.

Upon her return, Nzinga found her father talking to the guard at the gate. He looked at Nzinga's car, which was covered in mud.

'Where have you been?' he asked in anger.

'To Kawempe,' she replied softly.

He looked at her and spat on the ground. Then he got into his car and drove off, a wounded bull ready to kill in revenge. I am going to teach that sonofabitch, slum filth, good-for-nothing scum boy a lesson he will never forget! he said to himself. He was going to see WaMwago.

7

Rough Road to Paradise

The screaming headlines in the special afternoon edition of the local daily read, 'Petro Mpendwa Murdered'. Petro Mpendwa was the minister for Culture, Women and Youth Affairs. The indefatigable middle-aged man had given new impetus to the nation's culture through festivals, youth centres, women's projects and sports. He was a personal friend of Vice-President Hon. Fikira. It was widely argued that if other honourable ministers had the same commitment to duty, Kuzania's woes would be a thing of the past. What endeared him to the people was his humility and honesty. His popularity was becoming a bush fire throughout the land and people were openly saying he should be vice-president if Fikira became president. Rumours were rife that he was associated with a clandestine movement whose aim was to wage a guerrilla war should Hon. Tumbo corruptly take over the presidency. He was regarded as a champion of good, while Tumbo was the prince of evil and darkness, a demon in human flesh.

Hon. Mpendwa's body was fished out of a disused quarry, in the suburbs of Glitta, which had become a lake with the rains. The official version was that he had been seen driving in the direction of the quarry with a woman passenger on the night of the murder. The pathologist's report indicated he had been hit with a blunt object on the head, which cracked his skull. He had deep cuts in the throat and abdomen. Neither the car nor the woman had been recovered but they were suspected to be submerged deep in the quarry. Official investigations were continuing and the president would initiate a Commission of Enquiry into the murder.

Dark gloom descended over Glitta and by three o'clock, the city was deserted. Murder and assassination of able sons of Kuzania had been going on since independence. As a result, Kuzania's political ranks were decimated, leaving fools, psychopaths and idiots at the helm. People said this would not have been if so-and-so had lived. From the day of the betrayal and murder of Shaka's father to the death of Hon. Mpendwa, Kuzania had buried most of its able nationalist leaders. The vacuum created was a political void, which made Kuzania the laughing stock among nations.

Shaka, like everyone else, packed up and went to Kawempe, deep in thought. He remembered vividly Agu's words on the fight between good and evil and knew without a shadow of doubt that evil had claimed the life of one of the good sons of Kuzania.

The country was very tense, with anger unable to express itself. The University of Glitta had hardly resumed classes for a week. Somehow, the anger of the people found an outlet there. Students stormed from their halls of residence and invaded the deserted city. They sang near-forgotten liberation songs, smashed shops and stoned any car on sight. The unemployed and the street urchins took advantage of the situation to break in and loot shops. For a while, at least, some would

152

be rich enough to afford a square meal. Looting was no more than an expression of anger at hunger and deprivation in the land of plenty.

Nzinga, holed up in her room, could not drive to Kawempe as her father was in the house. He was celebrating with Kimondo, the minister for Internal Security, Hon. Nyoka and their foreign friends. Nzinga did not understand the reason for the mirth but she was disgusted, considering the loss to the nation of her father's colleague in the Cabinet. Her hatred for him was now a throbbing reality.

Information began to circulate in whispers that the government version of the cause of Hon. Mpendwa's death was a lie. The few who had seen the body when it was fished out reported that both his eyes had been plucked out and his legs and arms broken. He also had two bullet wounds to the head. Some of those who had seen his body had been picked up by the police 'to help with investigations'; in reality, detained. The only car that had been seen in the vicinity on the fateful night was a police van. The neighbourhood had thought it was on patrol. Now they knew better. To render credence to doubt was the fact that no woman had been reported missing and the minister's car had not been fished out. In Kuzania, two plus two was no longer four, it was equal to any number the government agents pronounced. Lives, even those of prominent and good politicians, had become prime targets of the political madness reigning in Kuzania. For those who assisted, promoted and executed the inglorious acts, there was protection and rich rewards. Professional assassins were now wealthy members of high society. They were all from the organs of state security with Hon. Tumbo, the people's representative, as their godfather, and he was ruthless in his evil scheming for power.

In the hearts and minds of the ordinary people, meanwhile, Petro Mpendwa's name was painted in big letters in gold, and it could not rust or wear off. To them, he was a hero, like General Jongwe Mkombozi and others who had died trying to give the people a new meaning of life in the struggle for African renaissance. His death hung like the sword of Damocles over the evil political leadership in Kuzania. They now understood that when a regime rots, it rots from top to bottom. 'Some day,' people said, 'someone will answer for all this. We shall then build monuments in honour of the fallen heroes, the friends of the wretched of the earth.' This, however, remained more of a dream than a reality in the circumstances. Even to the most ignorant, the running of state affairs and the diabolical conduct of the leaders was a game whose rules were dictated by insanity, an abuse to common sense and an insult to conscience. The national leadership was in cahoots with criminals, psychopaths and opportunists. They stood exposed and naked. They were like the wall of Jericho with graffiti in broad letters written on it. What was inscribed read 'incompetence, corruption, abuse of human rights, murders, civil war, genocide'. There was also 'power, money and devil worship'. Unfortunately, unlike in Jericho, there was no Joshua to bring the wall tumbling down.

Hon. Tumbo was happily seated on his throne of chaos. He was perfecting his strategies and tactics in the season of change. To him and his supporters, the demise of Mpendwa had removed a major stumbling block but there were still a few more to go before the road to State House was pronounced clear. The death would serve as a warning to the incumbent vice-president, who was the biggest threat.

Hon. Tumbo's joy was, however, incomplete because his priceless Nzinga was behaving in a manner incompatible with his grandiose scheme. She was debasing herself, sabotaging his strategy for a political marriage. By associating with commoners she was his Achilles' heel. To his mind, she had fallen under an evil spell; had Kahindo the witch-doctor lived to this day, he would have her taken to him to have the spell cast out. The only way to bring her back to her senses was by dealing with the agent of evil, the village scum called Shaka. He was attending to the problem with his usual meticulousness.

Within a couple of days, the University of Glitta was reopened following the riots. Nzinga had just a few weeks to her final exams and she was working hard. The lectures from Agu had given her a deep insight into understanding anthropology as it related to her people. Her lecturers marvelled at the way she was handling issues in depth, with ease. They were encouraging her to take a master's degree and to join the teaching staff. She had two choices: either to undertake the master's degree or to join the National Youth Service in readiness for a working career. Taking a master's degree at the university would mean continued fights with her father. Going overseas would be running away from the reality of herself and her people, which she so much wanted to come to grips with. Opting for National Youth Service, on the other hand, would take her away from the clutches of her father and at the same time keep her in touch with reality. She made up her mind to join after graduation.

* * *

It was a Saturday afternoon when Shaka and Nzinga boarded a minibus at the university bus stop and went to Kawempe. They found old man Agu waiting for them. He had been pestering Shaka on the whereabouts of the 'beautiful girl'.

'My children, I've cheated life for far too long. These days, I hear the voices of those who went before calling me. Sooner or later I will answer the call and join them. Before that day comes, I want to give you the secrets of my heart because the good spirits have commanded me to do so.'

Old man Agu narrated to them his links with the celestial voice. They were told about the genesis of evil, how sin spread to the world and how Kuzania became the devil's workshop. Agu told them about the struggle between good and evil and how finally the two forces were destined to clash in the final Armageddon. What he did not tell them was that the good spirits had chosen the two of them as bearers of good in the struggle against evil in Kuzania.

'There is no immutable law that says our people's song will for ever be one of lamentations,' he continued, 'it is the game of power and money that has sapped our souls. Not so long ago, we all spoke with one voice asking for freedom and, in the next breath, we were divided with independence. Now the politicians are slitting each other's throats as they fight for the highest office in the land. Evil is eliminating good before our very eyes. Soon, the same devils will come to us asking for votes in elections. We, like hapless zombies, will dutifully elect to parliament and State House the very worst of them that cajole the population with money. Even worse, the emerging regional and tribal alliances will be used to set one tribe against another. They too, will be slitting each other's throats and shooting one another with bows and arrows. It is no longer love your neighbour as you love yourself, it is butcher your neighbour before he butchers you. The tribal leaders claim victory after genocide; celebrations are held over the stench of the decomposing bodies of their neighbours with whom they shared a calabash of porridge only yesterday! It is a game and the victors who count the numbers of the dead, the mutilated and the displaced will tomorrow be counted themselves as losers, in another victory, in another clash. And in this chaos, Africa still dreams of finding her rightful place in the sun! Yet Africa will rise after the present evil has been eliminated. The battle between good and evil has already begun and you, my children, are now privileged to witness this battle from a position of knowledge, armed with the vision of a better tomorrow. Give me your hands.'

Shaka and Nzinga gave old man Agu their hands, which he held together. As the warm intensity of a celestial presence spread over him, he spoke to a being they could not see. 'I've fulfilled my duty, let it be as I have seen.' When he loosened his grip they felt a strange warmth engulf them. They looked at each other, lost in the awe of the old man, the sage, the seer, the prophet, the man who communicated with gods and angels of good.

'My children, go in peace and brace yourselves for the tough times ahead.'

'Thank you, Great-grandpa, and may God be with you,' Shaka said.

'Thank you, Great-grandpa,' repeated Nzinga.

Shaka and Nzinga left Agu's house in silence. Shaka escorted his friend to the bus stop, both without speaking a word. The weight of what they had heard hung heavily on their hearts.

That night, Nzinga did not go home, but slept in the halls of residence at the university.

Nzinga was awarded a first-class honours degree. Her father, who was in the thick and thin of political campaigns, gave her a bundle of money to buy anything she wanted. She called Shaka and the two celebrated her graduation with ice-cream. It was as they were seated that Nzinga broke the news to Shaka that the following week she would be reporting to the National Youth Service camp, four hundred kilometres from the city. Shaka felt as if an old friend was deserting him.

'Will you come to visit me in the camp?' Nzinga asked. 'Give me your address and I will write to you when I get there.'

As they parted, Nzinga gave Shaka two envelopes: one addressed to Agu, the other to his mother. 'Shaka, I don't want you say a thing! My father gave me money to buy a present. You and I have celebrated my graduation with ice-cream, the rest is for my friends to celebrate. Please deliver these envelopes and tell them I will see them as soon as I can.'

'But...'

'I said, not a word, remember!' Nzinga, radiant with happiness, held Shaka's hands. With a final promise to keep in touch, they parted company.

Agu was surprised to receive so much money from Nzinga, but he accepted it. 'The gods choose those with big hearts for their work.' Shaka could not fathom the meaning but he knew that these were very kind words. Shaka took the second envelope to his mother.

'Mother, why are you crying?' he asked.

'Shaka, these tears are for you. First, I had the pain of losing your father and soon I am going to lose you!' she cried.

'No, Mother, I will always be by your side. Nzinga is only a friend, and she is a good person. She is not the type who would drive a wedge between you and I and, after all, she is only a friend and not a girlfriend!'

'Shaka, you are too innocent and too naïve to see life as it is,' she said steadily, 'but, let me tell you, innocence is the mother of misery. Ever since I learnt that she was Tumbo's daughter, I've not slept a wink. The daughters of such men are not supposed to mix with the likes of you. To her father, you are worse than a leper and he will kill you! Leave that girl alone.'

'Mother, you don't understand . . . '

'Shaka, a mother feels pain long before the child is hurt, be warned,' she said. 'Don't misunderstand me, I like Nzinga very much but there are dangerous consequences for your friendship. Please explain it to her. I am sure she will understand.'

'I will, Mother, and I want you to know that she kindly asked me to say goodbye to you,' he reported.

'Where has she gone?'

'She has graduated from university and gone to the National Youth Service camp.'

'The daughter of a minister has gone to the National Youth Service camp? Her father agreed that she should go to the National Youth Service camp?' she asked again. It was only the children of the non entities who went; the children of the rich went abroad for masters' degrees.

'No, Mother, Nzinga and her father are not on speaking terms. It was her decision.'

'That girl is a very special child. She will go very far in life. Why is she not talking to her father?'

'I don't know, Mother,' he lied.

'Well, just take care my son and tell her that, because I like her, I have accepted the gift. Otherwise, you would have returned the envelope to her,' she smiled. They parted company.

His mission accomplished, Shaka retreated to his humble dwelling, a little wiser and more confused. He recalled the anger Tumbo had shown and the abuses he had unleashed on him. He knew his mother was right, in a way. But Hon. Tumbo would surely not think of harming him simply because he was a friend of his daughter. The night was long and it wore away very slowly for Shaka.

Nzinga packed her bags and was driven secretly to the National Youth Service camp. As the sleek BMW left the city all she could think of was how she was going to miss Shaka, his mother and Agu. The roads were filled with throngs of gloomy faces walking aimlessly in all directions. Probably they were still mourning the death of the late Minister Petro Mpendwa.

Old man Agu was very happy with himself. He had offloaded the heavy burden he had carried for days. In Shaka and Nzinga, he had deposited the secrets of life and he knew they were safely stored. In bed that night, he said a prayer: 'The white man's book says there will be heaven and hell after death. Heaven for the good and hell for the bad. We will see. In all my life, my deepest preoccupation has been over my existence as a man on earth. I have a right to be here, otherwise why was I born? Nobody has more right to be alive than another because at birth we are all equal. In the capacity of a man, I have humbly and honestly preoccupied myself with my personal welfare, that of my family, my society and my nation. I have never done anybody any harm. My main concern has been how to make life better. It has not always been easy, with evil men establishing themselves as more equal than others, believing they were born to lord it over others. I've tried hard to understand the basis of their greed and irresponsibility in the name of leadership. At the twilight of my life, I have been assured of light at the end of the tunnel.

'I've seen generations of leaders come and go but none like this one. They are so drunk with power that they are completely lost in their self-importance. With an aimless leadership, the people are lost like sheep without a shepherd. The package of independence handed to us carried hell. I am ashamed and amazed by the willingness and vigour with which the people's representatives enforce the package on the people. As old as I am, I will shout freedom even with my sapped energy and frail breath, to my last heartbeat! Grant me strength, oh Lord. Some day, the gods of good will deliver us from the power of evil, and the time is not far. Amen.'

Agu covered himself with the warm blanket Shaka had bought him and went straight to sleep, as if he had the assurance that his prayers had not fallen on deaf ears.

With the words of his mother's warning weighing heavily on him, together with the revelations from Agu, Shaka felt his life was getting out of control, like a whirlwind. Nzinga was gone and he felt as if a part of him had gone with her. He was confused and unsure of himself. He tried to find solace in books but anger boiled inside the more he discovered the root causes of the ills affecting Kuzania. He was reading Nkurumah's

Neo-colonialism, the Last Stage of Imperialism. When he finished the book, he had a clearer picture of the struggle between good and evil, which Agu had so ably traced. Thoroughly exhausted in mind and body, he decided to take a break.

His new routine crystallised in the old company of Musa and Apunda in Vuruta Bar. They were happy to welcome him back. They noticed he had become reticent, quiet, more mature and he drank very modestly. He was like a man with a mission in life, a mission they did not understand. What the three had in common was hard to comprehend. Apunda was a graduate from the University of Glitta, Shaka was an upstart trying to better himself and Musa was a carefree, self-employed slum dweller. There was no doubting the depth and warmth of their friendship, though. Their company was also enjoyed by two journalists from a local daily who fed them with scoops yet to appear in the newspapers.

Around this period, an old friend of Musa who went around by the name Brother Music arrived from Mimosa, where he had been working as an entertainer in a nightclub. Brother Music had returned to Glitta to sign a recording contract with an international company. However, the deal had fizzled and he was roaming the streets, entertaining passers-by with his guitar. He had not found a hotel contract and his contract in Mimosa had expired. For long, he had harboured the dream of becoming a recording artist. With his advanced age and his kind of music, that dream was no longer realistic. The music he played belonged to a bygone generation, the songs he had composed rejected as unmarketable. His best days were behind him.

Brother Music had no left leg and walked with the aid

of a crutch. He had joined the King's African Rifles and was trained in artillery. During the Second World War, he was deployed in the North Africa campaign. In one of the many engagements, his artillery piece was knocked out by a German mortar shell. By the time he regained consciousness, he was in a military hospital minus a leg. It was during convalescence that he met a friend in the hospital, who had a guitar. As they sat idly, his friend taught him how to play. By the time they parted, Brother Music was doing wonders with the instrument. Upon his return to Kuzania, he was declared unsuitable for the King's African Rifles and abandoned with a small monetary reward with which he bought himself a guitar. That was the beginning of his recording dream, which never materialised. Now that his dream was up in smoke, he was quite happy collecting coins on street corners, singing to any idler who cared to stop by and listen. Brother Music enriched the diversity of Shaka's group by adding humorous stories and music to it. He travelled with his old guitar hanging from his right shoulder. Every time he started singing, people would pull seats closer and, in the process, get to talk to one another. Shaka made a lot of friends from the crowd in the bar in this way.

Nzinga had not written and Shaka was feeling lonely. He had never thought seriously about a girlfriend, but Nzinga had awakened something that had lain dormant in him: the need for companionship from the opposite sex. Shaka was not a virgin, though; no child over ten was a virgin in Kawempe. In the slums, sex was regarded as a game among the young ones and as a trade among the older girls. However, these chance encounters were casual and involved no lasting obligations.

He feared city girls whose interests were movies, coffee-houses and discos. They were quite a drain on the pocket but they were always readily available as long as you could afford to keep them happy.

'You can exchange them like shirts or socks! I call them "come easy, go easy",' Apunda had briefed Shaka. 'Even married women are yours for the asking, though you have to date them during office hours.'

Shaka was getting wiser on the generosity of women in Glitta as dictated by the size of the pocket. The range was there; it was up to him to decide which one of the categories he wanted to hook himself to: schoolgirls, secretaries, Ms or 'miscellaneous', married women, harlots, or any combination from the mix.

Somehow, he felt Nzinga had awakened in him something more beautiful than the women in Glitta could ever offer. He was not in love with her, but he liked her very much and their relationship was based on mutual respect and understanding, clean, natural and unselfish. But they were from two separate worlds and the words of his mother kept ringing in his ears, despite nature and the chemistry of his body ringing another warning. He was torn between the desire to be closer to Nzinga and the limitations imposed by his background and social status. But surely, he lamented, the two worlds could be bridged?

Apunda was sitting opposite Shaka in Vuruta Bar and had been watching him closely.

'Shaka,' Apunda called, 'it is obvious that you are under some kind of stress or in trouble. Maybe we can help. You know, when men resolve to kill an elephant, the elephant will fall! There is no problem too big to solve – what do you say, Musa?'

'Apunda, when a man decides to kill the she-elephant leader of the group alone, that man is as good as dead,' Musa said.

Shaka raised himself sharply and looked at Musa straight in the eye. Musa's eyes were full of pity and understanding and Shaka lowered his own.

'What do you mean by that, Musa?' Apunda asked.

'The good book says whatever is done in the dark will come to light! The story is all over town. The touts know about it and the minibus drivers know about it. Shaka, why don't you tell Apunda what is eating your heart?'

In all his life, Shaka had never been in a situation like this before. He thought Musa was trying to trick the truth out of him, but here was neither the time nor the place. Musa, the doctor in rags, had many ways of diagnosing problems but there was no way he could get to the root of this one.

'You seem to know a lot more than I do. Tell him!' challenged Shaka.

'He is madly in love with a minister's daughter,' Musa whispered to Apunda.

'What!' shouted Apunda.

Musa took his bottle of beer and drank it slowly, his head tilted backwards, closely watching Shaka.

'You, madly in love with a minister's daughter!' Apunda laughed. Musa did not join in; Shaka had frozen in his seat.

'Musa, some jokes are in exceedingly bad taste —' Shaka tried to talk but was interrupted by Musa.

'Shaka, you have never known me to joke over a serious issue and I won't start now. What I have said is true, is it not?'

'Well, not exactly,' Shaka said quietly.

'When the honourable minister gets wind of what is going on, you will wish you were never born. Haven't you heard of stories of young men disappearing without trace? Nzinga belongs to the world of the precious, the protected, insured by the security of guns! This is Glitta and things happen in a flash. Do you value your life?'

Musa was so serious that Shaka felt as if the day of judgement had come. He did not say a word. He kept fingering his bottle of beer on the table, turning it around. He was shocked to know the details Musa had, including Nzinga's name.

'How did you come to know about it?'

'Small men look for big stories to tell. When Nzinga visited your place in a big glittering car, whispers reached the ears of those who make gossip their business, those who eat by selling the blood of others. How many young girls drive BMWs in this city, tell me? There is only one and she is the envy of every young man, the angel in the dreams of touts and minibus drivers, university students, lecturers bachelors and married men! They are envious of you. My fear is that someone will tell her father in return for a favour and that will be the day!'

'He already knows,' Shaka heard himself say, like a man in a trance.

'And what did he say about it?' Musa asked in amazement.

Shaka kept quiet, the picture of Hon. Tumbo chasing him away from his house dancing before his eyes. He was in pain and trapped. His friends could see Shaka was in deep trouble.

Apunda broke the silence.

'Shaka, I thought we were good friends and yet you

166

did not tell me about it! Where the hell did you find the guts to drive yourself into the arms of a minister's daughter – and Hon. Tumbo's daughter at that! Man! You have more courage than I gave you credit for.'

Shaka at last found his voice. If he had to perish, then he had better perish as a man.

'Let me tell you people, innocence is the mother of misery, and the good man shall perish together with the wicked. The road to hell is crowded with believers, people who lived like moles out of their burrows, as blind as bats, marching to eternal damnation.' Shaka's eyes stayed fixed on the bottle as though he were reading his own words on it. 'Musa, may I have a cigarette?'

'Sure, Shaka, go ahead. Since when did you start smoking?'

'From now on Musa, with this very cigarette. If life is worth living and life is short, then it must be enjoyed to the full, cigarettes included!'

In between puffs at his cigarette, Shaka told them the story of how he met Nzinga.

'We are only friends, not lovers! Now that she is gone, I do not see what the fuss is all about. There is no danger at all,' he proclaimed, puffing away the last remains of the cigarette.

'My friend,' one of the journalists who had arrived in the middle of the story spoke up. 'A story has just arrived from one of our stringers informing us that Hon. Tumbo has beaten and sacked the policeman at his gate because he had allowed into the compound an unruly hemp-smoking boy from the slums whose intention had been to rape his daughter. We have been looking for the policeman but he has vanished. Could it be that you are the slum boy mentioned in the story?'

167

'Does he look like a rapist?' Apunda interjected angrily.

The journalist continued, 'I do not think that even if we had all the facts the newspaper would have been courageous enough to publish the story. Nobody messes with Hon. Tumbo and gets away with it. We were told the hon. minister was raving mad, swearing that this boy from the slums would suffer. He swore that he would protect Nzinga with all the means at his disposal. He is going to wrench the neck of the vermin who intruded unceremoniously into the forbidden world.' The journalist spoke like a prophet of doom.

'Supposing all this is true, tell me, what is wrong with me falling in love with Hon. Tumbo's daughter, tell me!' Shaka insisted.

Musa pondered the question for a while and replied, 'Shaka, you understand the beauty of love, which I must confess I don't. My mother abandoned me as a child and I have never known what it is to love or to be loved. I have no respect for women, be they mothers, whores or daughters of ministers. To me, they are all sources of pain and misery like Eve in the garden of Eden. But you know very well we now live in a divided world in this country; ours is the world of beggars. In the eyes of the demigods who live in Happy Valley, our world exists purely to serve their world. What you have done has violated the laws of this existence, like Prometheus stealing fire from the gods. You see, the poor have no right to fuck the rich but the rich have a right to fuck the poor. Until good overcomes evil, the poor must not have an erection in the territory of the demigods or they will have their penises severed! Do you understand?'

Like a man carrying the weight of the whole world on

his shoulders, Shaka left Vuruta Bar and went home. Once in his house, he lay on his bed. His thoughts raced through his mind. He realised how precious Nzinga was to him, and it seemed that the more society fought against his relationship with Nzinga, the more it strengthened his resolve for defiance. His father had carved his name in golden letters in the hearts of the people. What of himself? Were he to die now, would he be remembered only as the poor young man who lost his life and his soul because of a woman? No, he was not going to die like a dog without a name. The issue was bigger than just the relationship between a man and a woman; it was one of dehumanisation and rejection. The fight was for himself, for Nzinga and for millions of others in Kuzania who were no longer living but merely existing, waiting to be rescued from misery by death. He felt the rebellious spirit of his father and Agu guiding him. They were going to win a victory over bigotry and ignorance. With Nzinga and Agu on his side he could stave off the threatened nemesis by Tumbo.

This is another weekend and we will drift to Vuruta Bar and drink as if we were paid to do it; then we will stagger home like lost babies without mothers. Men without aim or a purpose in life. But I have fears for Shaka, for by then they might have broken his limbs and fractured his skull, abandoning his body in a forest, to be eaten by hyenas and jackals, and Tumbo will be celebrating his pyrrhic victory. This is Kuzania, where life and death are judged on the pedestal of money and power. Where wisdom and justice are equal to one's bank account, and those without it can drink themselves to the grave. So long live the man who invented

169

beer, or how else do we drown our sorrows? Indeed, he is the saviour of the miserable and voiceless majority. Do me a favour, if you ever find his name, send it to me via the Drinkers' Congregation, Private Box Hangover, Broken Town, Glitta City, Kuzania. I am obligated to send him a message of congratulations for his philanthropic act of salvation. Your kind action will be greatly appreciated and please accept my thanks in advance. Oh! you say it would be more prudent to send it through the local primary school or church or hospital! Listen, my friend, in the slums, there are no schools or hospitals any more! The plots on which they had been built have been grabbed by politicians and their friends. I do confess the church still stands, though with reduced acreage, on account of greed, but we don't go to church any more for we have no sins to confess. You ask what about all those thieves, pickpockets and harlots in the slums! They are not sinners at all, they are only earning an honest living in the only way they can, the best they know how! I thank you for your understanding and I can see you are better material than Mr Tumbo, for a ministerial appointment! We will meet again soon.

Rev. Mwago had not informed anybody about his return. He took a taxi from the airport and went to his house. He found a maid cleaning the house. She was very surprised to hear that he was the husband to Jennie WaMwago.

'I thought she was not married,' she commented.

Upon further enquiry, he was told that Jennie WaMwago had left in the morning and it was not known when she would be back.

'Sometimes she is away all day and all night,' the simple girl informed him.

Rev. Mwago took a minibus and went to visit the bishop, his father-in-law. He found him in the house, reading a Bible.

'Welcome back, my son, how was your trip?'

'Very successful indeed! I am now armed with another degree. I must thank you very much for the scholarship,' the reverend said.

'Well, to tell you the truth, you should thank Hon. Tumbo, who was responsible for your nomination. I was only a messenger,' said the bishop.

'Hon. Tumbo? The offer came from Hon. Tumbo?' the reverend asked, raising his voice.

'Yes, my son, what's wrong with that?'

'Well, I came to let you know that my wife has become Hon. Tumbo's concubine. He has cuckolded me ever since I left – even before I left, according to my cousin, who told me the whole story in a letter while I was away. I seek your understanding in the matter because I intend to sue for divorce.'

'I see, so this is the source of her newly acquired wealth? I had wondered how much money you were sending to her!' the bishop said. 'What can I say! First you rescued her from the cold in Britain and now, when you are about to shine, she does this shameful thing. This is the second time she has brought disgrace to my house and to the church. I will never have anything to do with her again! Never!'

At midnight, Rev. Mwago heard a car drive into his compound. He was seated in the sitting room charting a new course of life without his unfaithful wife. As Jennie inserted the front-door key, she was singing a rowdy song about circumcision. That she was drunk, you could tell from the way she was fumbling with the key. At last she let herself in, staggering, her eyes half closed.

'Why are the lights still ... oh!'

Seated on the sofa was her husband Rev. Mwago, looking murderous. Instinctively WaMwago retreated, got back into her car and drove off. Rev. Mwago did not move from his seat, neither did he close the door. He sat there like a mad man, gazing at the darkness outside, until daybreak. He then packed every item belonging to his wife, hired a pick-up and took them to the bishop's house. He narrated to the bishop and his wife the episode of a drunk WaMwago arriving home at midnight, and how she had left without a word, not to return. He left both father and mother on their knees, in tears, asking God what they had done to deserve this abominable calamity. He walked away from the pitiable sight, never to return.

Jennie WaMwago took refuge in Hon. Tumbo's house and, that night, she got the promise of her own furnished apartment. Tumbo was having the time of his life, with WaMwago ever present to relieve the tension of the heated political campaign and Nzinga's unceremonious departure to the National Youth Service. He could not care less whether Rev. Mwago was back in town or not. He was only an insignificant fly that could be pulverised with the pressure of his little finger.

Rev. Mwago (B. Comm. Hons.) now found himself in a most unenviable situation. He was too ashamed to explain to his close associates the exact details of what had come to pass; he merely told them he wanted to divorce his wife because she had had an affair with Hon. Tumbo. He was cautioned against it with a warning that if he valued his life, he should forget it. But for Rev. Mwago, the fight was not over yet. If the judges and courts could not handle Tumbo, then he was going to handle him alone! The church offered him an unassailable weapon: the pulpit. If Hon. Tumbo and the other demigods thought they could get away with corruption, murder, torture, detention without trial and the cuckolding of husbands, they were mistaken. The day of reckoning had come. He would not divorce his wife, he would let her melt out his existence. Marrying her had been a raw deal in the first place. He would also punish her through the pulpit. He recalled how Jesus Christ had whipped black marketers in the church. He, too, was justified in whipping Hon. Tumbo and Jennie WaMwago with his tongue in the pulpit.

Jennie WaMwago's tale of rags to riches spread like bush fire, helped by the fact that she was now openly wining and dining with Hon. Tumbo. It was known she had ditched her poor husband in search of greener pastures and, with Hon. Tumbo as the most eligible bachelor in town, marriage was quite possible. In the event that Hon. Tumbo became president, Jennie WaMwago would be first lady. Opinion was divided on whether what she had done was right. Some called her a fool and a harlot who would be dropped by the hon. minister when he had had enough of her. Others called her a brilliant woman, a strategist who knew how to strike while the iron was hot. So there they were, each a champion of their cause, with Tumbo busy putting final touches to the succession programme and using WaMwago to relieve his tension; Jennie WaMwago having the time of her life making hay while the sun was shining.

Rev. Mwago, meanwhile, meantime, was burning candles late at night, preparing his lethal sermons. On this earth, one dreams one's own dream. If a single dream should be different from the others there will be tears. When Lucifer dreamt of leadership, he caused chaos in heaven and on earth. One day, when we all dream the same dream, there will be harmony and peace on earth. It is hard to see how Rev. Mwago, his former wife and Hon. Tumbo could ever be persuaded to dream the same dream. An Armageddon was inevitable, and hell would be waiting to receive the losers in the battle.

Whether it was the return of Rev. Mwago or the intensity of the campaign that was affecting Hon. Tumbo, Jennie WaMwago could not tell. Hon. Tumbo had become very scarce. She would not mind if their love-making hit an all-time low, as long as he continued to meet the demands of her financial well-being. But he did not seem to care. She was grateful for what he had done so far but a lot remained to be done before she could stand on her own feet. Her lifestyle had changed and her upkeep required a lot of money if she was to maintain the high standards of the elite circles in which she now belonged.

Had she wronged him in any way? The answer was no. She had promised herself never to punish him again when making love; she had promised herself never again to bite the hand that fed her and had been extra good to him in all ways. He had not complained about their relationship, not once. She feared that Tumbo might be having an affair with another woman. She concluded that something serious must be the matter.

It was in this mood that she drove to the golf club to have some fun. She found Kimondo, Tumbo's campaign manager, seated with a white man, whose name she was to learn was William Stans. She had seen him before at a distance in the company of Tumbo.

'May I join you?' she asked them with a charming smile.

'Sure, sure,' said Kimondo, motioning her to a chair next to him. 'What would you have, a screw?' he asked.

'Right now, I could do with a double!' she said, tilting her head sexily backwards, as her hands ran through her hair.

'Beautiful lady, what's your name? Mine is William Stans.' They shook hands.

Kimondo started his dirty jokes and Stans put in a few of his own. WaMwago, not to be left out, told the dirtiest of them all, the ones she had learnt in Soho as a whore. There was a lot of laughter around the table as though life was one big picnic. When William Stans went to the bathroom, Kimondo seized the opportunity.

'You are so sexy and beautiful and I swear the day I lay you, I will not wash my body for a week.' His hand lay on her thigh.

'Kimondo stop it!' she said harshly. 'You are so ugly and stupid! When will you grow up?' she hissed. 'The only thing you ever think about is fucking WaMwago! You never stop to think about what she eats, what she wears. If you cared like Tumbo does, you would have laid me ages ago!'

Kimondo sat there grinning, pretending not to have heard the insults.

'Where is your bastard friend of a minister?' she asked tersely.

'Hon. Tumbo has gone to the game parks in a private plane. He wanted to get away from the heat of the campaign for a day or two.'

'The bastard! Why didn't he take me along? He knows I am always there for him!'

'Because you are not the only one!' he replied.

175

The words of Kimondo cut her like a sharp knife.
'What?'

'I haven't said anything,' said Kimondo defensively. He immediately cursed his loose tongue. A man does not betray his friend even in moments of weakness, and a slave must always be loyal to its master.

'Kimondo, I want the truth!' said WaMwago.

'Look, you are a woman! Use your sixth sense and don't bother me!'

The two figures sat there in silence until William Stans returned to the table.

'You are very pensive!' came his deep American voice, addressing WaMwago. 'Why have we never met? I find your company most thrilling!'

'I find yours very interesting, too,' she said with a sweet smile.

'You two cut it out,' Kimondo said.

'Why? Are you jealous?' asked Stans.

'WaMwago is Hon. Tumbo's woman.'

'Kimondo, sometimes you should make an attempt to be a gentleman! Why do you address me as just "Tumbo's woman?" I am Jennie WaMwago, full stop. Tumbo is my business partner.' WaMwago had the airs of a queen and her brilliant smile said it all.

'He is my business partner, too. He seems to have a lot of business partners who do not know one another! I guess we should meet more often and exchange notes,' Stans suggested.

'Why not, that's a good idea,' she said.

'You two are playing with fire,' Kimondo warned.

'Why? Do you think he will swallow me alive?' WaMwago asked with a sneer.

Stans knew that Kimondo could be silly and dangerously careless when drunk. He felt it was time to go.

176

'Lady, it was my singular pleasure to meet one as beautiful as you. I sure look forward to meeting you again soon. Here is my business card. Call me and we can exchange notes over lunch.'

WaMwago took the card and put it in her handbag. With an electrifying smile, she said goodbye.

8

The Rising Spectre of Armageddon

Nzinga's arrival at the National Youth Service camp raised eyebrows, though it gave her great relief. She was free from her father and she resolved to live a balanced, realistic and meaningful life. As she settled down she went out of her way to make friends. She was soon jolted by the rumour that her father was suspected to have had a hand in the murder of his colleague, Petro Mpendwa. It made her life miserable and she did not know how to face this disquieting development. She became a recluse once more, a caged bird wishing to fly. She did not have the same vigour she had shown upon joining the camp. She had friends and sympathisers to talk to but her spare time was spent thinking about Shaka and Agu, both of whom she missed dearly. She knew that her rebellion was closely related to her friendship with Shaka, who had opened her eyes. She was not an object and she would fight her father's hold on her, tooth and nail. In this fight, she needed Shaka and Agu.

Meanwhile, Nzinga's feelings towards Shaka were

changing. Every time she thought about Shaka, she felt warm all over and her heart beat faster. She could no longer sit still when she thought of him. These were feelings beyond friendship and Nzinga knew she was in love. At night she found herself exploring the wonderful feeling, spending sleepless nights, tossing and turning, with her heart throbbing like an overheated engine; her mind whirling like a hurricane. Yet she knew these natural feelings spelt danger and doom, if not for Shaka, for them both. She cursed her father and a society that erected barriers against nature, against love.

Shaka tried, in the face of the warnings, to forget that Nzinga had ever existed. It was a futile exercise and the more he thought of her, the more he was deeply bound by their relationship. He realised, finally, that he was in love with her.

And so it was that two healthy seeds, planted in the fertile garden of love by two innocent hearts, promised only the bounty harvest of agony, as one was uncertified, from the slums, and they had pollinated each other. The two young souls found themselves, unknown one to the other, united in purpose, nurtured by love, in hastened maturity, challenging the established order. Verily, verily, I say unto you the man with good intentions shall perish together with the wicked on the day of judgement, in the year X, in the Armageddon. The road to hell shall be crowded with the broken hearts of those who lived their lives like moles out of burrows, as blind as bats, marching to eternal damnation. Show me the single camel that will go through the eye of the needle and I will worship it beyond doomsday. What heroes shall we sing if we fear the size of the eye? We have become docile, dispirited, exhausted and damned because not a single one of us has

179

the courage to cut the Gordian knot. We waste our time in prayers, which are never answered, dancing around our foes, making threatening noises, till we drop down, dead! Ah! but the demigods who control our lives, the people's representatives, they have thrown the needles into the haystacks of power and money and they have become immortal in their own eyes.

'Between Nzinga and I, we shall rake the haystacks until we find the needle and we shall march through its eye hand in hand. That will be the first day of salvation,' Shaka swore.

Brother Music was trying to get a contract in Matunda Bar, to entertain the revellers in the evenings. Matunda Bar was a low-down joint; there were no seats, tables or glasses. People sat on empty crates of beer, and drank straight from the bottle. But it was always full, which was a good indication that in this world of cut-throat competition, simplicity had not entirely died. Musa, Shaka and Apunda were seated in the rear of the bar, between the toilets and the kitchen. There was an acrid smell in the air that made one want to vomit immediately upon arrival. Eventually, one adjusted to the stench. Discomfort had come to be accepted as part and parcel of everyday life, and no one complained.

That day, Shaka had received a letter from Nzinga, about life in the National Youth Service camp. She said she missed him and the letter ended with the most beautiful words he had ever heard; it was signed off 'Love, Nzinga'. Shaka was feeling elated, nine-feet tall. He had not told a soul about it, and he was not going to. It would only compound an already complicated situation.

'Shaka, I am so happy to see you relaxed,' said Musa.

'It is a sign that you've recovered from the affliction of love.'

Before Shaka could respond, Musa was on his feet, hailing Brother Music, who had just entered.

'Over here, Brother Music, over here.'

Brother Music sat on an empty beer crate and leant his crutch next to the wall beside him.

'Brother Music, I want you to do me a favour. You must compose a song based on the story of a slum boy who fell in love with the daughter of an honourable minister. The minister threatened hell and brimstone if the slum scum did not leave his priceless jewel alone,' Musa said.

'You say this is a story?' asked Brother Music.

'Yes, as true as we are seated in Matunda Bar.'

'What makes you think it will sell?'

'Everybody has been waiting for a challenge to the established order! People are happily talking about the affair and I bet you they would happily sing about it!' said Musa excitedly.

'She is the daughter of which minister?' asked Brother Music.

'The daughter of Tumbo!' answered Musa.

'Musa, they say, "Give a fool a rope and he will hang himself." Tumbo will not give me the rope, he will hang me until I am truly dead! No, my brother, such a song would lead to my death. I do not wish to take Tumbo head on.'

'This joke has gone too far, drop it!' said Shaka, who had been listening to the conversation in stupefied silence.

'Come on, my boy, why do you lose your temper over such a trivial matter?' asked Brother Music.

'He is the slum boy in love!' put in Apunda.

'I said, stop it!' said Shaka once again, raising his voice. 'Some day, I will tell you when to sing the song and I will contribute to the words, but that time is not yet, as Brother Music has wisely cautioned. It is not just yet.'

Brother Music started tuning his guitar in preparation for his first audition, which would culminate in a contract if he were lucky. Long ashes from the cigarette in his mouth dropped through the strings into the gaping hole in the middle of the guitar. It was not a very impressive show for one about to sign a contract but it was absolutely normal for Matunda Bar and hardly anybody noticed. You could not blame him, he had only two hands, one twanging the strings, the other turning the keys, and there was no third hand for the cigarette that was still hanging from the corner of his mouth. It was something he had done many times before and it was part of his trademark. As soon as the guitar started wailing in tune, he put it aside, satisfied. The music would come later, when the crowd was a little more drunk.

Musa, in the meantime, was talking to Shaka in low tones. 'You see how calm and composed he is; this man is a walking time bomb. His songs rebuke man's inhumanity to man. He sings against corruption. He sings for us and for the millions in the world who are disinherited. He is a revolutionary, fighting in bars. Not everybody likes him, though, and that is why the music industry will not have anything to do with him. They are scared stiff. This man has read Mao, Karl Marx, and another one he calls DeGrassi. If he were younger with both legs, his passion would lead him to start an uprising against tyranny.'

Shaka kept nodding his head intently listening to Musa. He had not read the books Musa had mentioned but he promised himself he would. He was dying to hear the message from Brother Music. Brother Music, the hero of the drunkards and the enemy of the corrupt regime in Kuzania, sipped his beer.

One could tell from the huge crowd in the bar that, while the political parties and the church had lost many followers, the bar had not. In the bottle people had found an answer to their growing problems. They were drowning their sorrows, and from the look of things, there was a lot of sorrow in Glitta.

'You see,' Musa was telling Shaka, 'his message is true to those who can see further than his moving lips and wrinkled face. He talks of better days to come, with the coming victory of sanity over insanity.'

Shaka was surprised by Musa's words. They sounded identical to Agu's. Brother Music called attention to introduce himself to the revellers.

'My name is Brother Music and I was in the world of music before a lot of you were born. My music cuts across generations. This stump of a leg is the history of my services to the British Empire. My leg was left in North Africa. In those days, we had a different anthem, which called upon God to Save the Queen, I don't know from what, maybe from the king! After beating the hell out of the Germans and Japanese, we came back home to bondage. The queen and her people were free, but we were not. We engaged them and almost beat the hell out of them too but that is another story.'

He took his guitar and started to sing:

> How I wish
> The queen was dead
> and I was free
> with my two legs!

I lost my leg
To save the queen
of some distant island
How shall I dance
Who will dance with a cripple
When the bongo drums
sound in the air
In the year X, the year of our total salvation?

It was a short song, full of agony.

'Encore! Encore!' shouted the crowd.

'What is this about the year X?' Shaka asked Musa.

'It is the sacred year in which our people will free themselves from tyranny. The year when we shall break all
barriers and live a free and proud people,' Musa
answered.

'And do you believe in this kind of an eventuality?'
asked Shaka.

'Of course I do! The days of thieves are numbered and
so are days of tyranny,' said Musa, looking
Shaka in the eye. 'Do you think life will continue like this
forever? Put an animal in a cage, then whip
it and starve it and you will see what happens. It
will free itself and eat you. That is the truth. We are
caged, we are whipped, we are starved, just you wait and
see!'

Musa took a sip from his bottle. He was wearing a
look of deep pain, one Shaka had never seen before.
Shaka took a long gulp of his beer and swallowed hard.
Events were conspiring, washing away his ignorance,
educating him beyond his age faster than any book he
had read. People he had hitherto considered ignorant
had a deep understanding of the social and economic
dynamics of life. Probably they were not ignorant; they

were trained and cowed to look and behave as if they were. It was no wonder that seemingly ignorant natives had driven colonialists out of the continent. There was still hope for Kuzania, he thought.

Brother Music spoke. 'We have been cheated for far too long. We were enslaved, colonised, made to sacrifice our lives to save other nations, but we are still suffering! What do I have to show for my leg? Nothing. What do I have to show for independence? Nothing! My music, I am told, is too inflammatory because it talks about the suffering of the people! How long can we live a lie? How many tormented souls do we have around us singing sad songs because those are the only songs they know! Sad songs when they are awake and terrible dreams at night! They cannot conceal pangs of hunger, they cannot satisfy pains of poverty and disease beyond endurance, and yet a people with a flag and a national anthem to call their own! We have lost limbs, dignity, souls and lives in silence. I tell you what, a change is going to come!' he roared.

'When?' asked one of the drunkards.

'In the year X,' replied Brother Music. They roared in laughter.

'Today,' continued Brother Music, 'a small change will come to my life. If we get along tonight, I will be here tomorrow and the day after and the day after! Are we together now?'

'Yeah, together for ever,' roared the revellers.

Shaka realised it was like a political rally, as if the year X had already come. He prayed that the so-called year X arrive sooner than later, so that he could look Hon. Tumbo in the eye, victorious. Yes, if it was the year X he would take Nzinga's hand and they would dance to the beat of bongo drums and tom-toms without fear. The year X will come, just you wait and see, he consoled himself.

Shaka's thoughts were terminated by the voice of Brother Music, who had started to sing a song about the year X, ending in victory of good over evil, a billion voices rejoicing in freedom. When the song ended, the cheering was deafening. Someone was shouting, 'I will be there too!' and it was picked up by others, who kept repeating, 'me, too', 'me, too'. Shaka was shouting 'me, too, and Nzinga, too!', his voice inaudible, drowned in the din of drunkards, in the celebration of an imaginary victory. The huge loud applause accompanied by whistling was abruptly silenced by a stampede that began in the front section of the bar, near the main door. Revellers were running to the back near the toilets, dropping beer bottles that exploded like mini-grenades, as they jumped over beer crates. There was confusion and cries of agony everywhere in Matunda Bar that night. Men and women were scaling the security wall, falling into the street on the other side. Police and special branch wielding riot gear, batons and guns had invaded the bar. It was learnt later that someone had telephoned police headquarters reporting an illegal anti-government rally taking place in Matunda Bar. Police and other agents of government had responded with their usual efficiency and brutality. Most of the people escaped but Brother Music was found calmly seated on an empty crate of beer, puffing a cigarette. The police descended on him. Some worked mercilessly on his body while others had fun smashing his guitar and crutch to pieces. Unconscious, he was dragged into a police van and whisked to the central police station where torture awaited him.

Shaka was panting as he ran from the bar. Once out

of danger, he sat on the pavement, catching his breath. It had been a close shave and he wondered what would have happened if he had been caught. He had no idea what had happened to Apunda and Musa but he was sure Brother Music could not have scaled the wall with his one leg. To his mind, Brother Music was safe because the police could not possibly harm a cripple.

Once in his house, Shaka went over the words in Brother Music's songs, especially the long one about year X. He could swear that the song and the counsel he had received from Agu were identical. How long can this go on? Shaka heard himself ask. The swelling of a new vision, the desire to mould a new society is in the air. I see it; I feel it on the bodies of half-naked and starved men, women and children. I see it written in the bitterness of each dehumanised, exploited and disinherited soul. I hear it in the wail of unwanted babies in the slums. They are all crying for change, for dignity, for a share of the fruits of their labour, the fruits of independence, the fruits of national wealth. God, there must be a way out of this hell! From this mess, a new Africa must rise in which everyone will be his brother's keeper but, first, we must do away with this selfish, cut-throat and parasitic order of things, which is crippling the soul, mind and body.

Shaka knew what Brother Music's words and those of Agu and the books had done to him. They had opened his eyes to the reality of the looming struggle. He knew that his conflict with Tumbo over Nzinga was in the context of a bigger battle and that he could not win the battle for Nzinga as long as the status quo remained unchanged. The spirit of his father, the great freedom fighter, enveloped him with a clearer vision and strength, in readiness to face the coming challenges. He was a changed man and he could feel it. He had discovered a new side of himself, a fighting man. Heavy in thought he fell into deep slumber. He did not think or dream of Nzinga that night as other matters, urgent and weightier, had come to claim priority over everything else.

News of the arrest and beating of Brother Music were splashed in the local daily. The breaking of his guitar and crutch was taken as the highest possible form of police brutality. The beating and torture was described as barbaric. 'Why arrest a harmless cripple? Why torture a defenceless cripple?' were the questions asked. 'What is wrong with the police? What is wrong with our government?' They were questions without answers. Such is the nature of tyranny. Those who had heard the songs of Brother Music approached the issue from a different angle. They asked, 'Has the government truly lost its senses? Is the regime feeling so insecure that it has to maim, torture and kill because of simple words of a song or the demonstrations of students hardly out of their teens?' The frustration was the planting of seeds of defiance and eventually, rebellion. Civil wars in Africa are not engineered overnight. They are products of years of corruption and incompetence at the highest level.

Hon. Tumbo and Hon. Nyoka had their ears to the ground. They were happy that the popularity and credibility of the government was low, both in Kuzania and overseas. The strategy for 'managing change' was working like clockwork. William Stans warned Tumbo and his supporters that the strategy could very easily lead to a breakdown of law and order or even worse, an armed uprising as had happened in several neighbouring countries. Tumbo dismissed the fears.

'I know these people very well. They are like children on a merry-go-round. It is the operator who decides how many times and at what speed the children will go round. I am the operator of the merry-go-round and you have absolutely nothing to worry about. All these talks about police brutality, torture, detention without trial, and murders are nothing more than hot air, the noise of over-excited children. These people are not capable of organising their own homes; they don't think! They are fools to be led, to be organised when the need arises, and your role is to keep me in the driving seat.' Tumbo had a big grin on his face, very satisfied with the wealth of his experience, wisdom and strategy.

William Stans looked at Tumbo with pity. He recalled words he had read somewhere that 'the African is a child ... to be led.' He wondered whether Tumbo's observations of the situation were right or whether Tumbo himself was not a big child who needed guidance. Stans was merely interested in making money and enjoying life and the status quo suited him perfectly. He had hoped to guide Tumbo to eventually take over the presidency, but Tumbo, like a naughty child, was acting in haste. If the president saw through the veil, heads were going to roll or there would be a big split in the government. Meanwhile, Tumbo and the minister for Internal Security kept the president 'well briefed' on 'an underground movement of dissidents and enemies of the state bent on destabilisation and making the country ungovernable'. They had pledged their direct loyalty to him with a promise to stamp out the rebellion and to restore the name and image of the country. Tumbo had also briefed the president on the activities of one called

Brother Music, who had been recruited by the anti-government movement and was spreading disaffection with the state through seditious, inflammatory and treasonable songs in bars, streets and market-places. The president was assured Brother Music had been arrested and was very satisfied that the situation was under control.

Shaka, Apunda, Musa, the journalists and a few others organised a meeting to discuss how to bail out Brother Music. The venue was a high-class bar, one in which they would not be molested by the police. Their first shock came with the price of beer and an order of three plates of meat.

'I know the man who owns this place,' Musa was saying, 'he frequents the brothel next to my house and his girl-friend drives a Honda Civic.' From the prices it was obvious he ran his high life from the pockets of others. He drove a Mercedes-Benz and had a house in Happy Valley. His children went to boarding school overseas.

'Well,' Musa said picking a piece of meat, 'the pleasure is his and the agony is ours. Gentlemen, let's get on with business.'

The journalists gave an account of what they had gathered. Brother Music would not be taken to court because there were no charges against him. However, being a 'threat to state security' he had been placed in protective custody, incommunicado. They also heard that police had received firm instructions from the minister for Internal Security to arrest those in Brother Music's camp of dissidents. Hon. Tumbo had an interest in the matter and was keeping the president briefed.

They all wondered what madness had gripped the

people's representatives. In the circumstances, it was agreed there was nothing they could do to bail out Brother Music, at least not for now.

At the mention of Hon. Tumbo, Shaka had frozen. 'There must be a way out of this mess,' he whispered rather too loudly.

'Shaka, why are you talking to yourself?' Musa asked.

'Listen, people,' Shaka started, 'my father died fighting for the independence of this country and a better future for all. What has happened since independence? Oppression, tyranny, exploitation and greed have become the hallmarks of leadership. Simple people have no rights and no voice. They are there to be misused, to be seen and never to be heard. The crime of Brother Music is that he tried to speak, to be heard! What am I worth if I cannot build on the inheritance of my father? What kind of a son am I if I cannot protect that which he held so dear and died for? And what is my inheritance but the continuation of the struggle!'

Shaka had spoken more to himself than to the others but they had all heard. They had never before seen him shaking with rage and anger. This was a different Shaka from the one they knew, a transformed man. They exchanged glances. Matters were coming to a head. They were very difficult and dangerous matters. It was Musa's turn to speak.

'Shaka, you have been with us for quite a while now and we trust you. You have revealed yourself very freely to us. All of us here in fact belong to an underground movement that is trying to find a solution to the problems facing our country. Brother Music is not one of us, not just yet. Gentlemen, Shaka needs to belong!'

And it was agreed that Shaka would be introduced to the chairman of the cell to which they belonged and pay his membership fee in the National Redemption Movement.

Shaka could not believe his ears. The struggle had already begun! He was going to join the movement and devote all his energies towards achieving its goals. With the memory of the police brutality in Matunda Bar still fresh in their minds, they parted company.

Jennie WaMwago was not born to take humiliation sitting down. She was the fighting type. She picked up the telephone and called Hon. Tumbo, demanding that they meet that evening. As Tumbo listened to her harsh voice, anger built up inside him. Nobody gave him orders, nobody!

'WaMwago, it looks as if you are growing horns! May I remind you of your place in society? If I had not picked you from the gutter, you would still be wallowing in garbage like a maggot! From now on you do not call me, you wait to be called!' He banged the telephone down on her.

What WaMwago did not know was that Tumbo had just had a row with the vice-president, who had accused him of being in cahoots with the minister for Internal Security to destabilise the government in a strategy to take over the presidency. Tumbo had been warned that although the president was swallowing the lies they were feeding him, sooner or later the truth would be told and Tumbo was going to face the music. 'People are not as blind and foolish as you think,' Hon. Fikira had added.

Tumbo had replied: 'Your sole interest is to take over the country by force and you do not have the interests of the nation at heart. There is no way we are going to let a bunch of dissidents destroy what we have built over the years. Do you want this country to go to the dogs like Somalia or Liberia?'

'You have been warned,' replied the vice-president.

A slow puncture was threatening to destroy Tumbo's strategy in 'the season of change'. To lessen the heat, he called the minister for Internal Security and advised him to release Brother Music. Tumbo also wondered whether he should heed the words of William Stans and ask him to work on an alternative strategy.

WaMwago was a bundle of resilience. When one plan did not work out she tried another. This made life very simple, and she thought the weakest of all creatures was man. Stories told of how Eve had led Adam by the nose to bed, how Delilah had shaved Samson and destroyed his strength, how the Queen of Sheba had disorganised King Solomon and his harem of a thousand wives and concubines. And history will tell of how Jennie WaMwago rose to the stars by destroying many men, she promised herself.

She raked through her handbag and found the business card William Stans had given her. WaMwago left her name and number on the answer-machine and requested Stans to call her back. Barely half an hour later, her phone rang. It was William Stans.

'Hi, beautiful, what's up?' He was unable to hide his excitement.

'I am fine! I thought I should call just to confirm this number you gave me is not a fake!' WaMwago charmed. 'Listen, can you spare the time? I want to see you,' she said, leaving Stans with the benefit of doubt as to why.

'Any time, baby, any time! Who would turn down an offer from one as beautiful as you!' he laughed, laying his cards on the table.

'Some fools who do not know the value of beauty might do just that!'

Stans felt a change of mood in her voice, some touch of anger.

'Is everything all right?'

'We shall talk when we meet,' she said in a friendly tone.

WaMwago arrived at Stans's house dead on seven that evening, as planned. They sat joking and drinking wine. After dinner they sat on a settee in front of a log fire, drinking brandy. The brandy was getting to their heads and soon, they were exchanging long, passionate kisses. WaMwago loosened the buttons of her blouse, complaining of the heat from the fire. In no time at all they were making love, WaMwago's body shaking like a reed in a storm. Maybe it was the sexual starvation she had been subjected to by Tumbo, the special way William Stans caressed her, but the lovemaking had never been so thrilling.

Stans was stunned. He had made love from Vermont to Chile, in the Caribbean and to many women in Kuzania, but none compared with WaMwago. She was the greatest screw he had ever had. They made love again, and Stans suggested that she spend the night but she declined. In the ensuing conversation, Stans told WaMwago that Tumbo was extremely busy and would be for some considerable time to come. However, it was true that he had another woman on the side. 'All politicians are like that,' he concluded.

'Stans, Tumbo has been shunning me and I have suffered sexually and financially. I turned to him because I wanted to set myself up in business but one thing led to another. Now, he doesn't want me and I am not yet in a position to run my life independently. I need some help, Stans.'

'I could help but Tumbo is a friend and a business partner. There is a lot at stake and we have to be extra careful,' Stans cautioned.

'I promise to keep my lips sealed,' she said.

By the time WaMwago left, she had a cheque in her name, and the amount was quite substantial. Stans had made easy money through corrupt deals alongside Tumbo and others. To him, money was not a problem. It was his honour and pleasure to help WaMwago, which also gave the guarantee of many more nights like this one. He was left feeling like a conqueror that had taken over a kingdom at a small price.

The next morning, WaMwago handed a letter to Hon. Tumbo's secretary with the words, 'Give this to the bastard.' She stormed out, barely suppressing tears. The secretary was not surprised at WaMwago's anger. She had witnessed many incidents like this and even worse, between Tumbo and his women.

Hon. Tumbo read the letter:

Your Excellency
You drive me to a little corner deep inside my heart that stores only pain, hate and anger. Way back when I was younger, I suffered these feelings when I lost my way and bastards like you fucked me for money. I am used to being misused, but the difference now is that I won't let you get away with it.

I will remember you like an old wound that will not heal and, as it pains, I will remember who was responsible for it. Some day, you will lick the wound with your tongue.

Have lots of fun with your harlots,
Ms Jennie

Well, he smiled to himself, it will only take a few shillings to calm her down. He put the letter in the shredding machine.

'Women,' he said aloud, 'are never satisfied.'

This led him to think about his rebellious daughter Nzinga. Now that she had graduated from the university, it was time for him to look around among the families with a name, for a man to marry her. Her wedding would be a political alliance between two powerful families, with guaranteed maximum returns. The marriage would be a national event; he would invite everybody who mattered, including H.E. the President, and use the occasion to further his political strategy. Bulls, goats and chicken would be slaughtered in large numbers and beer would come from the breweries in a chain of lorries and trailers. On that day, people would truly know who he was, as he would feed a multitude, like Jesus Christ had. To ensure that Nzinga did not stray again before the day, he would deal harshly with that boy from the slums, as a lesson to others with ill designs on his prized Nzinga, on whom so much rested for his political future.

9

Between the Devil and the Deep Blue Sea

After the long rains, the biggest scramble among the leadership was for contracts to resurface roads and rebuild bridges. The contracts were highly inflated and the jobs so shoddy that, come the next rainy season, havoc would reign again and more contracts would be awarded. To the leadership, it was a profitable game; to foreign investors, it was a nightmare; and to the people it was a complete waste of resources.

When the honourable minister for Justice died in a road accident, the nation was shaken to the core. Most infuriating were the different versions of the accident. The official version had it that the minister's car had entered a main road without due care and had been rammed by a lorry. Other reports said the car was on the highway and the lorry came from a side road. Within minutes of the accident, the scene had been cleared. Such efficiency was not usually known in Kuzania. The driver of the lorry was not charged and his version of the accident was endorsed by the police.

It was not lost to the people that he was an ex-policeman. The minister, his bodyguard and the driver had died on the spot.

A couple of days earlier, the minister had issued a stinging attack, castigating policemen for their lack of judgement and sense of duty. He had harangued them for arresting and harassing innocent people while the crime rate rose to unprecedented levels. They were accused of arresting people, including cripples, for crimes that could neither be proved nor prosecuted. He had strongly advised that if the rule of law were to be maintained the police had to pull their socks up and, above all, respect the habeas corpus.

'I cannot preside over the rule of the jungle,' he had warned.

The honourable minister's attack had received mixed reactions. While the population, the Law Association of Kuzania, human rights groups and the press both local and international had poured accolades on him, calling him a voice of sanity and reason, it had raised great fury from Hon. Tumbo and the minister for Internal Security, under whom the police portfolio fell. Hon. Nyoka had called on the minister for Justice to resign, accusing him of undermining the very government in which he served. He had called him 'a wolf in sheep's skin, a dissident and a traitor, working to please his foreign masters'. Hon. Tumbo had strongly supported this position without making it known who the 'foreign masters' were. It was a commonly used, meaningless phrase.

As expected, there were riots in the streets of the major towns. Government property was set on fire. Policemen, students and civilians died in the mayhem. The president was alarmed by the fury and the magnitude of the riots. His government received the harshest criticism imaginable from both friend and foe. Most worrisome was the strand that the government was at war with itself and that it had lost touch with reality. Some called the president 'ill-advised' and 'under siege of evil powers'. They said he was ignorant of what the nation was going through. He read that his ministers were eliminating one another in a battle for succession and others were busy siphoning money from state coffers and grabbing public land. Farmers had not been paid for milk, tea, coffee, cocoa and rubber, which had been delivered to the cooperatives over a year ago. The cooperatives were broke because the managers and ministers had given themselves huge loans without security, leaving nothing for the farmers. He heard that political leaders were crooks first, business magnates second and least concerned with the welfare of the people and the state. Kuzania was suffering from mismanagement, insensitivity and bad political leadership. It was on the brink of both economic and political collapse. Uncertain times ahead were predicted.

H.E. the President saw this as a smear campaign. The enemies of the state were taking advantage of a mere accident to tarnish the good name of Kuzania, which he had so painfully nurtured over the years. Of course there was discontent here and there but you cannot satisfy everybody, he reasoned. Hon. Nyoka had reported the accident to him and Hon. Tumbo, one of the most senior Cabinet ministers, himself had confirmed the sequence of events.

The president then received a disturbing report from the head of Intelligence on the nature of the 'road accident'. The report implicated Tumbo and the minister for Internal Security. He dismissed it and called an urgent meeting of the Cabinet, warning his ministers about 'washing dirty linen in public'. They all vowed to protect the name and image of the government from further ridicule – and especially from themselves.

At the end of the meeting, something at the back of the president's mind warned him to keep an eye on Hon. Tumbo. He had noticed Tumbo had acquired airs of superiority and arrogance, the reason for which he could not understand. It was as if Tumbo had become some sort of president himself. He had to put Tumbo in his place, otherwise such arrogance could complicate matters and result in grief. If indeed Hon. Nyoka and Hon. Tumbo were implicated in the murder of their colleague, it was a very serious matter. It meant that he, the president, was no longer sure of his personal safety. He recalled that Hon. Tumbo had won a medal during colonial days for his contribution in the fight against 'terrorists', or freedom fighters. It was as a result that he had quickly risen in the ranks as a key figure in colonial public administration, a position he held after independence before plunging into politics. He knew Tumbo had no scruples and his main goals were money and power. He had made Tumbo minister of Commerce because of his business connections with British and US businessmen and investors. He did not understand why the press in both countries was pointing an accusing finger at Hon. Tumbo as the author of the political and economic mess in Kuzania. If Tumbo were indeed a rotten apple, he would be removed from the bunch one way or the other. For the moment, though, he decided to have complete faith and trust in him. He argued with himself that he was not scared of death but was concerned with how history would remember him after he had gone. He wanted to leave a good name.

For quite some time, the president had considered Hon. Tumbo favourably as his heir apparent. Although they were not from the same tribe, he had seen in him a person who could work with men from all tribes and races. The only weakness he had seen was that Tumbo was rather shallow-minded. His catholic outlook at times appeared as a tool in the service of his personal ambitions. This, however, was better than the antagonistic power base of some of the other potential candidates, who were guilty of gross nepotism and embezzlement. True, he had appointed a lot of key members from his tribe but could he have trusted other tribes to toe the line with the same level of obedience? He doubted it. The fact that a lot of his appointees were semi-illiterate was unfortunate but one need not have a PhD to run a public office. They all had most able staff who were educated.

'Such are the trappings of power,' he justified. 'First, you look for the most faithful, and merit is not a strong point in such appointments.' Hon. Tumbo would have a chance to appoint his own team but he was sure he would not overhaul the system. Tumbo would follow in his footsteps.

Maybe the vice-president would be a better heir to the throne. There was no love lost between the vice-president and Hon. Tumbo. He was certain Tumbo would be thrown to the dogs if Fikira took over. The man would also overhaul the system and eradicate corruption and nepotism, which would mean the end of everything he had so painfully built with the help of Tumbo over the years. Even more alarming, the British, US and Indian interests would be thoroughly scrutinised and this would unsettle members of his family, who had many joint ventures with them. It would result in a national catastrophe, one which would leave his name and that of his family highly exposed to ridicule. There and then, he decided that the vice-president would be eliminated in the party elections as a guarantee to future stability and the interests of his family. Then who else was there? It dawned on him that over the years, the most able of Kuzania's leaders had met deaths in various ways. Among the remains, the best was Hon. Tumbo. Yes, Hon. Tumbo was the best leader to carry on his good work with only minor cosmetic changes, without rocking the boat. It looked like a bad choice, but it was the best in the circumstances. Satisfied with his wisdom, he poured himself a Johnnie Walker to celebrate.

In Africa, the season of gales, hailstorms, thunder and lightening brings with it many things. It is the season for cursing, it is the season for pledging vows, for settling old scores, for washing away old ills, for sowing blessings and seeds. It is the season in which the Good Lord created the earth and the garden of Eden.

The claims manager of Kuzania Insurance Company sat glued to his seat, his eyes fixed on the front page of the local daily. Normally jovial and composed, he resembled one who had seen a ghost. He was a wealthy man by any standards, with a stable home and his children were doing well at school. He was neither a drunkard nor a womaniser and was an elder in his local church. He was a contented man.

Shaka noted that his boss was perspiring, although it was a cool morning. He turned to Apunda. 'What is wrong with the boss, today? He looks sick. Have you noticed he has not turned a page of the newspaper for the last thirty minutes?'

'He is moody and unapproachable this morning,' Apunda replied.

'I wonder what is in the paper!'

Shaka reached for the daily he had bought but had not had the time to peruse. Both looked at the headlines.

'Look at this!' Shaka pointed at the picture of a ghastly road accident in which thirty people had died, involving a lorry and a bus. The registration number of the lorry was quite visible and so was the name of the company owning it. It was a company that insured with Kuzania Insurance Company. 'But this lorry was involved in an accident and written off two weeks ago! I personally handled the case on instructions from the manager and the cheque was released yesterday!' Shaka informed Apunda.

'Get the file,' Apunda requested.

'No, we will look at it at lunch-time,' Shaka cautioned. 'Someone has eaten a cool half a million shillings but failed to obey the rules! A written-off vehicle must not move until it is registered again, right?'

'It is going to be a dangerous half million, a disaster,' Apunda concluded.

The claims manager laboriously got off his seat with the newspaper in his hand. He walked out, never to return again. He was being sought by the police with his picture in the papers, under a heading 'Wanted'. He had touched the cake of the demigods in a big way, and he was going to pay for it most dearly.

The newspapers splashed news of frauds in the insurance industry as an example of the moral decay which was threatening all sectors in Kuzania. The story was that the claims manager and the owner of the lorry had conspired to defraud the insurance company. The police was involved and an accident report written. An assessor had given his report, indicating the lorry and trailer were damaged beyond repair and they had been written off. The claims manager had speeded up payment, and the cheque had been given to the claimant and deposited with special clearance instructions. The agreement between the claims manager and the owner was that the vehicle would be off the road until it was given a new registration and re-insured. Unfortunately, the owner thought he could do business in a neighbouring country with his lorry in the meantime. The driver had been instructed to stay across the border. He in turn got a lucrative deal to ferry smuggled coffee and had planned to make one or two quick trips secretly into Kuzania. It was on one of the trips that the lorry was involved in the accident. He had since disappeared.

Investigation teams raided the insurance industry. More cases were unearthed and policemen and assessors arrested. Shaka and Apunda escaped the dragnet by the skin of their teeth. They agreed never to play the game again. This upset Shaka's plans to buy his mother a piece of land and build her a house. From now on, he would not be in a position to frequent bars as often as had been the case. He decided it was time to try the market for a better-paying job.

In Kuzania, only those in positions of power are allowed to steal and embezzle funds with impunity. Lesser mortals, especially if they act independently, do so at the peril of their lives. The claims manager went underground but, sooner or later, he would be unearthed and thoroughly punished for challenging the rules of the established pecking order. Worst of all, he had touched one of Hon. Tumbo's pies.

Later in the week, Shaka received a letter. The handwriting was familiar and, as he opened it, his hands were shaking.

It was from Nzinga. He had not expected a letter from her that soon. He had sent a letter earlier, in which he had revealed his concerns over the fight between good and evil. Nzinga's letter read:

Dear Shaka

Your letter came as a godsend, relieving me from mental anguish over the state of affairs in Kuzania. I want to thank you for taking me in your trust and for the weighty words that freely flowed from your heart. It was heartening to hear that all is not lost.

My dear, ignorance is a bliss enjoyed by a great many in the political leadership. Their crusade is one of self-strangulation but they are blind to it. It is unfortunate that they will take multitudes with them when they sink. As the old saying goes, 'The king does not sigh alone,' and so it is in our case.

There are very few people who can sacrifice their lives for a better tomorrow. They are in constant danger of elimination and, as you put it, from 'muskets' and 'cannons' in the hands of the evil. I believe you and I have opted to face the fire, though we may perish. The words of old man Agu are very fresh in my mind. Evil cannot triumph over good, though its kicks are lethal.

The madness in the political circus has come to a head over the struggle for succession to the presidency. Those involved are like a pack of mad wolves on the trail of a wounded animal. As the scent gets stronger, they become more selfish and they are now mortally wounding one another as the strongest wishes to claim the carcass alone. They call it a fight for leadership.

In their myopic, cut-throat scheming, they have

forgotten that the pack must hunt together, defend as a team and live in harmony. As a result of the in-fighting, the political jungle is littered with the smell of death. What has become of our national pride? Who takes care of the people as leaders butcher one another on the road to a false heaven?

I am delighted that you have looked into these matters with the seriousness they deserve and, no doubt, old man Agu with his deep, searching eyes and wisdom has given you invaluable guidance. We must put our trust in this ray of hope, otherwise we are all condemned to eternal damnation.

As soon as you can, please visit me so that we can discuss these and other matters in greater depth. I miss you.

Love,
Nzinga

Shaka felt renewed, aware there was a divinity of some sort that was shaping his growing relations with Nzinga. Though he could not pinpoint the source, he prayed that it carried the matter to logical conclusions, both in the fight to save Kuzania and in his special relationship with Nzinga.

10

The Power of Love

The National Redemption Movement was taking shape. Its cells were holding serious debates on the future of the country. The leadership was aware of the dangers involved and that Special Branch knew of the existence of the clandestine movement. As the local saying goes, 'The eyes of frogs do not deter cows from drinking water in the river.' They were prepared to treat Special Branch in like manner and drink from the cup of victory. Victories of similar movements in neighbouring countries gave them hope that theirs, too, was not a plunge in the dark.

In the meantime, Shaka had applied for a job in a leading bank and, with the help of a key member of the movement, he had succeeded. He was now a bank clerk and his salary was much higher than before. He hoped to secure a loan to buy his mother a piece of land once his probation period was over. Apunda also left Kuzania Insurance Company to set himself up as an insurance broker. Shaka was pleased that he had severed the shameful link between himself and Hon. Tumbo. He felt independent and free, working with the First National Bank. Things were moving in the right direction. He was grateful that he had not been cowed into dropping Nzinga. He felt tied to Nzinga like a barnacle is to rocks in the depths of the ocean. Their relationship would grow, he told himself, till the sun cooled with age or the oceans ran dry. When all else in the world had lost its shape, form and meaning, he knew his relationship with Nzinga would still be going strong. Nzinga was not an object, she was not just another human soul, she was his alter ego and he knew that this feeling was mutually shared. In the year X, they would dance to the rhythm of bongo drums and tom-toms, transformed into one. He prayed that this was not another castle built on the sand, to be blown away by the wind. Time would tell.

Fire keeps burning as long as the fuel does not run dry, for when it does, the fire dies. When the paraffin dries, the wick flutters and dies. Shaka needed to fuel the fire in his heart. Consumed by love, he wrote to her:

Nzinga, dearest
Do you remember the day
by Kahindo Falls, when
We watched the moon
kiss the sun, a total eclipse
and daylight gave a wink
in half darkness?

Do you remember, the lone eagle soaring high
that evening
And how we wondered
by what compass she would find her nest?
Then as sure as the bright sun
will rise tomorrow

And as sure as the lone eagle
will find her nest again
I will come to you
next Saturday

Show me that man strong enough to sail against the
tide and I will worship him for the rest of my days.
Nature dictates and we submit. Shaka and Nzinga at
the bottom of it all were only a man and a woman,
with hearts that ached for human warmth. Nature is
very strong, stronger than the barriers created by
man, wealth, power and law. But these barriers have
their strength, too, and the good and clean-hearted
will perish with the wicked when calamity strikes.
They will be like moles out of their burrows, marching
to hell and eternal damnation. Believe you me, heaven
and hell are here, on earth, and each day is the day of
judgement.

Shaka, wearing his Sunday best, arrived at the
National Youth Service Camp on Saturday afternoon.
Nzinga had been waiting for him under a tree, reading
a book, her eyes frequently on the gate. It was not the
Shaka of old that she saw, but a transformed man, tall,
stately and as good as the best Kuzania ever produced.
She did not walk to meet him, she ran. Shaka saw her
coming and he ran, too. He lifted her from the ground
and turned two full circles before he put her down.
Instinctively, they kissed. There they stood looking
simply wonderful, like Adam and Eve before sin came
to the world. Nzinga had tears in her eyes. Shaka
muttered, 'I am so happy to see you, Nzinga, so glad,'
and Nzinga was responded, 'I missed you, Shaka, oh,
how I missed you.' With kisses, embraces and sweet

words, they consummated the longing for togetherness, which had been eating them for days on end.

They retreated to the shade of the tree. They talked and talked, freely holding hands and caressing one another, their eyes full of warmth, their hearts full of love, their bodies on fire. Every dream is a balloon, light and very delicate. You must blow it very carefully and, once airborne you must fly it with a strong string attached. If the string snaps, the balloon is gone and, once beyond control, it will be blown aimlessly by the wind until it bursts. They were tying many strong strings to the balloon to ensure it was under control. Tell me, who can bring back a balloon once it takes to the sky?

Near the camp there was a hotel and a lake. Shaka suggested they go boating on the lake first and then share a meal in the hotel before he returned to Glitta. They hired a boat. Each took an oar and they paddled into the calm waters. At first it was difficult to steer and move the boat but they soon found their rhythm. Once away, Shaka told Nzinga about the Movement and all else that was happening in Glitta. Nzinga listened attentively, her eyes fully fixed on Shaka with great admiration. They could not tell how long they were on the lake before the thunderbolt rocked the earth. The clouds were moving fast, pregnant with rain. The first raindrops caught them as they turned the boat around. By the time they anchored, they were drenched. They ran into the clubhouse and took seats by the fire, their bodies and clothes smoking with vapour as water evaporated.

'Nzinga, I want to buy you a drink to celebrate our friendship,' Shaka said.

'OK, I will have a Fanta.'

210

'No, no, have something else like gin and tonic or brandy and coke,' he insisted.

'No, I don't drink that heavy stuff,' she said and then added, 'what will you have?'

'I will have a beer.'

'I will try one, too,' responded Nzinga. At first Nzinga did not like the taste of beer but soon settled down to it and enjoyed it, as the evening wore on.

Shaka suggested having dinner at the clubhouse. They ordered dinner and ate by the fire, discussing innocent things such as Agu and Shaka's mother. The name Tumbo was avoided. Lightning was streaking everywhere in the skies, while the sound of thunder shook the earth to the roots of its foundation.

'Old man Agu says that in a night like this many things happen,' Shaka told Nzinga.

'Like what?' Nzinga asked.

'Old people die, people make vows and such like.'

'Let's make vows,' Nzinga said with a smile. She lifted her glass and made her vow. 'I give my life to Kuzania. Now it is your turn,' she challenged him.

Shaka lifted his glass and made his, too. 'My life to Kuzania and my heart to you.'

'My heart to you, too!' exclaimed Nzinga as they touched their glasses and drank to the vows.

'When I was a little boy, my mother warned me not to sleep on my back on a night like this because lightning could split my body into two. Now, when it rains, I still find myself struggling not to sleep on my back. I long for the day you will be back in Glitta,' Shaka said, suddenly changing the topic.

Nzinga took some time to respond.

'That's one way of looking at it but there are two sides to a coin. I miss you, that's true but then, I am very happy to be away from my father. Have you heard all those rumours about him? I hate him!' she said almost in tears.

'Nzinga, please take heart. These things will come to an end and there is no need to talk about your father like that. Trust me, everything will be fine.'

Nzinga rested her head on his shoulder. As hell broke loose outside with high winds and hailstorms, they sat there like people in a trance, oblivious to everything else except their dreams. They were rubbing shoulders with all that is pure, majestic and beautiful in nature: rain, lightning, wind and the deep sound of a thunderstorm. It was an extraordinary, mysterious moment and one they were bound to remember for the rest of their lives.

Shaka smiled.

'What is so funny?' Nzinga asked lightheartedly.

'I have this dream that, one day, I will dance with you in complete freedom, to the beat of tom-toms and bongo drums!' he said with a smile.

'Yes, in the year X!' she replied, holding his hand.

'There will be trumpets made from impala horns and there will be a new song to sing when the old order is gone. We shall tame the wind and, with a single command, we shall stop the fight for the sun. There will be no more rivalry, greed and selfishness. We shall uproot all dead wood and in its place, plant fruit trees and everybody, the people of the slums, the parking-meter boys and the street urchins, will eat to their full, in the year X.'

Nzinga did not comment but kept her gaze on the fire, teardrops streaming down her cheeks.

'Nzinga what is wrong? Have I offended you?'

'No, Shaka it is not you, it is my father! You know about the assassination stories, don't you?'

212

'Nzinga ... there are so many things going on...' He did not finish.

'You know the truth! Tell me the truth!'

'I really don't know, love, honestly,' Shaka confessed.

'He is a brute! I wonder where he will be in the year X!' she paused. 'Cheers!' Nzinga was smiling once again, as their glasses touched. 'When you go back to Glitta, tell the Movement that I want to join.'

Shaka watched her tears, which were still rolling down her cheeks, as they reflected the flames from the log fire. 'You know, love, I would like to watch those teardrops on your cheeks for ever. They are like dancing flaming diamonds. In our new world, there will be no tears.' He took his handkerchief and wiped them from her face.

'I promise you, no more tears. There will only be a battle cry!' said Nzinga. They looked at each other, in love, united in purpose.

'Nzinga, there is no way I am going to go back to Glitta. It is too late. I suggest we spend the night here. I have enough money for two rooms.'

'Why waste money? We can sleep in the same room, I trust you!' Nzinga said shyly.

The season of thunder, lightning and hailstorms brings with it many things, as I have told you before, but the road to heaven is littered with sinners marching to the promised land. The story of Adam, Eve and the rotten apple will be told many times throughout the ages, because it was a rebellion. The story of Shaka and Nzinga will only be told once, as it was the beauty with which all other loves will be measured. Once is enough, as repetition can only take away from it. When two bodies are joined in love, they become one soul. They melt into each other, part by part as tongues are lost in mouths, legs are like ropes, arms like vices and their breathing becomes one. There is a softness and mellowing of all resistance as the union breaks all barriers in a sacred sacrifice, blessed by the gods, and virgins are virgins no more, as the seeds of life are planted in the most fertile of soils. And gales of wind, thunder, lightning and hailstorms come to witness the union, bringing with them many gifts.

It was not a night for rebellion, rather it was the night of rebirth, blessed by the heavens, of pure, selfless and purifying love.

When Hon. Tumbo left the golf club, he had one intention in mind; to make it up with WaMwago. He had neglected her for a long time but, even as heartless as he was, he felt one should not drive another to desperation. His new girlfriend, though much younger, was too loose and too demanding both in sex and money. WaMwago had a high level of maturity and understanding and that was what he needed. It was ten o'clock at night. He told the driver to take him to his suite at the Milton Hotel, from where he telephoned WaMwago. There was no answer. After several frustrating attempts, he gave up. What is this? he asked himself. The bitch, where can she be? He sat there wondering what to do next. He poured himself a drink and sat on the bed looking at the floor. 'Bastard!' he hissed, not sure whether he was addressing WaMwago or himself. He remembered she had warned him, but he could not recall the exact words. He had thought WaMwago was his, a toy to be used and stored away as he fancied. He had seen her like a puppet, made to dance by pulling this or that string. The beautiful doll was not where he had placed it, it had developed a life

214

of its own and walked away. 'Impossible!' he heard himself shout.

If she is screwing around, I will teach her a lesson she will never forget' he promised himself.

WaMwago lay naked besides William Stans in his house. They had had dinner and drifted to bed. Tonight, she was going to stay the night and give Stans the best time of his life, with every trick she had perfected in Soho. WaMwago had seen pictures of Stans's house in Vermont. She particularly liked the maple trees, which looked like they were on fire in autumn, before the leaves fell.

'Someday you will take me to Vermont, won't you?' she asked Stans, who lay lifeless in bed. 'And those pictures of Chilean women, you must have made love to them, too! They are beautiful!'

'Not as beautiful as you,' William Stans mumbled.

'They must have taught you a bag of techniques, Stans, you sure screw great!'

'You reckon so?' he asked with a voice heavy with passion.

'Yeah,' she whispered, and was all over his body, touching and kissing him everywhere until he was aroused again.

Stans could not understand where the strength was coming from but he found himself making love to WaMwago again, the third time that night. Her legs were on his back and her arms locked around his shoulders in a most pleasurable and thrilling stranglehold, like an octopus. His 'sweet octopus'. Afterwards, he lay on top of her, panting. She was deeply asleep, her body spread-eagled.

* * *

When Hon. Tumbo arrived home from the Milton Hotel, he was like a time bomb ready to explode. At the gate he rebuked the sentry for taking too long to open the gate. In the house, he told the cook he was not hungry and waved him away like a dog. He entered his bedroom, picked the telephone and dialled WaMwago's number once again. There was no response. Hon. Tumbo lay on his bed face down, feeling defeated and helpless. He began pounding pillows with his fists and soon became quite frenzied. He was sweating all over with his coat, tie and shoes still on. He got out of bed and changed into pyjamas. He turned on the radio to listen to Voice of America broadcasting to Africa. The radio was carrying a story of a gruesome massacre in a country in the lake region of Central Africa, in a struggle for power between two tribes. At two a.m., he dialled WaMwago's number yet again. Still there was no response.

'The harlot, bloody fucking whore, I will massacre her!' he shouted. Tomorrow, he would detail one of his henchmen to trail her wherever she went.

At seven a.m. in the morning when Tumbo woke up, he dialled her number again. WaMwago answered the phone. She had just arrived from Stans's house.

'WaMwago, darling, where have you been all night? I have been trying to reach you since ten o'clock last night! What's going on?' Hon. Tumbo asked in his usual authoritative voice.

'Where I go and what I do is none of your business and, incidentally, Your Excellency, never call me darling again. Have I made myself understood? You are nothing but a spineless motherfucker!'

'But my dear —' Tumbo was rudely cut off as WaMwago slammed the telephone on him.

Hon. Tumbo, the presidential aspirant, the minister for Commerce and Industry, the people's representative, could not come to terms with what had just happened. He was stunned. Nobody had treated him like that since ... he could not remember when. He felt belittled and abused.

'I will teach the bitch a lesson she will never forget!' he swore.

Hello, it's me again, I am sure you remember me well. This is Sunday the ... like hell, there is no calendar here, so how the dickens am I supposed to know the date?

Early each year, big corporations and governments distribute calendars to those who matter. Since I have never received one, I assume I do not matter. If you are a big man either in a big company or in the government, do me a favour, please make me feel I matter early next year, if only for once by sending me a calendar. I am sure your act of kindness will be specially rewarded in heaven. Calendars, diaries and notebooks are very important tools of civilisation. They help in the organisation of appointments. For example, today is Sunday because the ... well, forget about dates until I receive a calendar, but I do swear it is Sunday. I have seen the usual parade of sinners going to church to ask for forgiveness for wrongs committed since their last confession seven days ago. It is a ritual. It is in the morning, I swear, since the shadows are very long to the west. Together with the calendar, is it too much if I kindly request for a watch, so that I can keep our appointments to the minute? If you forget, I will continue to exist in the long list of those who do not matter, the scum, slum dwellers, the disinherited, the wretched of the earth, those who deserve nothing, not even free calendars at the beginning of the year or a watch for Christmas. No wonder their lives are so disorganised.

Those who matter, such as Hon. Tumbo, have a lot of calendars and watches. That is why this Sunday he is heading to the church dead on time. He has an important appointment, one he must keep in this period of change. He has been requested to deliver the first reading in the service, which to him is a very great honour indeed. To be associated with men of God counts for a lot of votes, you know. You can only ignore the church at your own peril. The church can also be used as a tool for political change. Tumbo had calculated well. He did not want to be in the church's bad books and that is why he was hurrying to cement his ties with the men of God.

Hon. Tumbo stepped out of his limousine immaculately dressed, his double-breasted coat nicely buttoned over his massive stomach. He was welcomed by the bishop. As they walked down the pews, Tumbo waved to the congregation, as if at a political rally. He sat on the dais, next to the bishop, with a huge smile on his face. He stayed transfixed, scanning the congregation until his eyes fell on Rev. Mwago, seated on the front bench. Hon. Tumbo saw the burning eyes of the reverend fixed on him. There was a visible expression of anger on Rev. Mwago's face and his mouth seemed to twitch. The huge grin died from Hon. Tumbo's mouth as he cleared his throat involuntarily. The church was very full.

Rev. Mwago continued to fix a steady and piercing gaze on Hon. Tumbo. Tumbo, however much he tried to avoid the reverend's eyes, found himself drifting back to them again and again. He felt very ill at ease, almost repentant. He composed himself and fixed his gaze on the floor. He did not understand how a simpleton like Rev. Mwago could make him feel so small in the house of the Lord.

The service continued until it was Tumbo's turn to read the verses. As he got up from his seat, he felt as if he were carrying a heavy load. He stumbled over a footrest and his Bible fell. He picked it up and placed it on the pulpit. Beads of sweat were forming on his face. The bookmark that had been placed on the page he was to read had fallen out and he could not remember the book, the chapter or verse. After fumbling for quite some while, he looked at the bishop appealingly. The bishop stepped forward calmly and assisted him by opening the book and marking the verses to be read. The hon. minister wiped sweat from his face with a spotless white handkerchief. Laboriously, he read the verses, repeating himself as though the words were dancing all over the page. He completely humiliated himself in the house of the Lord. Finally the congregation heard the words, 'There ends our first reading.' Some people chuckled but Tumbo did not hear them. He wanted to be far away, very far away from the presence of Rev. Mwago.

Rev. Mwago, his thick, black-rimmed glasses eating the rays of the sun like a Bavarian gentian, sat there absolutely composed, an executioner facing a condemned demigod. To the reverend, this was not a moment of victory, it was only an opportunity to test the waters. Deep down in his Christian heart, he felt great pity for Hon. Tumbo whom he regarded as a lost sheep. Two more songs were sung and the bishop announced it was time for the sermon, the message of the day, to be

delivered by a special guest, Rev. Mwago. Hon. Tumbo
sank deep into himself, feeling very small.

Like a star actor, Rev. Mwago took to the pulpit in
style. 'Brothers and sisters, I greet you in the name of
Jesus Christ our Lord and saviour...' He sounded a
man inspired. The theme of the sermon was 'All
have sinned and come short of the glory of God'. He
continued:

'Kuzania has become a replica of Sodom and
Gomorrah, and we have surpassed the evils of those
two cities, which the Lord destroyed in anger.' The
hushed house nodded in approval. 'We have let our
minds wander without the guidance of the Holy Spirit
and we have become hostages of the dictates of the
flesh. Evil reigns supreme in our hearts, our souls, our
minds, and in our bodies. We have created gods and
idols of worship. Power has become a god and its disciples
have ascended the throne and become demigods.
Today, we are sacrificing to the devil our sons, ministers,
lecturers, university students, peasants, workers, civil
servants, and even cripples! We have turned this
nation into a devil's hoodlum in the name of stability
and state security. We are paying lip service to the
sanctity of life and the protection of human rights.
Whoever heard of a state so hell-bent on self-destruction
as Kuzania? We have destroyed institutions, we have
destroyed the infrastructure, we have destroyed our
economy and we have destroyed a whole generation of
our most able sons, the leaders of tomorrow.'

Hon. Tumbo was perspiring profusely.

'Money...' the reverend roared on, 'money ... is the
junior god in league with the god of power. Dishonesty
and fraud have become sanctioned official channels to
riches. Corruption rules all government contracts.

Roads are built today and tomorrow they are washed away. Factories are white elephants even before they have made a trial run! Who can explain our huge external debt? People do not have clean drinking water, they have no decent homes, there are no drugs in hospitals, schools and institutions have no books and equipment. Unemployment has become a permanent feature and we have seen the crime rate soar to unprecedented heights. And who is to blame?

'The government says dissidents and their foreign masters are to blame for all the ills facing Kuzania! I tell you, dissidents and their foreign masters are in government offices, in the names of our leaders and their foreign advisers! Guided by the twin gods of power and money they have wrecked this nation! When you ask questions, you are branded a dissident, tortured and murdered. I ask you, are these the actions of people who believe in God or are they the work of the devil and his worshippers?

'Immorality is another god in league with power and money. The people's representatives and their lackeys have turned their lust on schoolgirls and people's wives. I am a living victim. To them, the common people are toys to be used and misused as the leadership dictates. They are objects of pleasure!' Rev. Mwago took a sip of water and continued.

'The name of the living God, in the name of Allah the merciful and benevolent I urge this nation to remove blinkers from the eyes so that we can clearly see the road to salvation, or the wrath of God will descend upon us mercilessly as was the case in Sodom and Gomorrah. We have strayed from the path of righteousness and there is no health in us. Repent for the day of judgement is near! The wrath of God and the anger of the masses will smite you! There will be gnashing of teeth and yells as judgement is executed.

'I tell you, "Though I walk through the valley of the shadow of death I will fear no evil for thou art with me." We shall rise up and sing, "Guide me, Oh thou great redeemer, pilgrim through this barren land."'

Outside the church, Hon. Tumbo said a hasty goodbye to the bishop and took off like a wounded bull. The congregation gathered around Rev. Mwago and congratulated him on his great message and prayed that it did not fall on deaf ears, especially those of the leadership of Kuzania.

Once in his private office, Tumbo called the minister for Internal Security. He warned him that the churches had been taken over by anti-government elements and had become political platforms. The leader of the movement, Hon. Tumbo informed, was called Rev. Mwago. If stern measures were not immediately taken against him, stability, peace and development in Kuzania were threatened. Hon. Nyoka thanked Hon. Tumbo profusely for the invaluable information and promised to take immediate action. He also promised to brief the president on this new front of attack. Hon. Tumbo felt reassured. He cursed Rev. Mwago: 'Who does he think he is? Just because I fucked his harlot of a wife, he has no right to abuse me like that in public. I will fuck his bitch again and again, and my wrath will descend upon him until he cries for mercy.'

Rev. Mwago's sermon made headlines in the local daily. It was extensively quoted in the foreign press; on TV and radio stations. He was called the most courageous man to have faced the evil and corrupt government in Kuzania. Some papers speculated that he had hidden political ambitions. Soon thereafter, he was arrested and detained incommunicado, said to be a threat to state security. Two days after his arrest, his house was broken into and his books and files taken away. It was said to be the work of a criminal gang from the slums. People were not fooled.

WaMwago knew she had hurt Tumbo's pride and she was very pleased with herself. She had hit back where it hurt most: his pride. She knew, however, that Tumbo was not the type to take matters sitting down and she was aware of the dangers of her action. Above all, she was living in a house and driving a car bought by him. She did not want to extricate herself from Tumbo, but she was not in a hurry to patch it up with him for a while. Stans was providing very well for her immediate needs, be they physical, emotional or financial.

She did not give a damn about Rev. Mwago's detention, either, although everybody said Hon. Tumbo was behind it. For all she cared, her 'husband' could rot in detention. He had no business talking about her affair with Tumbo in public because, as far as she was concerned, they had long ceased to be husband and wife. Had he learnt the art of living well and making money, they still would be together. Tumbo was not responsible for their separation, she argued, it was Rev. Mwago's stupidity that was to blame.

As she drove towards the city centre for a massage, she was aware that the car driving behind her had been parked not far from her house the whole morning. The driver looked like a man high on Indian hemp and he had on dark sunglasses and a baseball cap, the kind worn by Tumbo's youth-wingers. When WaMwago left the massage parlour late in the afternoon to go for her manicure, she noticed the same car parked not far away.

As she joined the highway, the same car followed her. This was too much of a coincidence: Hon. Tumbo had put someone on her trail. 'The bastard,' she hissed.

'Darling, how are you?' asked Stans over the telephone.

'I am fine, dear, but listen, someone has been trailing me the whole afternoon! I suspect it is one of Tumbo's henchmen. What do I do?'

'That sure is the work of Tumbo, I know him well. From now on, we had better be doubly careful. You haven't talked to him lately, have you?'

'I talked to him the other day and called him a spineless motherfucker!' she said with a laugh.

'Look, do me a favour, call him and apologise. You do not antagonise Tumbo and expect to get away with it, do you?' he asked harshly.

'Men! You are all the same, each and every one of you wants to be treated in a special way! All right, I will apologise. When will I see you?' she asked.

'Don't you realise that you've to make it up with Tumbo first before we can be free again? Get those hounds off your back first. Do it for me,' he appealed.

'All right, I will call him tonight and I will brief you later,' she replied.

'Don't call me tonight, call me tomorrow,' he requested.

Upon hanging up the phone, WaMwago called Tumbo's house. The houseboy informed her that the hon. minister had left for the golf club. She got into her car and followed him.

When Tumbo saw WaMwago, he smiled to himself. His hunch had been right, poverty would bring her back. 'Hello, my dear,' he greeted her with a huge grin.

'Hello, love,' she replied with a sexy smile. She joined the group and they spent the evening eating and drinking.

Later, in separate cars, they drove to Hon. Tumbo's house. Throughout the night, WaMwago apologised to Tumbo for her rudeness and made love to him very tenderly. Tumbo accepted the apologies and warned that such words should never be repeated again, otherwise he might do something she would live to regret. She knew Tumbo meant what he said.

'But promise me you won't send those scary men to follow me again,' she appealed coyly.

'As long as you conduct yourself well, there will be no need,' he said.

'I will be the best woman you ever had,' she declared.

'Then you will never see them again,' he promised.

As they parted in the morning, Tumbo gave WaMwago a bundle of money and the spare key to his suite at the Milton Hotel so that she could wait for him there if he was ever delayed in meetings.

WaMwago had scaled many hurdles. She felt very special, rich and loved. She felt powerful. At the back of her mind, however, she felt she needed Stans more. He was a good lover, kind and a gentleman. She knew that nothing could keep her away from him, not even Tumbo's henchmen. At the same time, she could not leave Tumbo without dire consequences. She felt caught between the two men. It was a game she had not played before but surely she could juggle two men and keep everybody happy? Her love kingdom was expanding both in size and complexity, and the financial rewards were doubled. These were the fruits of the power of her body.

Innocence, sweet innocence, the great mother of misery...

Hon. Tumbo sat in his office working out profits from a cargo of sugar from Brazil. There was a shortage of the commodity and, as soon as the vessel set sail, he would announce that anybody was free to import sugar duty-free for the next three weeks. He knew that only his consignment could enter the country within that period and he would make super profits. It was a plan he had used before to import rice, maize and beans. Sugar, however, gave the highest profits. Before he had finalised the calculations, his secretary buzzed him and reported that one of his youth-wingers had an urgent message to deliver.

The young man wearing a baseball cap sat down and delivered his message. Hon. Tumbo looked at him, his body shaking with rage. 'Are you sure of your sources?' Tumbo was sweating profusely and the youth-winger feared that he would soon suffer a heart attack.

'It is true, honourable. They spent the night at the sailing club and, the following day, they walked all over the National Youth Service camp, holding hands. He left for Glitta in the evening and they kissed by the bus stop. It is true, sir and, very serious.'

'You don't have to tell me it is serious, I know that!' Hon. Tumbo banged his table. 'The son of a bitch has used witchcraft on my lovely daughter! She is bewitched! First the brat comes begging for a job, then he invites himself into my house, then he lures my daughter to the slums! The boy is a witch-doctor! I will teach him a lesson he will never forget! The boy has to be stopped before he infests the whole place. Nobody is safe from such powerful evil!'

The hon. minister picked the telephone and called the managing director of Kuzania Insurance Company. 'The boy I sent to you for employment, I want him sacked immediately,' he roared.

'You mean Shaka?'

'Yes, that's him. Sack him!'

'Sorry, sir, the boy is no longer with us. I gather he got a better-paying job with First National Bank. As a matter of curiosity, what has he done? Hello ... hello.' The phone had been disconnected.

Tumbo dialled the general manager of the First National Bank.

'It is Hon. Tumbo here. How are you?'

'Fine, thank you, Hon. Minister, what can I do for you?' the manager asked.

'I want a favour.'

'All you have to do is ask!' said the manager.

'There is a young man by the name of Shaka who is working for you.'

'Yes, he is a brilliant man and I was thinking of sending him to London Institute of Bankers. He has a bright future in the industry,' the manager said.

'I want him sacked!' roared Tumbo.

'Why, what has he done?' asked the manager in utter confusion.

'Let's put it this way, you will be doing me a favour if you sack him,' the hon.minister said.

'It is not going to be easy. He has just gone through his probation and he is now in the permanent and pensionable scheme. Couldn't you at least give me a hint of what he has done?' the manager asked in exasperation.

'If you must know, the young man is involved in anti-government activities,' Tumbo lied.

'That is serious, but why don't you have him arrested?' the manager asked.

'The investigations are still going on and it would be easier for the government to track him down if he was free in the streets.' Hon. Tumbo sounded very convincing.

'OK, sir, I will do my very best but, as I said, it won't be easy,' the manager cautioned.

'You will be doing the government and yourself a great favour.'

As Hon. Tumbo sat there, he thought of an alternative plan of how to deal with Shaka. He had several options. Meanwhile, he felt that the ground he was standing on was not too firm. Firstly, the press had painted him black and the battle was continuing. Secondly, WaMwago had abused him and got away with it. Thirdly, Rev. Mwago had called him a devil's agent in the public, in the church and, finally, there was this peasant bum from the slums who had bewitched his daughter. For once in his lifetime, he felt things were getting out of hand. He decided it was time to share his burdens with his friends. The minister for Internal Security would be detailed to deal with Rev. Mwago; Stans had to come up with a new strategy on how to manage change; Kimondo and the boys would deal with Shaka while he gave himself the pleasurable duty of dealing with WaMwago. Division of labour, after all, is supposed to make work easier and give quicker results. He would no longer lose sleep over these small matters; he had enough friends to help him.

He turned to his calculator to finalise the computation of profits from the Brazil sugar imports. He needed money, lots of it, in order to keep things going in his favour.

Shaka's mother was talking to Agu about moving out of Kawempe.

'Who would have thought that one day we would be living like this, like animals crowded in a cage! I remember the days we used to grow bananas, sweet potatoes, yams, cassava, maize, beans, sugar canes, millet and fruits. What have we now? A jungle of hovels everywhere and not a lone tree in sight! my heart is sick and my soul is worn out. We have lost our children to vice and the older generation to cheap liquor. For those of us who can, we must move out of here to save the younger generations.'

Agu could not agree more. 'My daughter, you have spoken well. As I sit on the stool outside my house, my heart aches to see what I see, to hear what I hear. Our people are so lost that only a miracle can save them. I have long contemplated moving out of here to die quietly in a more serene atmosphere. But where can one go? The price of land is so high that one cannot afford a graveyard in the quiet of the countryside!'

'Old man Agu, don't lose heart. My son Shaka is now working in the caves where money is stored. I am sure he can get us a loan to buy land. He has been talking to me about moving out but I do not want to go alone. If we got together, about five of us, we could buy a large piece of land and share it. We shall be neighbours and in this way we shall not feel the loneliness of living among strangers.'

'You are a wise woman blessed with a big heart. I will talk to three of our close friends and see about buying land together. It is a good idea,' Agu said.

In due course, Shaka talked to the loans manager in his bank and an appointment was made for the following Saturday in the manager's house in Happy Valley.

Shaka, his mother and four friends took with them the gift of a fat goat as a sign of deference, friendship and goodwill. Agu did not go. They parked the vehicle in the compound and waited. After a while a heavily made-up woman came to greet them. She was wearing tight slacks that revealed the contours of her body.

'Please do come in. Leave your shoes outside the door, the carpet is new you know!'

Humbly, the team from Kawempe obeyed the instructions. The driver of the hired minibus, which had taken them to Happy Valley, accompanied them into the house out of curiosity. Once in the sitting-room, they marvelled at what they saw. Besides the new red carpet, the room had two leather sofas, and easy chairs were neatly arranged in the far corner, where there was a television with a massive screen, a video and a music system. There was also a computer and a fax machine, among other electronic gadgets. On the wall were pictures of horses, castles, animals, the president and Jesus Christ on the cross. They had never seen such tidiness and cleanliness in their lives. Each concluded in their hearts that heaven must be something very close to this. The house servant appeared and offered them tea with biscuits and bread. In the meantime, the woman had disappeared somewhere in the house. All they could hear was her voice and that of a man, talking excitedly. The visitors sat in silence with the awe of mortals before God appears. The owner of the minibus broke the silence.

'We cannot wait here all day. Don't they realise time is money?'

'Be patient,' Shaka's mother said.

'You paid me to bring you and to take you back to Kawempe, you did not pay me to sit here all day. You have to pay me waiting charges,' the minibus driver told them.

'This is why Africans will never go very far in life. We are always in a rush and in the process we never accomplish anything. We are here for something important, so please be patient and stop grumbling about time,' an elderly gentleman who was acting group leader appealed.

Just then, the goat tied uncomfortably in the boot of the vehicle started to bleat loudly. Either by coincidence or because of it, the loans manager came down the stairs. 'Sorry to have kept you waiting. My cat is giving birth and it has been a most fascinating spectacle to witness. I think we should have maternity hospitals for cats and dogs, they need care and attention.' They all looked at him in silence. 'Shaka, these are the people you talked to me about, right?'

'Yes, this is my mother and the rest are members of the group,' said Shaka.

'You are most welcome. Where do we begin?' the manager asked.

The leader of the group took over.

'Sir, first, we brought you a goat as greetings. Secondly, and as Shaka has already briefed you, we want a loan to buy a farm.'

'He tells me you want three hundred thousand shillings?'

'Yes, the land we have in mind will cost that much.'

'And you will give the title deed of the land as collateral?'

'That is so.'

'You are aware of the other terms, are you?' the manager asked.

'Which other terms?' the spokesman replied.

'That I need ten per cent of the amount either up front or when you get the loan, in order to speed up matters,' the manager said, his eye fixed on the carpet.

'How much is ten per cent?' the leader asked.

'Thirty thousand shillings.'

'But that is a lot of money. Can't we settle for, say, five thousand shillings?'

'No, that is the standard procedure nowadays.'

'Sir,' the minibus driver intervened, 'fifteen years ago, I got a loan from a bank to buy that vehicle you see outside. Since then, I have secured two other loans and nowhere have I been asked to cough up ten or even one per cent. If you want to eat, please eat that goat in the minibus, but, for Christ's sake, save these poor folks from your so-called standard procedure. Thirty thousand shillings is a lot of money. They will not see it and yet they will have to pay it back at thirty per cent interest. It is daylight robbery! Soon, they will be unable to repay the loan and you will auction the land. Maybe yourself or one of your friends will buy it at a throw-away price. Can't you see what you are doing? You are making it impossible for this poor lot to move forward. You are impoverishing them, you are killing them.'

The woman in tight slacks came down the stairs from the labour of the cat and her newly arrived kittens. 'Darling, what is the racket?' she asked haughtily.

'Nothing, dear! I have a wiseacre of a junk driver who thinks he knows banking more than I do.' They exchanged glances with smiles and the woman retreated to take care of the kittens and the mother. 'Listen, you people!' the manager said angrily. 'Unless we overcome this atmosphere of suspicion and mistrust, I am afraid we cannot strike a deal.'

'Suspicion and mistrust my foot!' the driver said. 'You are a bloody double-headed crook! It is because of people like you that Kuzania has gone to the dogs!'

'All of you, get the hell out of my house and I don't

want you to ever come pleading again! Get out!' The manager was on his feet, shaking with rage and pointing to the door.

'This man is not one of us, he is not in our group...' the leader of the group pleaded with the manager, pointing at the minibus driver.

'Get out now before I call the police.'

'Let us go,' pleaded Shaka's mother.

'Yes, we will go, but remember this, your wealth stinks! You are anti-people, anti-progress, you are evil! One day, you will pay for your ill-gotten wealth. Do you think we fought for independence to be treated like this? Like scum? Today we are beggars, tomorrow you will beg for mercy, I swear!' the minibus driver threatened.

'Get out! Get out!' the manager continued shouting, as the group boarded the minibus and headed for Kawempe, the goat bleating in the boot of the vehicle.

On the highway to Kawempe, the leader of the group spoke. 'We have to brief Agu about what has happened. Secondly, as tomorrow will take care of itself, I suggest we celebrate our victory by eating this goat in Agu's house. We have lost nothing, and we have gained a lot.'

It was so agreed and they headed for Agu's house. The goat was slaughtered and as they ate, Agu congratulated them on their bravery and wisdom and told them that theirs was a victory of good over evil. The search for a loan to buy land would continue.

When Shaka reported to work the following morning, he was ill at ease. He did not know what the loans manager was going to say to him. He felt no need to apologise over what had happened. They avoided each other like the plague. The loans manager reported the incident to the general manager. They always shared the ten per cent. The general manager was not happy with Shaka. As the day wore on, he was wondering what to do with Shaka when the phone rang.

'This is Hon. Tumbo. Have you sacked the boy?'

'Not yet, sir, but I thought he was very close to you, a relative of some sort?'

Tumbo was infuriated. The reference to relative could infer potential son-in-law. It was an insult! 'It looks like you are very slow at carrying out orders! I will have a word with the minister for Finance about your inability to —'

'No, sir, please, Honourable, I will sack him right away,' the general manager pleaded.

'That's more like it,' said Tumbo as he hung up the phone.

Within an hour, Shaka received a letter on his desk terminating his employment because he was 'not capable or suitable for the job', as his overall performance fell far short of expectation. Shaka did not believe his eyes. Only the other day, he had been praised as 'a brilliant worker whose future was very bright' in the industry! He stormed into the general manager's office. 'Sir, I want an explanation as to why I have been sacked. The reasons given in your letter are far from the truth and you know it!'

'Why don't you go and ask your godfather Hon. Tumbo, the hon. minister, the people's representative? Is that a good enough explanation?' the general manager asked, puffing his cigarette in fury.

'He is not my godfather! The man is after my neck because I love his daughter. He hates me because I am from the slums. Sir, I am sorry to tell you that you have been used like a piece of toilet paper!' Shaka said, in a very controlled voice, not betraying the deep

234

anguish and anger that was threatening to burst out.

The general manager looked at him blankly, his mouth half-open. At last, shaking his head, he found his voice. 'I have detailed the accountant to give you your salary for this month and three months' salary in lieu of notice. Go and collect your money.' The general manager turned to a file on his desk. Shaka left the office more calmly than he had entered, satisfied that he had fired a salvo, and, in his estimation, scored a direct hit.

It took the general manager a long time to digest the full meaning of Shaka's words. If Shaka's story was true, then Tumbo was the meanest low-down rat he had ever come across. Did he have to bend that low over an affair between two young people, regardless of who they were? He agreed with Shaka; he had been used like a piece of toilet paper, dirtied and discarded with no feelings. He was very angry with himself but there was nothing he could do about it. 'Next time,' he promised himself, 'I will not allow myself to be used. Zombie!'

Shaka took the minibus to Kawempe and briefed Agu about what had happened. Agu listened to Shaka with a lot of pain, his sunken eyes seeing further than one could imagine. He knew that Shaka was being shaped for the battle ahead, the battle between good and evil. He was an angry man with plenty of time to plan his moves.

Shaka went home and wrote an application for admission to the school of journalism at Glitta University. He knew that the time had come to hit Tumbo and others, and the chosen weapon was the pen.

11

The Hunters and the Prey

Genuine, unselfish friendship is a priceless gem. To Shaka, he had lost only part of his world in losing his job. He felt convinced of his ability to face this cruel life. He was no longer the desperate village boy who once went begging for a job, but a mature man who knew that though money was important, it was not everything. To him, self-respect and courage were what made life meaningful. Beyond that, he valued the friendships with his mother, Agu, his comrades and, most of all, Nzinga. With them on his side, and with the added mission of the National Redemption Movement, he had a full life, regardless of Hon. Tumbo's persecution. He knew that sooner or later, he would get a steady source of income to satisfy his modest needs.

When Shaka stepped into Vuruta Bar, he was wearing a worn-out face. It was early Friday evening and the crowd was thin. He found Musa devouring a plate of roasted goat meat, washing it down with a *muteta* soup. *Muteta* is a bitter native herb believed to prevent excess drunkenness and hangovers. It is also said to be a sexual stimulant. Seated next to Musa was Brother

Music, who had been released from detention. He was set free with no explanation and no apologies. Musa and Apunda had bought him another crutch and they were organising a fund-raising to buy him a guitar. Tonight, there would be no music from him and people were amusing themselves with the music from the jukebox. Apunda and the two journalists were seated in a corner, engaged in a serious discussion. Shaka took an empty crate of beer and sat in the company of Musa and Brother Music. 'Brother Music, I am very glad to see you again. Welcome to the world of the free! And Musa, how are you?' Shaka enquired.

'Shaka, we are celebrating the release of Brother Music! Join in, have some meat. Brother Music can't chew because his jaw is hurting. They almost broke it you know!'

'They may break my jaw but they will never break my spirit!' Brother Music said defiantly.

'Brother Music, have a mug of *muteta* soup, it will do you good,' said Shaka.

'I have already had some,' he replied.

'Then have a beer,' offered Shaka.

'That's more like it!' said Brother Music.

Shaka ordered beer for the three of them. Brother Music narrated the conditions in the police cells and the torture he had gone through. Shaka sat there wondering which was more painful, physical or mental torture. Apunda joined them and tapped Shaka on the shoulder.

'When you came in, your face looked like of one who had seen a ghost! You scared the daylights out of me. Is everything all right?'

'I am fine, Apunda. Let's put it this way, it could be worse,' Shaka said.

'I take it that there is something the matter?'

'One thing at a time, Apunda. First, we celebrate the release of Brother Music and then we shall moan or celebrate whatever else,' Shaka said without elaborating.

'Shaka, answer my question. Why do you look so crestfallen?' Apunda insisted.

'My brother, wonders will never cease in this land. I have been fired from my job on orders from Hon. Tumbo!'

'Fired?' Apunda asked in alarm.

'Yes, I am now a man on the tarmac, but don't worry, the Lord will provide.' He briefly explained how Tumbo must have threatened the general manager in some way.

'Shaka, although I admire your courage, to be unemployed is a curse. There is no dignity in unemployment, in fact, just the opposite,' said Brother Music.

'What do you contemplate doing next? You could take up the matter with the industrial court on grounds of victimisation,' Apunda advised.

'No, I will deal with the Hon. Minister in my own way, when the moment is ripe. This afternoon, I visited the school of journalism at the university and filled in admission forms. They looked at my grades and wondered why I did not take law or another degree. I told them I am interested in justice, not law. You know what, I was admitted on the spot! The course is only nine months and I can meet the bill,' he said proudly.

'And you will use the papers to hit back, will you?' asked one of the journalists.

'Precisely,' replied Shaka.

'It is a fifty-fifty chance. The editorial board might refuse to use any of your materials if they know you are involved in a personal vendetta,' advised the other journalist.

'Gentlemen, I have thought about these things and I believe I have come up with a workable strategy. First, I will begin a column called "The Way We Were" and use those wonderful stories of Agu. They will sell. Slowly, the column will progress to the way we are!'

'Brilliant!' said one of the journalists.

'Wonderful!' said Apunda.

'And I will give you stories that have never been told,' said Brother Music.

When Tumbo told Kimondo he wanted an urgent meeting to review the strategy for 'managing change', he gave him specific names of those to invite. Not everybody previously involved was invited and there were new names added. The additions included heads of Organisations dealing with oil, cotton, sugar, cocoa, tea, wheat, coffee and milk. They also included members of the armed forces, police and public administration. Kimondo was baffled, but he did not question. On the appointed night, they assembled in Kimondo's house in Happy Valley and as usual, there was plenty to eat and drink. Hon. Tumbo went straight down to business.

'Our strategy for managing change is suffering major hiccups. First, my faith in the president has waned as he appears to operate a one-man show and I do not trust the outcome of his intentions. One of the consequences might be that instead of calling party elections first, in which we are assured victory, he will call snap general elections. Our enemies seem to have made a lot of ground and we need time to undo the damage or people will vote most of us out. It will be a disaster for us and for the nation.

'I have thought about an alternative plan, which will

buy us time by making it impossible to hold the elections. As we are constituted today, we have the means to delay the elections. Firstly, I want all payments to farmers in the cocoa, coffee, sugar, oil, wheat, cotton and milk industries withheld indefinitely. The farmers will protest and hold demonstrations and we will infiltrate their ranks, urging more militancy. In the chaos, I want vital components of machinery in the factories removed and safely hidden. We shall then accuse the farmers of having wrecked the factories. The cost of repairing the factories should be inflated tenfold and deducted from the dues owed to them. This will cause total paralysis for as long as we want it and no elections will be possible. We shall refit the parts to the machinery when we deem it appropriate.

'Secondly, I want plans on how to initiate ethnic tension. One way is to organise cattle rustling between the pastoralists and to burn houses and food stores in farming areas. We will initiate action and withdraw. The rest will be achieved as communities rise against each other. We shall step in to stop these clashes once we have achieved our goal. There is no way the president can call for elections in the middle of a crisis. In the meantime, we shall reorganise ourselves with the assurance of sweeping the boards come the elections. I want special attention paid to the vice-president, who is our main threat. I want his name tarnished beyond repair. He should be associated with the crisis and driven deep in the mud.

'I will be issuing tenders and duty-free importation for several items including milk, sugar and wheat. As usual, you have first priority. I suggest you embark on dividing between yourselves who is to import what and let me have the allocations agreed upon. Gentlemen, we should relax and enjoy the fruits of independence!' concluded Tumbo.

At the completion of her course at the National Youth Service camp, Nzinga packed her bags and returned to her father's house.

'Nzinga,' said her father, 'welcome back.'

'Thank you,' she said coldly.

'I think you are a big girl now and we should start planning your future. I do not want you to devalue your worth by fraternising with the scum from the slums. I want you to keep friendship with the families of my peers. I also want you to think about marriage and to consult with me so that I may give you parental guidance. I have set aside a lot of money for your wedding, and the sooner you think about it the better.'

'Father, may I say something?' she asked.

'Of course, my dear, of course.'

'I wish to thank you very much for everything you have done for me over the years. Secondly, and as you rightly put it, I am a big girl now. May I kindly ask you to give me freedom to choose what I want in life and who should be my friends. As for marriage, I will leave that to time, chance and God. All I am asking is to be left alone. Is that too much to ask in this day and age?' Nzinga could not hide the anger bottled up inside her.

'Child, you do not know what you are asking. All these years, I have nurtured you and protected you as a very special child. I've planned a very bright future for you, in which you will never suffer from want. If you don't agree to my guidance, if you rebel against me, you will fall into a bottomless pit or you could end up in the slums, in the gutters! Is this what you want?'

'Father, you cannot treat me like a child and I am not

an object! I've an independent and sound mind and you must not try to lead me by the nose. I respect you and that is the bottom line,' she said, restraining herself from shouting.

'Your maturity, independence and education are nothing to me! They have already shown you the way to the slums and who knows where they will lead you next! I fear you have been bewitched. If you disobey me, I will not take it sitting down. A lot of people will suffer. Do you hear me? A lot of people!' Hon. Tumbo picked up his coat and left, heading for the golf club.

Nzinga unpacked her bags and retreated to her room. She did not feel angry with her father, she felt pity for him. She would defy him and there was nothing he could do. In her loneliness, she dearly missed Shaka. Over the last month or so, Shaka had neither visited nor written. She resolved to call him in his office the following day.

When Nzinga called the First National Bank, she was informed that Shaka no longer worked there. Frustrated, she decided to go to Kawempe. She arrived on the plot in which she had visited Shaka. She counted the doors as she had been shown and knocked. A strange face of a pregnant woman with a child holding on to her skirt showed itself.

'Hello, I am looking for Shaka,' she said.

'There is no Shaka in this compound.'

'But I am sure he lives in this compound, in this house!' Nzinga insisted.

'You must be mistaken. Try the next plot. This is my house and there is no Shaka in this compound!'

'Perhaps ... when did you move into this house?' Nzinga asked.

'A month ago,' came the short answer.

Nzinga headed for the house of Shaka's mother. The door was locked and there was nobody around. She turned and headed for old man Agu's house. She found him seated outside his house, basking in the sun. 'Good morning, Great-grandpa!' she greeted him with excitement, extending her hand to him.

'Good morning, my child. Which one are you? I seem to recollect your voice and face but not your name.'

'You don't remember me? I am Nzinga!'

'Oh, Nzinga, blessed one, it is good of you to remember the old man. Get a stool and sit down.' Nzinga got a stool and sat next to him.

'How are you keeping?' she asked him.

'I have no complaints, the gods have been kind to me though age is wearing me down,' he said.

'I have missed you very much. I hope Shaka told you I went to a youth camp very far away,' she said.

'Aye, he did. He brought me your greetings on several occasions. I am very grateful,' he said with a smile. 'And how is your father?'

A chill came over Nzinga. 'It is hard to tell.'

'I understand,' said Agu. 'I fear he is driving himself into a bottomless pit. If I were he, I would quit politics. I wish he could find time to come to me, I would counsel him on the dangers ahead, but they don't want to hear the truth, they are blind. You are a big girl now, take good care of yourself and don't let anybody stand between you and the sun,' he said seriously.

'Yes, Great-grandpa, I will be guided by your great words. Tell me, how is Shaka? I went seeking him at his place of work and I was told he had left, and at his house I was told he had moved.'

'Shaka is all right in body and soul, though he is much

243

tormented, sorry to say, by your father.' Agu spoke quietly, like a man announcing death.

'By my father? What has happened, Great-grandpa, what has happened to him?'

Agu explained how Tumbo had ordered Shaka's dismissal and hired thugs to do him harm. He was now living in another slum area with some friends. Unfortunately, he did not know where.

'So I cannot reach him?' Nzinga asked in desperation.

'Nzinga, my child, there is no hurry. Soon, he will know you are back in the city and he will get in touch. He is very fond of you and he always sings your praise. It is good to see two young people caring so much for each other these days. It reminds me of the good old times and the lost beauty of life. When he comes next, I will tell him to get in touch with you. Don't despair, he will come to you,' Agu assured her.

12

What is That Stir?

The announcement came on the national radio station in the one o'clock news bulletin. The ruling party would be holding party elections in a month's time to be followed by general and presidential elections shortly thereafter. It caught many people by surprise, including Hon. Tumbo. The president had several objectives in mind. Firstly, he wanted to seek a fresh mandate for himself. This would be his last term in office and he would use the opportunity to bolster his image, both locally and internationally, as a champion of democracy and progress. Secondly, he would rid the leadership of the growing array of sycophants surrounding him. They were becoming a weighty burden on him and a source of incessant embarrassments. Thirdly, he would get rid of those who had overstepped the boundaries and grossly misused their positions and, worst of all, his name. In the name of stability, security and the protection of the status quo, they had caused a lot of suffering to innocent people. It was as though they had a vendetta against the general population, something he could not fully fathom. The biggest culprit was the minister for Internal Security, Hon. Nyoka, whose conduct bordered on lunacy. It was these actions that had raised a furore with human rights groups and the US Congress. The man was recalcitrant; having been cautioned several times, he continued to behave defiantly. Also in this group were those who had enriched themselves by bending regulations, importing luxury and consumer goods without paying duty and lately forging his signature to grab public land in towns and the countryside. Worst of all, they had sold the land to foreigners. He hoped that his successor would bring all those involved to book and return the land to its rightful owners, the local people. He did not have time and energy to see this task through, but he could stop the damage by weeding out its key players. At the moment, he could not openly confront them because they still occupied influential positions of power, plus they were hugely rich and had international connections. A move against them would wreck the economy, so he would subtly ease them out in the elections.

Medical specialists had warned the president that he did not have long to live. The last thing he wanted was to antagonise anybody, which might lead to his assassination. He was treading very cautiously, aware of the dangers surrounding his intended sweeping changes. He knew there were those who would be planning pre-emptive action in order to better their positions. He would put his trust in his good friend Hon. Tumbo, because nothing escaped his attention. He was a good source of sensitive information, though rather ambitious and greedy. Lately, though, Tumbo had become aloof – or was it that he himself had isolated Tumbo? He would soon bring him back into his confidence. He had heard that Tumbo had acquired a new hobby of snatching people's wives and wining and dining in clubs and people's houses. He was human, after all, but these were not the qualities of leadership expected of him.

Hon. Fikira, on the other hand, advocated development based on the needs of the people; things like better roads, school, hospitals, shelter, water, employment and other simple things of life, of a civilised society. Western capitals were uneasy with the vice-president, whom they viewed as too independent and difficult to work with. They were seeking his eclipse from the political map of Kuzania. Tumbo believed in the creation of massive wealth, even if it were concentrated in the hands of a few individuals. He believed in foreign capital and external funding 'to make Kuzania as powerful as Taiwan, Singapore, Indonesia and other emerging tigers', whatever that meant. For this, he was going to compromise with foreigners by swallowing the bait, hook, line and sinker. He was the darling of western finance capital magnates and they were backing him to the hilt.

These were the options for succession that the president faced: Tumbo with the foreign powers versus the vice-president with the masses. The president could have openly campaigned for Tumbo in the slums and rural areas to tilt the balance, but the story of Tumbo's harassment of a slum boy who had slept with his daughter was both embarrassing and counter-productive. The president argued with himself that Tumbo could have made political gains by giving the hand of his daughter to the peasant boy, which could have put the vice-president in a fix. But that was not Tumbo's style. He had lost a golden opportunity due to his stupidity and short-sightedness, the president concluded.

Having made no definitive conclusions on a choice between the two contenders, he turned to his own

247

future. He planned to have elected a leadership that would uphold his name, hail his achievements and record him heroically in the annals of history for posterity. He admitted having made in his long rule several mistakes out of bad advice, errors of judgement and, lately, out of poor physical and mental condition. But to err is human, he consoled himself.

Shaka, upon the advice of his friends, had moved to Komoro. The area was chosen for several reasons: it had many members of the movement who would be in a position to protect him from Tumbo's henchmen and it was close to the city centre. Because of his zeal, Shaka, had been given special duties. He was the contact man, the overall coordinator of communications between members. His role was becoming vital with the announcement of the dates for elections and the heat it was generating among the political leadership and the masses. The Movement was determined that, whatever else happened, Tumbo had to go. At the same time, it was throwing its weight and resources behind the vice-president, who had to win; failure meant an armed uprising.

Another advantage of being in Komoro was that it was a no-go area for the police. It housed hard-core criminals, pickpockets, thugs and harlots. In the kiosks in Komoro, you could order a gun of any calibre and, within a week, you would receive it. It was like a republic within a republic. As busy as a beehive, people went about their business without fear. It was a safe place to hide. Having come from another slum area, Shaka fitted into the crowds like a fish in water. However, aware of the long hand of the government or, to be more precise, of Hon. Tumbo, he gave himself the name 'Porojo', which simply means 'Mr Chit-Chat' in the language of the slums. True to his name, he became quite chatty and made many friends from all walks of life. His knowledge of the problems teeming in Kuzania became encyclopaedic. He was so engrossed that Nzinga became pushed into the background with the justification that the separation was temporary and necessary for a better tomorrow for all. For fear of exposing himself, he had not called.

Shaka reported to the school of journalism and the Movement paid part of his bill. Other than essay writing, all else was easy and he had a lot of time to spare. He embarked on the stories told to him by Agu. The two journalists assisted him initially and also introduced him to the editor of the local daily. After reading the first few stories, he gave Shaka his weekly column, 'The Way We Were', under the written pseudonym 'Matata'. Letters to the editor were written in their hundreds praising the column and the column generated debates throughout Kuzania. Sales of the paper went up by leaps and bounds and, on each day the article was carried, the paper was sold out before offices were open. To maximise sales, the column was shifted to Sunday and sales promptly doubled. People demanded to meet 'Matata' and his hero 'Agu'. There were growing demands for both to appear on national television. When Agu was informed of the possibility of appearing on television, he did not understand as he had never seen a television. Shaka explained what it was, and Agu eventually decided to think about it.

A woman had rented a room next to Shaka's. Her name was Nyabo. From her looks, he knew she was a twilight woman. He had not heard her arrive the previous night but, that Sunday morning, her presence was everywhere. She was making love to a customer and, besides the creaking bed, she was crying uncontrollably. He had noticed that at times she made love to more than one man in a night, but this was something else. The whole building was shaking. She must be making love to a baby buffalo! he thought. Soon, the noise crescendoed into loud moans and groans before she shouted, 'I am coming.' And it was all over.

Shaka could not sleep. He was suffering from an acute hangover because the previous night there had been a meeting between the Movement and an emissary of the vice-president. Beers had been served generously, but no meat or *muteta* soup. His stomach was grumbling and his head was spinning. It was as though he had slept in one position throughout the night; his neck and ribs were badly aching. He heard the door to the woman's room open and the customer went, whistling in the morning mist. Shaka wondered about the woman contracting VD or Aids and passing it to a multitude, or whether the men used condoms. In which case, Hon. Tumbo should do well to open condom factories and modern brothels for the money-spinning industry, he concluded.

Shaka felt tension in his groin. He was the victim of some unspecified demon as his penis worked itself into an erection. He felt the need for a woman. It had been quite some time since he last made love but, when you are hunted, unemployed, involved in the future of the nation, such things are forgotten. He thought of Nzinga and longed for her. Tumbo had caged him like an animal. Perhaps he could meet her at night. But neither he nor Nzinga was an owl, to be confined to moving at night. It would be accepting defeat in the face of tyranny. He would wait until such a time as freedom was unrestricted. Nzinga was not just another woman like the one next door, she was very special. She had a big clean heart that broke barriers. A heart that saw and recognised the good in humanity, even from the slums, among the poor, the dispossessed, the desperados. Such a heart was rare and could not be confined. She had freely given him friendship and her body and asked for nothing in return, except the warmth of friendship. Yet he could not reciprocate this simple request. Her beauty was reinforced with the golden gift of selflessness. She had made possible the meeting of two worlds that were not supposed to communicate, let alone meet and love. Besides his mother, and maybe Agu, the other person he felt he could die for was Nzinga. He swore he would never leave her. The pain of injustice, torture and neglect of his whole generation, which had suffered untold miseries as the country slid to the brink of collapse, ate through his heart. Every sinew in his body became taut with tension and he began to manufacture possible strategies for dealing with the mess in Kuzania.

Next door Nyabo was making breakfast. There was a strong smell of bacon and the sound of sizzling eggs. Shaka was rudely reminded of the acuteness of his hunger. Tumbo had tried to ensure he remained in the throes of hunger and degradation, eventually to wither away. He would not wither away, he promised himself; whatever else happened, Tumbo had to go.

There was a knock on Nyabo's door. God, not another customer, Shaka cursed.

'Nyabo,' a voice called, 'we are late for service.'

'I won't be a minute, I am getting my Bible,' Nyabo responded.

They were going to church to confess their sins and that very day in the afternoon, in the evening and at night, they would continue with their sins. For now, they were going to join the congregation of sinners in search of a ticket to heaven after death. With Aids in epidemic proportions, the ticket would be needed sooner rather than later. Shaka closed his eyes and wondered how the Good Lord, the generous redeemer, could cope with the immorality and hypocrisy in Kuzania, whose levels had long passed those of Sodom and Gomorrah. Deep in thought, he fell asleep.

He woke up in the afternoon. The headache had disappeared but the hunger was still there. He lay on his back looking at the underside of the rusty iron sheets that made his roof. His attention was drawn to a flat, silver lizard that was advancing on a buzzing fly. The wings of the fly appeared ensnared by a loose thread from a spider's web. The fly was just out of reach of the lizard's tongue but if it continued struggling, gravity would lower it within reach. The lizard rested on the beam below, waiting. The spider advanced from its web towards the fly below. Not far from the fly, it noticed the waiting lizard and stopped to weigh up the danger. The distance was none too safe and it decided to wait until the lizard moved away. The trapper was trapped. Another loose thread fastened itself to the buzzing fly and immobilised it further. The lizard rested on the beam, its eyes rotating. Its movements were like that of a sloth, slow but very calculated. It was an insatiable goblin, very ungainful. Its hunting tactics were no more than halting movements; its tongue would do the rest, almost effortlessly. Its neighbour, the spider, was an aerial hunter. It overtaxed its saliva glands, excreting mucus with which trap threads were made. The web was the centre piece of an elaborate architectural network that connected aerial highways, beautifully woven, including escape routes.

To the lizard, both the fly and the spider were potential meals. The spider in the centre of the web was also out of the reach of the lizard's darting tongue, but the lizard was not discouraged. It knew that the spider would approach the beam below to strengthen its web at some point. Each had its natural wits and limitations. The only hopeless creature in the situation was the trapped fly. It was still buzzing; the more it buzzed, the more it was immobilised.

Shaka concluded that some situations are so helpless that any effort to escape makes things worse, like one sinking in quicksand. Nature in its kindness dictates the destruction of some for the survival of others. It was only among human beings that one sacrifices one's life for others to benefit. His father had done it and now he had opted to do the same. He looked at the fly. Its own kind would not benefit from its death. That, he observed, was a wasted life. Human beings should do better than to be caught in such a situation. Our stubborn leaders are as greedy as lizards, and not as hard-working as spiders. But people are not trapped flies, they can neutralise the darting tongues and traps of tyranny through rebellion, Shaka thought.

The struggle for succession was like the cunning scheming between the spider and the lizard. The lizard, slow and overfed, was like Tumbo and his ilk; effortlessly milking the country. The spiders were the vice-president and the Movement, establishing an intricate web of traps with escape routes. The general population was trapped like flies, helpless, but soon to transform themselves into wasps.

The spider moved forward and, by some stroke of bad luck, the thread broke from the web and hurtled to the floor, with both the spider and the fly. The spider had its prey. Shaka felt satisfied that the lizard had not benefited from the labour of the spider. Some day, he thought, the spider would build a trap to capture the lizard. All that was needed was an architect, the redeemer, and the masses would sing, 'Feed me till I want no more.' The Movement was meeting again that evening.

On Monday morning, the nation woke up to a great shock. The minister for Commerce and Industry had increased prices of virtually all basic commodities in what was said to be a 'mini-budget' agreed between himself and the minister for Finance and endorsed by the president. There was the lame explanation that prices of crude oil had gone up by a dollar or so and the factories would be threatened with closure and retrenchment due to the corresponding rise in the cost of production, as a result of higher energy costs. It was a lot of jargon that meant nothing. The president should have opposed it. Some speculated that the government was trying to raise money to fund elections. The population was withering away, emaciated with hunger; it was national genocide. It was then announced that payments due to farmers would be suspended because the state was spending all available money to meet the huge oil bill. In the past, the masses could have swallowed this jargon without questioning, but that time was now past. How patient can you be with a rumbling stomach, with children threatened with starvation and expulsion if school fees are not paid on time; with coffee, tea, cotton and cocoa pickers threatening to burn your house unless their wages are paid in full?

How long can a situation such as this hold before it bursts?

Factory workers, bankers, teachers and civil servants demanded a three hundred per cent wage increase and were threatening to strike because their salaries could no longer meet their daily needs. Landlords were hiking rent and the transport industry had increased fares because of higher petrol prices. The country was very tense, like a powder keg needing just a spark to explode. The president, holed up in State House, was working on his only concern - his succession.

When Hon. Tumbo cajoled the president to sign the measures to increase commodity prices, he had not envisaged that people would react the way they did. The consequences came crushing down on him like an avalanche. There were rumours of nationwide demonstrations expected to lead to riots. He was scared. He called Hon. Nyoka to gauge the threat. The words of the hon. minister did not reassure him. He was informed that even the police force was asking for a pay rise. He was warned that the situation might get out of hand and that the strategy for 'managing change' was threatening national anarchy. To Tumbo, the situation resembled the period just before independence when he and others, who had served in the colonial administration, were scared for their lives. He had been relieved when he heard the announcement, 'We shall forget the past and work together,' to which the masses applauded, signifying consent. Had the people disagreed, many traitors, including Tumbo, would have been lynched within minutes of independence. He needed another stroke of good luck. He was now frantically looking for William Stans, whose phone was off the hook as he occupied himself with WaMwago. Tumbo was sweating, dreading most of all a call of summons from the president, whom he had assured of the wisdom and benefits of the measures now threatening a national explosion.

The chaos in Kuzania came to a boil. As the general population was seething with anger, voices of reason called for a cautious assessment of the situation. People knew there was a sinister hand at play. It did not take long for the Movement to see through the ploy: Hon. Tumbo and his group had engineered chaos so that key players in the vice-president's camp could be eliminated before the start of political campaigns. At once, the Movement sent word to its cells calling for maximum restraint in the face of this provocation; this was not the time to take the bull by the horns. It was not wise to lacerate the whole body to get rid of a boil. What was needed was a carefully planned surgical removal of the agents causing the inflammation. The masses agreed to a tactical retreat, to attack at a more advantageous time in the future.

Hon. Tumbo was not happy with the failure of the strategy but on the other hand, he knew just how dangerous some of his manoeuvres could be. He had to tread cautiously, relying more on his good friend William Stans. Because of the easing of tension, he could now face the president and tell him that they were now in a position to finance both the party and general elections. Tumbo marvelled at his luck. He seemed to stand to benefit whichever turn events took. Assured of his political future, he decided it was time to celebrate. He called WaMwago. She was there, ready, willing and able.

Nzinga had enrolled for a master's degree in anthropology at the University of Kuzania. Lecturers and students asked why she had not gone to Harvard, Oxford or Cambridge for her MA. Surely it was not a question of money. She responded that there was no place like home; she had no desire to see other lands. She also argued rather convincingly that her course was based on data in Kuzania and it would be more convenient for research purposes to be in her own country.

Her close friends asked her about her love affair with a slum boy. She laughed and told them it was true, adding that he was a human being, just like them all.

'But why doesn't he come to visit you?' some would taunt her.

'He will,' she would reply, painfully aware that Shaka had disappeared, incommunicado. On the subject of her father, she would say that he had his life to live and she had hers, and that she was not his spokesperson. What surprised those close to her was her simplicity and clarity. She was mature and resolute. In the students' leadership and in debates, she cut for herself an enviable position as a voice of maturity and reason. She got involved with organisations assisting orphans and street children, which helped ease the tension in her life. At times, she wondered by what power she maintained her sanity. Often, she saw herself as a sacrificial animal and wished she could melt away or simply disappear without a trace. Then she would think of Shaka and the will to finish what they had started would rekindle afresh a new fire in her, to live on, day by day, hoping for what ... she did not know, but she knew it would be rewarding. If only Shaka could come out of hiding, it would strengthen her immensely. But old man Agu had assured her that he would find her by and by, and she lived by his word. She would wait, even if it took for ever. She had a very strong long-

257

ing for Shaka, to talk to him, to hold him, to reassure him, to make love to him. All she dreamt of was him, praying that the spirits and powers invoked by Agu would keep him safe until they met again.

On her way back to the women's hall of residence, where she was now living, Nzinga bought a copy of the daily paper from a street vendor. The headlines were on the struggle for the vice-presidency. There was a picture of her father and that of the incumbent vice-president. Once in her room, she read the section that talked about her father: the article accused some members of a certain church of having put their weight behind him and called them devil worshippers. Backing him also were certain multinationals, foreign governments, the CIA, Mossad and MI5. The writer described Tumbo as 'semi-illiterate, selfish, a murderer, immoral, bent on anarchy and power-hungry.' A person of his calibre was not fit for a ministerial post, let alone the position of vice-president or, God forbid, the presidency. 'Kuzania deserves better than Tumbo,' the writer concluded. Nzinga agreed with everything the writer said. She felt very detached from her father and she knew that, had she been the writer, she would have painted him far worse. She felt pity for him no more.

While she was perusing the other pages over lunch, she saw an article on Agu by someone called Matata. She went through it, her heart throbbing with every line. It was a very beautiful and well-written article but, above all, she saw the hand of Shaka in it. Nzinga did not finish her food; pushing the plate aside, she walked to the office of the local daily. Pretending to be an innocent student merely wishing to discuss an article with him, she requested to see Matata – or Shaka. She was told she would find him at the university.

The lecture over, students came filing past. Along came Shaka in the company of a lecturer and at once his eyes fell on Nzinga.

'Nzinga, I don't believe it.'

'I will see you later,' the lecturer told Shaka, leaving the two lovers alone.

'Shaka, oh Shaka!' Nzinga cried as she held him close to her.

Over coffee, they talked and talked; their stories were endless. Nzinga narrated to Shaka how she had gone to look for him in Kawempe and Shaka gave the reasons for his silence and for moving. They sat there for hours, not wishing to part. Late in the afternoon, Nzinga suggested showing Shaka her halls of residence. They climbed the hill to the women's halls. They were virtually empty as students were in lecture theatres or in the library.

Love is like dew. It forms slowly in the mist but, by the first rays of the sun, it has covered every blade of grass. In Nzinga's room, bottled flames of passion broke loose. The dew began to fall, slowly and freely. The lovers kissed and moaned with pleasure.

'Promise that you will never leave me,' Nzinga said.

'I swear I never will,' Shaka responded, holding her tightly as if his life was protected by her breasts.

Voices in the corridors signalled students returning. Nzinga's room-mate would be back soon.

'Well, I guess it is time to go,' Shaka said.

'Yes, and thanks a lot for coming. I really missed you, Shaka.' Nzinga held Shaka closely as they stood near the door.

'It is me who should thank you, Nzinga, I owe you a lot!' he replied.

Nzinga escorted Shaka to the bus. As they waited for the bus to arrive, she looked him straight in the eye and announced, 'Shaka, I am not on the pill.' She had an angelic smile on her face. In contrast, Shaka's shock was registered in a stern gaze, full of surprise and anguish.

'Nzinga, why didn't you tell me before? I hope it is your safe period!' he fumbled in alarm.

'Does it matter?' She held him by the waist and squeezed him.

'Nzinga, I would love to have your baby one day, but a lot remains to be done before we are free and able to—' he was cut short by Nzinga.

'I know, Shaka, I know. The Lord will provide.' With a dazzling smile Nzinga kissed Shaka as the bus came into view.

Nzinga turned and walked back to the halls. As she went, her beautifully curved body in the splendour of youth swayed in rhythm with every step. Those she met marvelled at the beauty of her face and the gaiety of her body. She was like an angel on earth. Blind to their eyes, she felt a thrilling feeling within her body, full of warmth, the kind of warmth that invites fertility. Her feelings for Shaka were overwhelming as she climbed the hill towards the halls of residence and she heard herself saying:

> I planted
> a little flower
> and with time
> it grew to bloom

> Its sweet fragrance
> fills the air
> and I am drunk
> with her nectar.

There are things
not to be improved
for nature has made them perfect
like Shaka
my sweet flower.

Nzinga was feeling wonderful. The tension that had
threatened the very locus of her sanity was gone; true
love was its therapy.

Innocence, sweet innocence, the great mother of
misery...

Shaka sat in the bus heading to Komoro. He was greatly
perturbed by Nzinga's words that she was not on the pill.
To love Nzinga was one thing, but to make her pregnant,
at this time when her father was still on his trail, was to
invite death. Tumbo had ceased hunting him as he
concentrated on critical political matters but, should the
worst happen, Tumbo would drop everything and come
after him personally. Nzinga did not seem to see the
danger or care at all. He was a student, living in the
slums; he had no income and the Movement needed him
most at this critical time. He simply could not meet his
obligations as a father. He felt as if his head were about to
explode. He thought of the slums of Kawempe, where
wails of unwanted babies in every other house cried
shame to careless sex. But now, if his worst fears came
true, what guarantee did he have that his own child's
voice would not be added to the wail of starving
babies? Love is stupid and lovers are blind! he said to
himself. But he knew that what he had with Nzinga
was wonderful, blessed by Agu and the gods. Oh
Nzinga, sweet Nzinga, what a wonderful woman! he
corrected himself. Love is wonderful and when it is

ripe, lovers embrace and whisper sweet things. They promise heaven and earth to each other though they can't lay a legitimate claim to an inch of either. All they can give freely are their hearts and bodies and even then... He was both happy and angry with himself, a very good man in a most awkward position, like the fly caught in the spider's thread.

When Shaka joined the Movement little did he know of its strength – or his own. He since learnt that the Movement was indeed a very elaborate political organisation with cells throughout the country and that its leader was no less than Hon. Fikira, the incumbent vice-president. When a people is faced with a situation such as was the case in Kuzania, they establish a common bond to fight it. The movement had penetrated the armed forces, the civil service, and was well supported by the teachers' union, the Law Association, the Medical Association and the university students. Once a government or a regime has outlived its usefulness, it is beset with paralysis. Its leaders, blinded by years of falsehoods, do not wake up to realities of the changing situation. The Movement was operating right under the nose of the organs of the decayed regime, whose main players were too drunk with power and money to fathom the implications of the anger of the people. Shaka reflected that historically the first strikes by liberation forces always caught colonial powers in similar situations of inertia. It was as if nature willed change and numbed those who had to be displaced. A people, dismissed as incapable of thinking or organising themselves, all of a sudden seemed to acquire new qualities as they smashed the old order. These changes do not occur overnight and every instance and act of injustice contributes to the awakening. Shaka also saw that the blindness of the leaders was brought about by the fact that, over the years, they lose touch with the people and become alienated. They concentrate on personal interests, those of their tribe and business connections.

The Movement had grown consequently from strength to strength almost unnoticed. In the planned elections, it would show the sharpness of its teeth and no amount of rigging would save undeserving leaders and their lackeys. Judging from its present network of cells, the Movement was capable of paralysing the operations of the regime if it so wished. The major handicap was that it had not developed an armed wing and this called for utmost caution should the regime resort to brute force, as was its usual reaction. The Movement would not take any rushed action that could give the regime an excuse to massacre innocent citizens and assassinate opposition leaders. It had been warned that entrenched foreign interests should be taken seriously into account. These interests were capable of tilting the balance by bringing in foreign troops and advisers to help the decadent regime. There were many cases cited where despots had been saved from popular uprisings. An old retired civil servant, meanwhile, had told the Movement that Hon. Tumbo had actually been defeated by his opponent in the previous elections, but the district commissioner had been coerced to destroy ballot boxes that held votes for the opponent. The district clerk had subsequently had an 'accident'.

A dossier on William Stans, who was working very closely with Hon. Tumbo and who was an expert in counter-insurgency, was available to the Movement. Stans, it concluded, was effective only as long as Hon. Tumbo held sway. Those close to the presidency informed that His Excellency did not seem to have a very close relationship with Stans, to whom he turned only as an adviser in defence matters, especially in the procurement of equipment for the armed forces. It was therefore concluded, albeit regrettably, that the physical elimination of Hon. Tumbo was a necessary evil, in order to neutralise William Stans and the dangers he posed. It was felt that if Tumbo and his close associates, especially Hon. Nyoka, the minster for Internal Security, were neutralised, there was a high possibility of the Movement working out a compromise with the president in order to save the nation from eventual collapse. The president would have to accept the registration of another political party, in the name of the National Redemption Union.

A select group of five was charged with eliminating Hon. Tumbo. It was headed by retired Colonel Shabaha Kali, who had represented the country in the Olympics as a member of the national shooting squad. The Movement had made its first urgent decision on the road to restoring dignity and sanity in Kuzania. Shaka approved the mission with no misgivings. This was one secret he could not share with Nzinga; it was a small price to pay for their freedom.

13

In the Season of Bloom

As the danger of a political explosion receded, the election campaigns got into gear. Through the cells of the Movement, people were united; a combined strength like the strands that tied down Gulliver. Singly, each was no more than the tiny Lilliputians but, united, they were a formidable force. Together, they were determined to uproot the mighty forces of oppression and unbridled tyranny. They began speaking openly against Hon. Tumbo, Hon. Nyoka and the minister for Finance. These three were seen as the main agents of the devil, with Tumbo heading the list. The clean-up operation would be an onerous and necessary task if Kuzania was to regain its sanity and respect in the community of nations. For a long time, people had cried foul play until their voices were hoarse but there had been no one to listen. It was a rough game, without a referee, a contest of unequals. People had lost the capacity to speak, let alone the capacity to be heard. This time round, they were going to make sure the game would be played on a level field and the rules of fair play would be strictly adhered to.

The Movement, with its reservoir of the most able

bodied in Kuzania, was working effectively and clandes-tinely, coordinating its tactics nationwide. The battle lines were clear but, as in any war, victory is never certain until there is surrender. One thing was for sure, the Movement would not sign any flimsy agreement with the enemy; it was going to be a war of attrition, a fight to the end.

Tumbo was counting on his many friends, both local and international. His team, headed by Kimondo, was the most ruthless machinery in Kuzania. It was short of ideas and common sense but it had other means to compensate; it had money and power and it could call on organs of state security, especially the police, through the ever-faithful minister for Internal Security, Hon. Nyoka. Besides them, there was William Stans, who formed the bridge for external support. Lately, though, William Stans had distanced himself, which was worrying Tumbo. He wanted Stans to work out clever campaign slogans that would neutralise the so-called intellectuals who were tarnishing his name and image. He also wanted Stans to engineer opinion polls to show that his lead in popularity was unassailable. These tools were necessary in order to bolster his image overseas, especially in London and Washington. A ruthless business magnate, Mr Patel, had made up for Stans's lack of enthusiasm by providing additional funds and the promise of a million campaign posters, t-shirts, matchboxes and buses. The t-shirts and matchboxes would bear the picture of a younger and smiling Tumbo. It was also planned that his campaign procession would have cars and motorbikes stretching for miles on end. His was going to be the campaign against which all other campaigns would be measured, including the American presidential race. It was going to be the biggest show on earth.

The campaigns opened with public rallies. True to his word, Hon. Tumbo's entourage turned out to be a spectacle unequalled in the history of Kuzania. Tumbo mistook the huge turnout, which came to witness the charade, for political popularity and support. He talked to the crowds about his achievements. He proclaimed that he had negotiated additional loans with the IMF, the World Bank and the European Union, and bilateral loans with Britain, Japan, Korea and the US with a view to revamping the economy, which was to record unprecedented growth, higher than the economies of Taiwan, Singapore, Indonesia and Botswana. Roads, schools and hospitals would be built anew. Huge industries were about to be set up, guaranteeing employment for everybody. To cater for the youth, new television and radio stations would be established with foreign shows and imported DJs. The country was also going to establish a powerful external broadcasting station, more powerful than Voice of America, which would bolster the image of Kuzania in all the corners of the globe. The list of marvels was endless and only 'the tip of the iceberg'. He was saving many great projects that would surprise the world. He urged the people to unite and vote for him, for their own good and for the good of Kuzania.

His opponents countered that Tumbo was a spend-thrift, a liar, immoral and a devil worshipper, and accused him of belittling the intelligence of the people. His programme was said to be a sham. Tumbo was exposed for having enriched himself through duty-free importation of basic commodities when the people were reeling from pangs of poverty. He was accused of having tried to create a wedge between the president and the people by implementing unpalatable economic and commercial measures, which only added to the misery of the masses and threatened peace and stability. It was also publicly confirmed that Hon. Tumbo had snatched the wife of Rev. Mwago, a helpless man of God. He had turned her into his concubine and given her a diplomatic passport, money and trading licences to be an international merchant. People heard that Hon. Tumbo had disowned his own daughter for falling in love with a slum dweller. He had had the poor man sacked from his job. Week after week, the campaign went on, more vigorous, dirty and violent. Though Tumbo used his thugs and money, people were not moved. They were going to use the opportunity like a broom to sweep the rotting mess of politicians into the waste-bin of history.

Shaka and Nzinga were playing critical roles within the Movement. Their hopes were for fundamental changes that would break down the artificial barriers created between classes; changes that would give equal opportunities to the people of Kuzania, releasing their full potential. They prayed that their children would not be subjected to the harrowing experiences of tyranny that they had gone through.

In the dim lights of a private suite on the seventh floor of Paradise Hotel sat two white men and an African engaged in a heated debate.

'Look, you have got to be honest! Do you know how much we have at stake in this country? Do you know how much we stand to lose by making a single blunder?' the US ambassador asked the African managing director of the local daily.

'I have done my homework and I know the terrain better than you do. I am warning you that you are backing the wrong horse. Tumbo is going to be trampled and he will not return to parliament, let alone this long shot of vice-presidency and his presidential ambitions. If by rigging or such other legerdemain Tumbo should be elected, there will be a civil war in this country,' the managing director warned.

He was a good friend of the US ambassador. They had attended Princeton University together as post-graduate students. He had come back to a country that had ceased to recognise academic excellence, but he had done well as a journalist over the years. He was at the forefront in his field and his role was important during the election period. A proud man, he had refused to be bought by Tumbo, whom he regarded as an 'overgrown child, playing with the toys of money and power'. Besides, as one who was not particularly happy with the way the country was being run, he knew time for fundamental changes had come. His strong sense of judgement told him that the Americans were making a big blunder in backing Tumbo this time round. It was not the first time their pride had taken over from sound judgement with disastrous consequences.

'Look, man,' the ambassador said. 'I want you to put your personal judgement aside and give Tumbo massive publicity. We have to change the image created by these unscrupulous rumour mongers, who are in the service of communism and anarchy. Tumbo has the unqualified backing of Washington and Whitehall. You will be handsomely rewarded. We are flying in two top-notch journalists to assist you, one from London and one from New York. They are propaganda gurus. It will make your work easier. Now, do I have your word?'

'At the pain of repeating myself, I am telling you

once again that if I were you, I would not associate myself with Tumbo this time —' the African said.

'In other words, you have refused to cooperate,' the ambassador asked bluntly.

'You may say so, yes!' said the African emphatically.

'Then the next board meeting of shareholders will have to reconsider your position in the company,' said the British high commissioner, who was also at the meeting.

'Are you threatening me? Do you know the government holds thirty per cent shares in the newspaper? You cannot threaten me!'

'Look,' the US ambassador said. 'You either play ball or you go. It seems you do not understand the value of the stakes! Your so-called thirty per cent shares will not help you. Around here, we pay the pipers and they play our tune. They are nothing but puppets. Now, do you understand?'

'You will not talk like that about our government! This is a sovereign and independent state...' he did not finish.

'It looks as though Princeton did not educate you enough. Wake up, man, wake up!' the ambassador shouted.

'Gentlemen, there is no need for such heat,' the high commissioner said with a smile. 'I recall that your paper was used by State House to cover up the first political assassination when you were instructed to break the news that the minister had gone abroad. You were a willing accomplice, directly or indirectly, were you not?'

'Who told you all that?'

'My dear friend, would you like to listen to the tapes of your conversations?' the ambassador asked with a huge grin on his face.

'This is blackmail,' the African protested, wiping sweat from his face. 'I am warning you! If you push through, you will have turmoil in this country and you will remember this day. You made mistakes in Cuba, Vietnam, Zaire and Angola. Do you want to make another mistake in Kuzania? The beneficiary of your action will be the Movement...'

'What movement?' the ambassador asked in alarm.

'You don't know? I thought you had your men every-where?'

'Speak, man, speak – what movement?' the ambassador asked again.

'I hear there is an underground movement, quite pow-erful, which is about to overthrow the government,' he said economically.

'How has this escaped our guys?' the ambassador asked.

'Because they are blindly concentrating on Tumbo.'

'Can you investigate further and give us a dossier on the movement?'

'I could try but it is going to be dangerous and difficult. I will need two things. Firstly, funding and, secondly, your commitment that you will not push me again to support Tumbo. As a compromise, I promise to see to it that there will be less attacks on Tumbo in my paper.'

'These sound like reasonable demands,' the British high commissioner said, as the ambassador nodded in agreement.

When the African left, the US ambassador turned to his friend.

'You know, he is not a fool! We have been caught napping again! Do you remember how we were fooled into supporting Idi Amin? We had better be careful this

271

time. I am convinced Tumbo has outlived his usefulness. With all these radical governments springing up
everywhere, if he proves to be a stumbling block to the
continuation of the status quo, it is time we worked on
an alternative strategy. We do not want to lose this
beautiful country, do we?' he asked seriously, lighting
his Havana cigar.

'I agree with you entirely. We cannot afford to lose
Kuzania. We have sunk a lot of money here and the
country is very strategic. We have to keep a tight grip.
But what shall we do with Tumbo?' the high commissioner
asked.

'Leave that to us,' said the US ambassador. 'Is he more
difficult to dump than Allende? The answer is no. Don't
forget William Stans is around. Tell your boys to work on
this movement and let's exchange notes on what it is
worth.'

Shaka woke up very early in the morning. He washed and
had his usual breakfast of bread and milk. He had an
early-morning lecture and, as usual, he would walk all the
way. Behind his room lived a woman with a withered arm
and leg. Her house was a makeshift igloo made from
discarded cardboard, paper and cartons. She lived alone.
Early each morning, she would wake up singing a sweet
song like the morning bird, as if the world were a beautiful
place and life were worth living. It made Shaka feel he
need not be angry with his own plight and should try to
be happy, too. Her sweet voice was now a part of his
morning routine.

Shouts of rioting and violence swept through Glitta
from the direction of the eastern slums. Soon, the mayhem reached the University of Glitta. Lectures were

suspended and students took to the streets. Shaka was with them. They were told that the city council had flattened the Komoro slums, that bulldozers had buried alive a child and a crippled woman, who could not move fast enough. Rioters started smashing the windscreens of cars and shopfronts. Shaka found himself picking stones mechanically and hurling them. If he had a gun, he was sure he would have used it without restraint on the enemies of the people. The dead woman was his neighbour; he would never hear that melodious voice again. They had bulldozed her to death and buried her in rubbish, together with a wailing baby. He took more stones and smashed anything that came in his way. He was in a rage, like a mad man. It was as though vehicles and shop windows were responsible for all the ills in Kuzania. By smashing cars, they were hitting out at tyranny. By smashing stores they were hurting foreign interests. He was lost in the frenzy.

Then it dawned on him. If they had bulldozed the igloo of his neighbour, where was his rented wooden room? He concluded that his room and all his earthly possessions had been bulldozed, too. His clothes were gone, his bed was gone but, God forbid, his books were gone! His anger multiplied tenfold. He had nothing left to lose except his life, and how much was it worth anyway? He picked up more stones.

The students gathered in their thousands. They joined the unemployed, the parking-meter boys and the street urchins. They were going to burn the city hall and if they found the mayor, they were going to necklace him. They carried an old tyre and petrol in a jerrycan for this specific purpose. Shaka thought the best strategy would be to lacerate the mayor's legs and arms before burning him, in order to fully avenge the woman with a withered arm and leg. They found the city hall ringed with armed policemen on horseback, backed by armoured personnel carriers. The city hall was empty, the mayor safe in his mansion in Happy Valley. Running battles ensued for three days. Shops were looted and burnt. An unemployed man looted a leg of beef from a butcher's, claiming his family had never eaten meat to the fill. A street hawker looted a telex machine, claiming it was for her daughter to learn how to type, as she could not afford fees for a secretarial course. Kuzania was tottering on the brink of collapse.

Hon. Tumbo rushed to State House and told the president that the riots were the work of an underground movement that was financed by the vice-president. This was betrayal of the highest order. He told the president not to lose his sleep over the riots because the minister for Internal Security was bringing the situation back to normal. He urged His Excellency, however, to punish the vice-president severely for his treachery. He further enlightened His Excellency that Komoro was a small place with a few cardboard igloos housing vermin and hard-core criminals. Nobody had died in the clean-up operation, he had assured him. What Tumbo did not tell the president was that out there in the cold, there were over five thousand families rendered homeless by an act of recklessness that Tumbo and his campaign team had conjured in their strategy to derail the election timetable. There had been no warning issued and very little had been salvaged. Many households lost everything and some human lives were lost.

'You see, Your Excellency, it is only the enemies of your good government who are trying to make political capital out of a minor incident. I leave it to you to deal with these dissidents, especially the major ones who are plotting your downfall,' he advised the president.

The president thanked him profusely for the detailed briefing, which reassured him that the situation was not as bad as he had been told by the head of Intelligence.

Since the departure of Hon. Tumbo, however, the president received very disturbing information. He was told of the senselessness and brutality with which Komoro was razed to the ground. He was warned to expect condemnation from within his own party, the government and from foreign circles. He was told that the demolition had been filmed by CNN and BBC crews. He was angry, very angry with the mayor and his team.

'Tell me!' he shouted at him. 'Are you the mayor of Glitta City in independent Kuzania or are you the mayor of a city in apartheid South Africa demolishing slums in Soweto?'

'I am sorry, Your Excellency, but —'

'Sorry! That is all you can say! What madness is this?'

'But Your Excellency, Hon. Tumbo told me you wanted the site cleared for the building of a new national stadium. I was only obeying your orders,' he said meekly.

The president slumped heavily into his armchair. He stared at the mayor blankly, unable to utter a single word. The mayor was rooted to the spot. They stayed like that, paralysed, for what seemed to the mayor like eternity. At last, the president recovered from the shock. He dismissed the mayor with a wave of his hand.

In the meantime, the University of Glitta was shut down indefinitely. Students were given two hours to clear from the campus. Riot police surrounded the area with orders to shoot anybody causing trouble. The orders came directly from the minister for Internal Security, Hon. Nyoka. In the confusion, Nzinga went to her father's house and Shaka went to live with Musa, in another slum area.

The figure of an old man seated neatly outside his hut cut a silhouette that was almost sculptural in the shadows of sunset. His head was clean-shaven and, indeed, he would complain most vehemently if his head were not shaved every other day. It was an old custom, one handed over the generations, and one he was going to keep to the end of his days, which it seemed, was not going to be for very much longer.

Agu had in his right hand some tweezers. He was running his left hand over his chin to detect any sign of hair that was once his beard. Once detected, he would pull it from the roots. Sometimes, it took several attempts to accomplish the feat because his hands were not steady any more. At the same time, he would amuse himself with one of those old songs that had lost meaning with modernity, civilisation, religion and education. He could swear, though, that they still carried a message for modern Kuzania. The song he was singing went something like this:

> At times I feel
> my heart too heavy
> And I have this urge
> to cry.
> Bursting with anger
> because the Mbuu clan
> has uprooted
> my sweet potatoes' plantation.

How shall they compensate me
these pig farmers
for I swear I don't eat pork.
How shall they pay?
And all they have are dirty swines!

Nyendaga kurira
Kieha gikanyingihira, ni mang'urika
Ma ngwaci ciakwa
Ciatarurirwo

Ni Mbari ya Mbuu
Ngarihwo naki?
Nandiriaga
Nyama cia ngurwe
Ngarihwo naki?

He knew there was a lot of compensation owed to him and
many others over ills they had been subjected to over the
ages. What they had suffered could be equated to farmers
having their sweet-potato vines uprooted, a senseless act
that denied farmers food. Those who had uprooted the
vines were many and they were the Mbuu clan of
demigods, who shamelessly raped and destroyed Kuzania.
But with what would they compensate the people,
since their world was artificial? Yes, the song had a
modern meaning, Agu concluded, as he struggled to
pluck out another wisp of hair from his chin. He was
waiting for Shaka and the men from the Kuzania
television company, who were taking him to the studios
for an interview. He had yielded to the clamour for an
appearance. Agu was very grateful to Shaka. In the
slums, people would buy newspapers and read Shaka's
articles to Agu. Agu was most thrilled when he saw his

photograph in the local daily. Tonight, he had a feeling of elation. He thought of Shaka: 'That man is cut out for greatness. To imagine that through his efforts my picture would be in the newspapers! And tonight, I will appear in homes of many people throughout Kuzania, in the glass boxes they call televisions! People will see me and they will hear me. Surely, if there is a day I have longed for all my life, just one single day when life would be meaningful, then this is my day!' For this special day, Agu had washed himself thoroughly, had his head shaven, plucked all the hairs from his chin (or almost so) and had worn his best blanket, the warm one that Shaka had bought him.

A vehicle bearing the writing Kuzania Broadcasting Corporation came to a halt outside his house. Out came Shaka and two men from the television station.

'Great-grandpa, I can see you are ready! You are looking wonderful. Need I ask how you are?' Shaka teased him.

'I'm fine, Shaka. I have been cleaning myself the whole day for the big show in the glass box. I do not want to make people's glass boxes dirty – they might hate me. I am ready, let us go.'

It was going to be a live broadcast. The panel was made of four people. As Agu faced them, his eyes hurt from the glare of the studio lights. He had never seen anything that bright in his life. The room was hot and he felt uncomfortable in his thick blanket. He decided the best thing was to forget about these minor disturbances and get on with the show. The cameras were not like those he had seen in the slums. These were big boxes, some fixed on stands and some on people's shoulders. There were at least four of them, just to take pictures of his one old face! He marvelled at the waste of modern life.

If this was the way the small glass box worked, maybe they needed a lot of pictures to send to each home. He also noticed that they were not taking just a few pictures, they were on him endlessly. By the end of it, he wondered if he would have a face left, as they seemed to take too much of it from all angles. If Shaka were inside the studio, he would have asked him a few questions, but he had been left outside. Well, he was man enough to go through it alone. Someone began to speak into a small object. It was as though he was addressing some invisible people. Three similar objects had been placed in front of Agu. He assumed them to be the instruments to take his voice. He heard his name mentioned followed by a brief history of his life. He listened carefully, they were correct in what they said. Shaka must have told them about him. He decided it was a great show and, since he knew the chance might never present itself again, he was going to make the best of it. As the old saying goes, 'A fruit is ripe only once and for a short while. If you don't eat it then, it will rot.' He was going to eat his ripe fruit here and now, when it was at its sweetest.

'Could you tell us, Great-grandpa, about your experience as a young man?'

Agu cleared his throat and spoke into the microphones as the panellist had done:

'Before the advent of colonialism, which were my days of youth, I was a young man grazing cows, sheep and goats; protecting them from wild beasts and neighbouring tribes. In those days, life was easy. We had plenty to eat. Forests were littered with beehives yielding fresh honey. They also brought forth wild fruits and fine wood. In the valleys, we had sugar canes, cocoa yams and sweet potatoes, while the highlands yielded tons of maize, beans, cassava, bananas and potatoes. People were happy and strong and nobody went hungry. We all cared for one another. I repeat, the hunger of an individual was unknown. In times of famine, which were few and far between, we all suffered together and, whatever little we had, we shared, beginning with the children and the elderly.'

'Could you compare those days with life today?' he was asked.

'My children, what can I say? It is like asking me to compare sleep with death. There is no comparison! Today, the population is very large and the land has shrunk. Land was grabbed from us by colonialists and the church and we were not compensated. The city also took most of the ancestral land of my clan and I am sure it is the same with other clans near big towns. Those in the highlands lost their lands to settlers. With independence, these lands were not returned to us. The population has exploded. We have been condemned as a result to small pieces of land enough for a house and a toilet. How do you keep a goat, a cow or a beehive in such a plot? What can you grow on it? Nothing! There is nothing to share and people – children, the youth, the middle aged and the very old – are dying of hunger. Today, nobody is spared, especially in the slums. I remember in the early days, we used to sing about the bounty and vastness of our land. We would sing:

> In the adjoining lands of Muthurwa
> which are ours
> should the need arise
> There is not a soul living there
> And we have left them to wildebeests
> to roam unhindered,
> until we need them.

Weru uria wa Muthurwa
Nduri kindu
Nduri kindu
No ngondi irarimutha

'Those big tracts of land, where are they now? We did not bequeath them to posterity, they were wrenched from us and turned into game parks for tourists, protected forests and high-cost estates. We lost everything and we were not compensated. A lot of water has passed under the bridge since those happy days, a lot of water and, today, even the water tastes bitter to the mouth! It has been a very long time since I last tasted honey. It has been a long time since I last enjoyed the ribs of a freshly slaughtered goat or the soup from the head of a ram, except the other day when my friends killed a goat in my compound and we really feasted! But, you see, it was unplanned; there was nowhere to keep it. It reminded me of the good old times, the way we were before we landed in this mess.'

Another panellist took over.

'We believe that every man has a mission in life. What can you say has been your mission and have you accomplished it?'

'My son, as you can see, I am in the final leg of my life, and the gods have been kind to me. They have given me long life and good health. Soon, I will be joining those who went before, to the land where there are no flies and bedbugs. When I meet them, they will ask me, "Agu, how is home? How did you leave our people? Did you give them good counsel?" And what shall I tell them? I will tell them tales of despair, destruction, betrayal and man's cruelty to man. You saw what happened in Komoro slums the other day. So what shall I report but the truth! I will tell them that we fought gallantly for independence but our hopes and aspirations were thrown by fools like pearls to pigs. I will tell them that independence was hijacked and derailed, leaving behind a trail of tears, hunger, death and destruction. But, as I go, let me also ask you a question. Have you been listening to the wind lately? It is carrying a new message of hope! Have you been listening to the rumbles in the slums, in the highlands, in the lake region, in the factories, in bars, in the streets, and everywhere else where two or more people are gathered? The nation is in despair. It is in an advanced state of decay. Do you know why our house is going to collapse? It is because it was built on sand. Someone stole the stones for its foundation! Listen to the wind blowing as it threatens the house, the house of Kuzania. It talks corruption, exploitation, murder, gross abuse of human rights – and all these in an independent and sovereign state. Do you think a house built on these can withstand the wind?

'Now, you ask me what has been my mission in life and whether I have accomplished it. I will answer you. In circumstances such as I have described, who, save for a mad man, can dream of a mission in life?' Agu appeared more angry than tired. At the same time, he looked very sad but dignified.

'Great-grandpa, what do you think should be done to save the house from collapsing?' asked another panellist.

'Thank you, young one. First of all, we must look at ourselves individually, very critically, and ask, "What have I done for Kuzania? How can I help Kuzania?" Secondly, we must accept each other as equal human beings, regardless of wealth and tribe. Thirdly, those who have taken food from the mouths of the needy must be punished. Fourthly, we must provide adequate food, shelter, clothing, medicine, schools and employment for all. We must learn to care for one another as in the days of old, the way we were. I hear that in Europe they provide for the unemployed. Is this communism? We must give those things we promised to the people in the manifesto of the freedom struggle. The national cake is big but it has become the preserve and property of a few fat-bellied leaders. This is the clan I call "Mbari ya Mbuu" and they should not be voted back in the forthcoming elections. How shall they compensate us for our wealth that they have stolen and squandered? I tell you, they must go so we can live whole lives.'

'As we are running out of time, I would like to ask Agu to leave us with words of hope,' the leading panellist said, signalling Agu to speak.

Agu took out his bottle of snuff and inhaled twice. He had two quick sneezes. When he spoke, his voice was more forceful and clearer.

'I will give you some encouraging words, words of hope but, first, I want to tell you this: there are times I wish I died a long time ago, not to witness the agony of the present times. Then I reflect that the gods and the spirits must have spared me to act as a bridge between the long past and the present. I have been a silent witness to the decay of our society. I am relieved to note that only a few in the society are completely rotten beyond redemption and so there is hope for tomorrow. The spirits assure me, "Don't worry, old man, things will turn out all right."'

Agu sat composed for a while, then, with a huge electrifying smile, said his last word: 'I have spoken.'

* * *

Hon. Tumbo, who had been alerted about the broadcast by Kimondo, stormed out of the golf club with WaMwago following. As he was driven to the Milton Hotel, he rehearsed what he was going to tell the president: 'Some mighty hand of evil was threatening the government. It has used beggars and now it using old men to spread false alarm. The minister for Information is in league with the vice-president, trying to bring down the government, and immediate action should be taken against both in the name of stability and state security.'

He washed his face with cold water on arrival at his suite, WaMwago having already let herself in with the spare key he had given her. 'Pour yourself a drink and pour me a strong brandy. I want to speak to the president.' With an air of arrogance and self-importance, he sat down, crossed his legs and dialled the president's direct line. It was picked up after one ring, as if the president was waiting for the call.

'Good evening, Your Excellency, it is Tumbo here.'

'Tumbo, you are the most despicable idiot that ever held a Cabinet post! You are working to undermine me, eh? You will see!'

The phone was banged down on him. Hon. Tumbo, his mouth wide open, slowly replaced the receiver on the hook.

'What is wrong?' WaMwago asked.

'Nothing, dear, nothing,' he said in a subdued, almost inaudible voice.

WaMwago had never seen Tumbo on the verge of tears before. He looked pathetic.

'Is everything all right, dear?'

Tumbo did not answer. He swallowed the brandy in huge gulps and told WaMwago to pour him another large one. He then drank himself senseless and collapsed in a heap on the bed. WaMwago was afraid. She left Tumbo asleep on the bed and drove to her apartment. She did not call William Stans; she just wanted to be alone. She knew something was wrong, very wrong.

Tumbo woke up the following morning, tired and looking ill. He did not even remember that WaMwago had been there. All he knew was that his world had come crashing in on him. He staggered into the lift and went to his car.

'Take me home,' he told the driver.

'Sir, you should go to see a doctor first,' the driver told him. 'You are not looking well.'

'Take me home, I said!' roared the hon. minister.

The minister for Internal Security had tried to reach Hon. Tumbo all night but to no avail. His contacts in State House had warned him that the president was very unhappy with Hon. Tumbo after the visit by the mayor of Glitta. Having been privy to the meeting that planned the destruction of Komoro slums, he was apprehensive that his standing was not any better. He was too scared to call the president to complain about Agu's 'inflammatory' show on the national television. He wanted to have Agu and the panellists arrested and detained. The way things were, however, he had to consult with Hon. Tumbo first.

Hon. Tumbo answered the phone in his residence.

'Boss, you sound awful, are you OK?' asked Nyoka.

'Things seem to have changed for the worse. His Excellency is very angry. I think the cat is out of the bag. We must change our plans.' Tumbo was no longer sounding sure of himself.

'I am calling you about old man Agu. Did you see him on television? I want to arrest him, together with the panellists. I believe these people are ringleaders in the so-called Movement. They could give useful information to assist in smashing it,' Nyoka said excitedly.

'Don't take any action against those people!' Tumbo cautioned. 'We need to buy time. We need not expose ourselves any further; we shall deal with them later.'

'OK, then, but what do we do in the meantime?'

'Let us bide our time for a while and assess the damage. Our next move should be without flaws and should be final. The way things are, there are more dangers than I had anticipated. Sit on the matter for a day or so and we shall see,' Tumbo advised.

Agu and the panellists escaped arrest only because of the heat and estrangement between the president and Hon. Tumbo. Who knows, Agu, who had cheated life for years, might have met his maker sooner via the police cells or torture chambers. The gods and spirits were indeed very kind to him and they kept watch over his safety. His interview set the nation on fire. People were singing his praise everywhere and clamouring for the programme to be aired again. The interview was also reproduced in full in the local daily and weeklies. He was quoted on CNN, the BBC, Radio Moscow, Radio South Africa and Radio China. Agu had become an international news item, an international star. His picture was later to appear on the covers of *Newsweek* and *Time* magazine. In Kuzania, Agu became a legend in his own lifetime. People wondered how a nation could have wasted such talent, wisdom and leadership. Some openly said had Agu been thirty years younger, they would have urged him to stand for presidency. He had shown the difference between natural leadership and the half-baked imbecility that had come to crown itself in the national leadership of Kuzania. It was like, as Agu had said, 'the difference between sleep and death!' People asked whether there were no younger Agus in Kuzania, who could make all the difference between life and death? They were there but the demigods had made sure they never got a chance, through arrests and detentions without trial, murder of the able bodied and the assassination of patriots. People swore to unearth more 'Agus' who would be given votes in the forthcoming elections. They openly abused the current leadership of demigods and the term 'Mbuu clan' became a new name for corrupt and insensitive leadership. A single one, like Tumbo, was now referred to as 'Kibuu' and more than one were called 'Mabuu'. It was the language of rebellion, the language of the fight between good and evil.

Agu was swept off his feet by the impact of his broadcast. People came from far and wide to pay him homage. Everybody wanted to be related to, or associated with, Agu, the new hero, the new star. Then one afternoon, no less a person than the incumbent vice-president drove to the compound of old man Agu, accompanied by Shaka, Apunda, Musa, Brother Music and others. Hon. Fikira had come to bring to Agu, 'gifts from the people', which meant the Movement. They included a video machine, a twenty-one-inch black and white television, two car batteries to be used to power the equipment as Agu had no electricity in his house, a huge fat ram, a goat and a gallon of fresh honey. They also brought a new blanket and an overcoat. They set up the equipment and the video started playing. Agu sat there watching himself. He was absolutely thrilled. 'Indeed, I have spoken,' he said at the end of it. As the goat and the ram were roasting on the fire, Agu enjoyed the taste of honey, licking it from a teaspoon.

'Honey will always be honey! It still tastes exactly the same as it did in the old days. Why can't we be like bees, preserving what is good in its purest form, for generations?' It was a question no one could answer and that everybody wished could be translated into practical reality in Kuzania.

Outside his hut, as dusk fell, was the silhouette of Agu and the vice-president. The evening air around them was ringing with rich laughter, a new language, a new feeling in the slums. Shaka and Musa stood close by, absorbing every word said. Three generations had found the meaning of life, in the slums, at dusk, as the dark figures of Shaka, Musa, Hon. Fikira and Agu reeled in genuine joy, guided by schooled wisdom, in the certainty of a better tomorrow for all.

Shaka wished Nzinga were there to complete the circle.

The president was alarmed by the reports reaching him. There was talk of an impending rebellion, not so much against him as against his regime. What was the difference? He either had to move quickly to implement his plans on the political future of Kuzania or he would be swept away by events. He did not want to end up like Mobutu. Already, he knew events were moving perilously close to rendering him redundant. He had to reassert his authority. Was this not what the presidency was all about, a game of survival? He owed it to himself to put the house in order. He felt tired and very weak. For once, he had doubts as to whether he was equal to the task. He convinced himself he was stronger and more of a statesman than Siad Barre and Mobutu put together. He would soon put the house in order.

14

Unclaimed Souls

Nobody could pinpoint with any degree of certainty the date of birth of the political malaise threatening Kuzania with death. The cancer had eaten into the political cohesion of the state to the roots. Of the myriad things going wrong, no one could tell whether the rot attacked each institution singly or whether they had been attacked in one fell swoop. Some blamed bad political leadership and economic mismanagement since independence. Others explained that the malaise was an extension of the oppressive colonial system that had not been dismantled with independence. A third school of thought blamed the advisers of the president, who were no more than a pack of incompetent, greedy liars. A fourth school of thought blamed the age, senility and sickness of the president, who was said to have lost control of the situation, leaving the nation to the mercy of plunderers such as Hon. Tumbo and Hon. Nyoka. The only point of convergence was that Kuzania was on the verge of collapse.

The president, it was generally agreed, was a good man at heart. However, nobody could absolve him from the ills of his regime. It was he who had named the Cabinet and the chiefs of the organs of state. His lethargy and irresoluteness had cost Kuzania dear. Both directly and indirectly he had a big share in the blame. There was no gainsaying the fact that he had surrounded himself with semi-illiterate sycophants who sang hollow songs in his praise, while behind his back their major interest was in lining their pockets. They did not want anybody to rock the boat. They were prepared to perpetuate the sickly nature of the state and even induce further decay if it would serve them.

A close look at Kuzania would reveal that there were two governments operating as one, but the demarcation line had been carefully camouflaged. However, the veil had began to split, exposing the divide. In truth, the nation had long ceased to have what one would call a political system. What was in place resembled more a political circus toying around with millions of lives. Twenty million people did not matter at all in Kuzania; what mattered were the interests of the twenty million-aires and their friends for whom, it seemed, Kuzania was specially created.

The birth of the Movement underlined one key factor: the urgent need for alternative leadership or, at the very least, a counterforce to halt the glaring excesses. The clamour for change started as a whisper, spread like a rumour, then transformed itself into a bush fire. It was a mass movement built on defiance and the dream of a better tomorrow for all.

The president felt very isolated and unsure of himself. He felt his head spinning and his temperature rising. He was sweating from head to toe. He tried to stand up from his chair but a sharp, deep pain in the chest crushed him back into his seat. With almost a superhuman effort, he pressed the emergency button on his desk as he collapsed into an unconscious heap on the floor.

Later in the day, the president was flown to London for treatment following a heart attack. In line with the provisions of the constitution, the affairs of the state were placed in the hands of the vice-president. Hon. Fikira continually briefed the nation on the state of health of the president. He assured the people that the president had only suffered a mild stroke, he was responding well to treatment and would be back soon. In the meantime, he ordered the reopening of the university and the suspension of political campaigns. One thing was very clear to him and the Movement; he did not want to be accused of having taken advantage of his acting position to bolster his political standing vis-à-vis other candidates. The people also understood that it was only logical for campaigns to be suspended as a mark of respect for the head of state. There would be no underhand schemings; he would hold the nation together and begin the battle from where he had left it, on a clean slate.

People did not understand this strange disease called a heart attack. The diseases they knew were malaria, pneumonia, cholera, typhoid, tuberculosis, gonorrhea and, lately, Aids. This new one baffled them. They asked if it only attacked presidents, others said the disease had something to do with the blood clotting. He had been bewitched, it was the work of the CIA, and the Americans had poisoned him with bacteria so that Tumbo could take over. In Africa, nobody dies a natural death. Terminal illness is seen as the work of enemies and evil spirits. The evil hand in this case was Hon. Tumbo and his American friends. Hon. Tumbo was evil and a thief, people decided, but concluded that the days of a thief were only forty. His number was up.

The president's illness took away the heat from the people's anger. It was a diversion that offered a period of adjustment. However, to the Movement, there was no cease-fire in the plans to rid Kuzania of evil. A new list of candidates was debated. It was also resolved that should the people's wishes be derailed through rigging, the country would be made ungovernable through a campaign of civil disobedience, while the Movement prepared its armed wing. The other important decision taken in the period was the shelving of the assassination of Hon. Tumbo. It would be seen as a cowardly act on the part of the Movement and would have counterproductive consequences.

The movement was spreading and entrenching itself in all corners of Kuzania. The doves in the Movement voiced the need to hold dialogue with the president and the ruling party in order to avoid bloodshed. The hawks, who were in the majority, overruled them, arguing that the ruling party was rotten through and through and that there was only a handful of patriots in the party who would be absorbed sooner or later. This was adopted as the Movement's stand on cooperation with the government and the ruling party. It was informed by the fact that if the Movement was registered as a political party, it was going to sweep the boards in the elections.

Hon. Fikira was a man in his late sixties. It was not lost to the people that he had actively fought for independence in the bush. To some, it was also known that he had been badly tortured when he was captured, and that his testicles had been crushed. It was the reason he did not have a wife or children. Sometimes, his colleagues teased him over it but he had learnt to live with it. He mixed freely with people of all classes and, if he had any weaknesses or vices, he did not expose them. He was fond of visiting all corners of Kuzania and participating in self-help projects. This angered his political adversaries who, basking in the comfort of the city, called him a 'political tourist'. His mantra was: 'We must be dedicated to the needs of the people.' The minister for Internal Security used to refer to him as 'the naïve eunuch'. He would tell Tumbo, 'This naïve eunuch is going to cause us trouble some day. Why don't you teach him how to eat! Doesn't he know that bread with butter tastes better than without!' The vice-president, however, knew that the struggle was not with individuals but with the system that placed them in positions of authority. He longed for the day he would see their backs as they were swept into the waste-bin of history. There was no doubt though that, had his acting capacity allowed him, he would have instituted investigations into Tumbo and Nyoka's involvement in corruption, embezzlement of public funds and assassinations. The day will come, he consoled himself.

The ailing president gave a new lease of life to Hon. Tumbo and his den of thugs. A short while after the president was flown to London, Tumbo reassembled his campaign team with a view to finding a new direction in his strategy to manage change. The routine was the same. There would be a goat-eating party in Kimondo's house in Happy Valley.

Many policemen were sent to guard Kimondo's house in advance and a number of patrol cars were in the vicinity. The neighbours wondered what the big occasion was. Had the acting president not announced the suspension of all political campaigns? They called the local police station, making enquiries as to what was going on. The officer commanding the station was equally surprised, because he had not released any detail to guard Kimondo's house. He took a patrol car and drove to Kimondo's house, arriving right behind Hon. Tumbo's brand new Mercedes-Benz. He saluted the hon. minister. 'Sir,' he said humbly, 'I am the officer-in-charge and I am here to enquire what is going on.'

'I think you should have a word with the minister for Internal Security,' replied Tumbo. He sent his driver to call the minister. The officer noted that the policemen were not from his station.

'There seems to have been some irregularity,' explained Nyoka when he arrived, 'in that you were not notified by the police commissioner that he would be sending a detail to your area from headquarters. Everything is in order.'

The officer was given a wad of bank notes and he drove away, very happy with his sense of responsibility. Back in his office, he dealt with all enquiries on the gathering most thoroughly and ruthlessly, knowing that both the commissioner and his minister were in command of the situation.

News of the gathering soon reached the ears of the acting president. He called Kimondo's house and demanded to speak to the minister for Internal Security, Hon. Nyoka. 'What is going on? I thought I suspended all political gatherings and campaigns until the president returns?'

'Who told you there is a political rally going on around here?' the minister asked with a sneer.

'Don't talk to me like that – as if I am your bloody wife!'

'What do you know about women – and yet you call

my wife bloody? For your information, Your Excellency,
Hon. Tumbo is thanking his campaign team for a job well
done. If that should cause you concern, it means you don't
have anything useful to do, Your Excellency!'

The acting president threw down the phone, shaking
with rage. Had he the power, he would have ordered the
immediate arrest of the whole group and charged them
with breaching the law. Even better, he would have
stripped them of their official portfolios. As things stood,
there was nothing he could do.

Early in the evening, the meeting came to an end. A
new strategy had been adopted. Everyone pretended to
one another that the campaign had gone well and that
power was within their grasp. They were told that the
president's impartiality was in question; he seemed to
be wavering in his support for Tumbo, mainly due to
his deteriorating mental state of health. For that reason, the campaign had to adopt a new strategy that
excluded him. It was decided that a coup d'état could
speed things up and ensure takeover. The minister for
Internal Security was to organise the support needed
among the different wings of state security. Kimondo
was to recruit thugs to beef up the operation. Hon.
Tumbo assured everyone that funds were available in
abundance, and that they could also count on his US
and UK friends to tilt the balance in case of difficulties.
He could see power within his grasp.

'Whether the coup is staged before or after the
president returns will depend on how fast we move.
What matters is that we succeed. All those earmarked for
elimination must be finished within the first hours of the
coup,' Hon. Tumbo stressed, talking more like a general
than a politician. No doubt, as the list of those to be

eliminated was finalised, Shaka's name would appear. He had caused Tumbo sleepless nights and his demise was vital for the complete happiness of the president-designate before he was sworn in. As the group drove from Kimondo's house, each felt there was something big coming his way. In the new government, they would form the inner circle, the Cabinet, and they would control Kuzania. Kimondo dreamt of a ministerial appointment. He wore a big grin as he got into his car to go to the golf club, to initiate his part of the grand new strategy.

Tumbo was very happy as his Mercedes cruised down the road. Soon he would be dining with the heads of states of America, Britain, France, Japan and Korea. This called for special celebrations tonight. He went to his suite at the Milton Hotel, poured himself a brandy and lit a cigarette. Once seated, he dialled WaMwago's number. The phone kept on ringing but there was no answer. 'Stupid woman,' he said. 'Where has she gone?' He dialled the golf club to enquire whether she was there but was informed she had not appeared that evening. He put the receiver down in deep disappointment.

'The stupid woman has grown wings! I will teach her who I am! I am the new president, I am His Excellency and commander-in-chief of the armed forces of Kuzania!' He downed the bottle of brandy and slept on the bed, fully dressed, his shoes still on.

What was going on in the city of Glitta was not ordinary talk, especially to those with ears glued to the ground. There was expectation of some dramatic event, but nobody knew what it would be or where it would come from. Everybody suspected everybody else of concealing the truth. Mistrust became the order of the day. Rumours started going around to the effect that the vice-president was about to move against Hon. Tumbo before the president's return. Others countered that it was Tumbo who was about to stage a coup with the help of US marines. The reported docking of a US aircraft carrier in the port of Mimosa only served to fuel the rumour further. The ship, however, was on a routine supply call. People decided that the acting president would have moved against Tumbo if it were not for the threat posed by the marines. They were there to protect Tumbo.

This being high tourist season, there were a lot of tourists in Glitta and Mimosa. Musa and Apunda were having a good time in Chakacha Nite Spot.

'These people you see here are not tourists, they are American spies,' Apunda whispered to Musa.

'No, they are just tourists!' replied Musa. 'They are ordinary folk, men and women enjoying the beauty of Kuzania! Man, relax!'

'Musa, in Kuzania today, there are foreigners who have come to support Tumbo in his campaign, women included. The Movement must guard against infiltration. Women, especially, are a powerful weapon and empires have been lost by the use of their charms,' Apunda said. 'I am going to point out this danger to the movement in our next meeting.'

'You are getting drunk, let's go home,' Musa said, pulling Apunda by the arm.

The return of the president put an end to speculation and rumours. It was time to get back to the drawing-board and plan how to win the political contest. He was greeted by a huge and tumultuous crowd upon arrival. In his short speech, the president touched on his joy at being back in Kuzania and thanked the vice-president for deputising most ably in his absence. He warned those scheming chaos from whatever quarters to desist, or they would face his wrath. 'I am not finished yet!' he added.

Hon. Fikira stood next to the president while Hon. Tumbo stood among his Cabinet colleagues. The president had greeted him with a cold stare, and Tumbo realised that the warning was directed at him and his group. It was time to show who was in charge of the situation: the president or Tumbo. Tumbo would not be cowed by threats.

In private briefings at State House, the vice-president warned the president that Tumbo was scheming a coup d'état.

'Are you sure about what you are telling me?' the president asked.

'Yes I am, Your Excellency. I have planted my men ... I mean, I ... I have learnt this from very impeccable sources,' he said, cursing the lapse in his concentration.

'Give me some time to cross-check on this. It is very serious.'

The president was tired mentally and physically and this was not the time to over-exert himself with serious state matters. He felt he needed a rest. What he did not tell Hon. Fikira was that, while recuperating in London, he had been informed that the vice-president was chairman of the Movement, which wanted to transform itself into an opposition political party. He had been told that the country was now divided into two antagonistic and increasingly belligerent opposing camps, as if he had ceased to exist. He remembered that his doctors had warned him not to involve himself in anything strenuous either mental or physical.

'I will see to these matters later,' he told the vice-president, who left with a feeling that the president was too far gone to handle the situation. There had to be another way out and the clock was ticking.

Shaka knew that Tumbo was in a fix. His unpopularity was spreading like fever and people openly talked ill of him. He had a hunch that Tumbo's days as a leader were numbered. Even if he had nine lives like a cat, this time he was on his last one. He felt hugely relieved for himself, for Nzinga and for the people of Kuzania. The struggle against evil will soon be over, he promised himself.

The last thing that Tumbo was thinking about was 'the scum from the slums'. His struggle now was for political survival through a coup and there was no alternative as far as he was concerned. This was his world, the shaping of his new heaven, his new garden of Eden.

Shaka and Nzinga were together almost on a daily basis and, like Adam and Eve in the garden of Eden before the fall, they were the happiest people in the world. Shaka was earmarked for a scholarship for further studies even before the final results were out. He was told that he would become a lecturer in journalism upon the completion of his advanced course. He was elated and it made him work all the harder.

Nzinga, relaxed and radiant, was also distinguishing herself. Her supervisors had talked of a PhD, thanks to the new ground she was breaking in the field of anthropology, with the help of Agu and other friends in Kawempe. She felt transformed both mentally and physically. Adding to her radiance was the fact that she was proudly carrying Shaka's baby. This was one of the reasons she kept her distance from her father. She knew that she and Shaka needed each other more and more and that their future was one. The world was changing, she knew, and the year X was no longer light years away. She could almost feel it! She eagerly awaited the day she would hold hands with Shaka in total freedom, dancing to the sound of tom-toms, bongo drums and impala horns.

Innocence, sweet innocence, the great mother of ... as I told you before!

15

Operation Black Pig

Hon. Tumbo's desperation grew by the day. He was losing his self-confidence. With the return of the president, the nation was waiting for the announcement of dates for the resumption of political campaigns. The road, Tumbo thought, was treacherous. His attempts to reach the US ambassador and the British high commissioner to warn them about the 'growing threat of communism' in Kuzania had been rebuffed and he did not understand why. His last resort was William Stans, who was an expert on security matters and counter-insurgency. Unfortunately, he was not accessible. Tumbo guessed Stans had hit yet another lucrative line of business. He partly blamed himself for having given Stans too much leeway, although both had benefited financially. He thought the Movement should be a high-priority security matter and Stans should drop all else to attend to it for the benefit of Kuzania and for the protection of democracy and western interests. Did the Americans want to see the emergence of a Castro in Kuzania in the name of the vice-president and his populist approach to politics? This threat could only be averted through a coup d'état, he planned to tell Stans, and all he needed was financial support from Washington and the promise of intervention by American marines should there be need to tip the balance. Was this too much to ask? He thought not. In his view, some of the US forces lying idle waiting to topple Saddam Hussein should be rushed to Kuzania for a day or two.

The group in charge of the coup was asking for funds to buy more support and to acquire the necessary equipment. Tumbo did not wish to use his personal money as he knew he was going to need it to buy popularity after the coup. Those in the army warned him that coup plans needed to be acted upon before the ink was dry. If the ink dried, the throats of the plotters could become pretty wet with their own blood, should the plot become uncovered. Tumbo was desperate.

When the president was abroad for treatment, the vice-president had taken the opportunity to reassure farmers that they would be paid their long overdue payments. He told them the government was in a precarious financial state and only the president could authorise the borrowing of the necessary funds to meet their demands; his return had therefore raised their hopes. The president had returned and still no payments were made, however. On the contrary, the local daily was carrying stories of the IMF, the World Bank and bilateral donors cutting aid because of rampant corruption, economic mismanagement and political repression. The financial situation was very bad and threatening to get worse. The economy was on the brink of collapse. The president avoided the issue like the plague. Matters would sort themselves out with time, he hoped. Had the nation not ridden over bigger storms in the past and come out unscathed?

In frustration farmers' unions turned against the

government. Added to the farmers' anger came the demand for compensation from the victims of the Komoro demolition. Factory workers, civil servants, teachers, doctors and nurses also made demands for higher pay, threatening nationwide strikes unless their demands were met. They channelled their grievances and support to the Movement, which promised them redress. There were loud calls for Hon. Tumbo to be stripped of his Cabinet post, expelled from the party and from parliament and put to trial. It was said Tumbo had single-handedly finished the economy. Tumbo's network countered that the accusations were the work of the Movement attempting to discredit the government and to seize power.

As the president listened to the debates, he became even more exhausted. He could not trust anybody. He promised himself to bring the situation under control as soon as he felt stronger. In the meantime, he had no choice but to watch as events unfolded, most unpredictably.

The president was a good man at heart, a God-fearing man, afflicted by fatigue, senility, sickness and old age. Brother, the road to hell is full of good people, marching to eternal damnation, singing songs of salvation.

Slowly, the government was getting strangulated. Powerful forces were on the move, heading God knows where, like bats flying in broad daylight. Kuzania was on the verge of a national disaster, drifting towards statelessness. As the local people say, 'If the head bull is limping, the herd will not make it to where the grass is lush.' The president appeared increasingly incapable of leading his people to the land of milk and honey, the promised land. They were lost in the wilderness.

Quietly, people started agitating for the president to retire honourably before things got out of hand. It was argued that, although he had good intentions, the world had greatly changed in the long period he had been in the executive seat. While his mental and physical faculties were grinding to a halt, the world, on the other hand, was moving at supersonic speeds with the advent of the new communication and information technology. He could not cope with the speed of events in Kuzania, let alone global issues. There was a new era dawning, one in which he had to be an observer not a key player. The nation had matured and it needed its able-bodied men to gather both the fruits of independence and of the global market, which had made the world one large village. There was no question that, if Kuzania searched deep within itself, it could come up with several names of able, educated and modern leaders, and the best among them would be chosen in free and fair elections to lead the nation. Whatever the president had done while in office had been his very best and he could only do worse or continue to paralyse the nation by his clinging to power.

The wishes of the people were reaching the ears of the president. Defiantly, he argued that he still had time to finish his mission of cleaning up the mess. He argued, 'He is a bad eater he who leaves the table littered with remains from his plate and is unworthy of the invitation.' However, the more he thought about his mission, the weaker he became. He was draining himself of any last ounce of energy with sleepless nights. He was not quite sure when the hazy disposition in his mind began to crowd his reasoning. It had alarmed him that there was too much left to be done in a too short a time. Things were becoming very complex, if not insurmountable. He could no longer distinguish between his true friends and his sworn enemies, even within his Cabinet of ministers. He had become distrustful and suspicious of every one of them.

When he was sworn in as president, he had promised himself that, unlike his predecessor and other African leaders, he would leave behind a legacy of impeccable leadership. He had reasoned that, after four hundred years in the wilderness, Africa owed itself one great leader to propel itself and its people to the heights of greatness and restore its lost glory. That leader, as he had seen it, was himself. Kuzania was the blessed nation to lead the march. Looking back, he knew he had fallen far too short of this historic calling. Now, he was being termed dictatorial by overseas commentators and his own people were clamouring for his political demise. His government was labelled ineffective and Kuzania was said to be on the verge of collapse. However hard he tried, he was unable to point to the specific period when his dream began to fizzle out. It was as if from the very start the dream had only been an illusion, a Utopia that had stubbornly refused to translate itself into concrete achievements. No, he could not have been this naïve! Then he remembered that his dream had been on line until the Yom Kippur war of 1973. Yes, that was when the woes of Kuzania began, with the rise of crude-oil prices. The oil bill guzzled all the national reserves and his grandiose schemes had come to a grinding halt. He had intended to provide Kuzania with a modern infrastructure: clean drinking water in all homes, free education, free medical treatment, shelter, better employment opportunities and many other things. He had also planned a social-welfare scheme for the unemployed, the disabled and aged and a special fund for the rehabilitation of street urchins and parking-meter boys. Those were his dreams until the Arabs used oil as a weapon but, unfortunately, they had shot his mission right through the heart. The finding of oil in Kuzania had come too late and too little, as there was then a glut in the market. The yields also fell short of the national demand. He concluded that he had not failed: the Arabs had betrayed him. The Arabs were to blame for all the ills of Africa, from the days of slave-trade and the distortion of the history of Egypt! If only his people could listen, and if only he could master the efforts, he could tell them of the genesis of the current mess. He congratulated himself on solving a very complicated riddle. His mind was still sound, he consoled himself.

The next morning, the president wanted to be alone. The pain in his chest had subsided somewhat and he felt the need to attend to several pressing matters. After breakfast, he felt the urge to drink a shot of whisky and soda. It had been a long time since he had felt this good and there was no harm in celebrating his remarkable recovery with a small drink. Sunday, after all, he mused, is the day devoted to the spirit, holy or alcoholic! He placed a pillow behind his back for more comfort. Somehow, he was not getting that special taste of whisky in his buds. Each sip was like a bitter episode in a story of misfortunes and failure. He looked at his picture hanging on the wall, the one inscribed 'President and Commander-in-Chief'. It was a powerful title, one that could move mountains, change boundaries and declare war, he thought. But with all these titles that conferred to him unlimited powers, what had he achieved in his long period in office, he wondered. The answer came back swiftly: Nothing.

Beads of sweat began to form on his forehead, growing bigger and bigger until they became drops and began flowing down his face. He wiped away the sweat with the open palm of his hand. Maybe it was the dim red bulb in the room that was creating an illusion, but he saw not sweat on his palm but blood. He was terrified. The sun shot its rays through the half-open curtains, and shadows of swaying trees outside his room played against the inside wall of his room. They fascinated him. As he watched, they took on what looked like human forms, at first grotesque and then clearer. Wiping his face free from sweat, again he saw blood. He switched off the red light bulb. Now he could relax and watch the images on the wall. But when he looked at the wall, his body went limp. Like everything else in the past, the sun, the wind, trees and shadows had conspired to mock him. Dancing on the wall was the picture of the first minister assassinated in Kuzania. His eyes were fixed sternly on the president. Then came the images of the two ministers recently killed. He could not stand it! He threw the glass of whisky at the wall. It broke into fragments that scattered across the room. The whisky spluttered on the wall, dripping like blood from images of the bodies on the wall. Their eyes, fixed on him, were crying blood!

He could not stand it. He cupped his face in his open palms and began to sob, at first softly, then uncontrollably. How long it lasted, he did not know. By the time he opened his eyes again, the sun had drifted further west and the shadows were gone. What remained of his illusion were fragments of glass on the floor and the stains of whisky drying on the wall. What went wrong? he asked himself, his eyes closed as if in prayer. Is this what I will be remembered for? No, I have got to set the record straight and leave behind a legacy with no blemish. I owe it to my Maker. I cannot face the day of judgement with a record like this. He went down on his knees and began to pray, 'Our Father in Heaven, you who sees...' His mind went blank. As his mind wandered in the darkness, he saw the face of Hon. Tumbo appear. It was a big face, filling all the space in the universe, and he was laughing a most wicked and loud laugh. Its echo filled the president's head, the whole room, the whole country, the universe. Tumbo's mouth appeared like a black hole and the centre was black. When Tumbo stopped laughing he said one word: 'Fool!' He disappeared.

The president opened his eyes and stood up. He did not know whether what he felt could be described as anger, defeat or madness. His mind focused on his minister for Commerce and Industry. Tumbo will never call me a fool again, he swore.

The president showered, dressed and went to his private office. He telephoned William Stans, his adviser on matters of security and requested him to report to State House.

Whoever lives by the sword must die by the sword, the president said to himself as he waited for Stans.

'Stans, how have you been?' he asked on Stans's arrival.

'Fine, thank you, Your Excellency, and yourself?'

'Could be better! I called you because there is an urgent matter I want you to discharge.' There was urgency in the president's voice. He braced himself. 'I gather your good friend Tumbo is no longer interested in the vice-presidency. Is this so?'

'Well, I have not talked to him for quite some while but ... when did he announce this?' Stan asked in surprise.

'Your friend is interested in State House. He wants to stage a coup!' The president was eyeing Stans very closely.

'God forbid!' exclaimed Stans.

'You know I have always had the welfare of Kuzania at heart, don't you?' the president asked.

'Yes, Your Excellency,' replied Stans.

'Kuzania is in danger from the stupid schemings of your friend. I want you to get rid of him, leaving no trace,' the president said coolly, without emotion. He continued, 'I don't care whether you put him in a drum of acid or dump him in the middle of the ocean but get rid of him.' He waited. Stans was stunned.

'Your Excellency, I understand your concern and your anger over his act of betrayal – it is high treason – but is there no other way out, such as trying him in a court of law?'

'I did not call you for a discussion on the matter! I called you to execute a decision!'

Stans considered the options. He had been in Kuzania long enough and the country seemed to be on the brink of something nasty. Maybe it was time to move on, to get out of Kuzania.

'How much?'

'Quote your price,' replied the president.

After haggling, a figure of half a million dollars in cash was agreed, fifty per cent was given over there and then and the other fifty after the operation. Stans coded it, 'Operation Black Pig' in his mind. Tumbo, he thought, would be a soft target. If parting company with his business partner was going to yield him half a million dollars, it was worth it.

Outside in the car park, Stans fumbled from pocket to pocket, looking for his car keys. He seemed to have lost all sense of touch and feeling. The president was watching him through the window, hoping he would not fumble the job. Stans got hold of himself and remembered the keys all along had been in his shirt pocket. He reflected that he had once read that, 'the African is a child, with no brains and easily manipulable.' He was not sure any more. As he drove away, he had a feeling he himself had been manipulated like a child by an African. Well, at least he was getting paid well.

He did not have to kill Tumbo himself, he would leave it to Scudulis. He reckoned that fifty thousand dollars was all that was needed. He would pocket the rest. He got home, deposited the money that the president had handed over as part payment in a safe, turned on the fan full blast and slumped on the couch. After a while, he started laughing. Shakespeare had said, 'troubles come in battalions' but, to Stans, it was fortunes that came in battalions. What the president didn't know was that Stans had already been detailed by the US ambassador to get rid of Tumbo. He was being paid twice! He tuned the radio to Voice of America broadcasting to Africa. He smiled in the foreknowledge that soon the station would be broadcasting news of Tumbo's assassination. He laughed as he listened to the gory news from Rwanda and Sierra Leone. There were great profits to be made from all this chaos. But, first, there was Operation Black Pig to attend to . This had to be a success and he hoped to be rewarded with the directorship of CIA activities in East, Central and Southern Africa with time. He felt the death of Tumbo was also necessary for his own release from their entangled business relations. He had played second fiddle to a black man for far too long. Now he was the master of the hand of destiny. It was good to feel so powerful. 'If only I had killed General Giap, the war in Vietnam would have been won easily! We lost Vietnam:

we are not going to lose Kuzania because of a stupid fat black pig! Tumbo is a dead man.' He picked up the telephone and called WaMwago. She had been waiting for his call.

Hon. Tumbo had a most sumptuous lunch at the United Africa Club that day. He went to the bar to wash it down with brandy. Scudulis, the errand boy for William Stans, was at the counter. They sat next to each other.

'The potential in tourism in this country is enormous,' Scudulis was saying. 'Imagine what interests a private nudist beach would generate! It would bring queens, kings and film stars!'

Tumbo was sure he would not venture nude on any beach to display his body but, if the venture was going to be a money-spinner, he was going to be a major shareholder. 'This is a brilliant idea. Consider the licence issued. What does Stans say about it?'

'I haven't talked to him about it but he will buy the idea, I am sure. I called his place a little while back but he was out. I need to call him again.'

'Tell him I am here and invite him for a drink so we can wrap up the deal right away. I also want to discuss with him some rather urgent business,' Tumbo said.

Scudulis went to the balcony and dialled Stans on the mobile. Stans was at home, waiting for WaMwago to arrive. 'Hi, Stans. I have been looking for you. We are at the United Africa Club with the boss and he wants to see you.'

'Boss? Which boss?'

'Hon. Tumbo!' replied Scudulis. They always referred to Tumbo as, 'boss' or 'big boss'.

'Tell the boss you caught me as I was leaving for a very important appointment. Tell him I've gone to see the US

ambassador and ... and ... I will call him in the evening.'
He hung up the phone. Scudulis went back to the counter
and relayed Stans's message to Tumbo.

Tumbo feared that there was something fishy going on.
He had tried to see the ambassador without success; he
had also tried to reach Stans several times but Stans was
evidently avoiding him. He wondered what business the
two had together.

'Scudulis, there is one thing I want you to do for me. I
want you to report on every move Stans is making; where
he is going, who he is meeting and why. The man has
started to forget himself! He has lost sense of time and
urgency. I am a very busy man with important things to
attend to, and he doesn't seem to realise that. Let me
have the reports regularly and I will pay you well. In the
meantime, work on the blue print for the nudist beach.
The title deed and land-use certificate will be issued in
your name within the week. We can manage without
Stans. About how many hectares are adequate and where
do you want it located?'

'Five hectares, twenty kilometres north of Mimosa. I
will give you the details of the site tomorrow,' Scudulis
responded excitedly.

'And the reports?'

'You can count on me, boss, you will get them to the
minutest of details,' he promised.

16

Hope by Fire

Brother Music had received a new guitar from the Movement. He sat on a stone outside his shack, reorganising the last chords of his latest composition. He felt great things were coming his way and that, after the year X, he would rise to become the greatest recording artist in the history of Kuzania. His songs would not glorify sex, no, they would glorify the Movement, the struggle for independence and the coming dignity of the black race. Regardless of the current plight of the race, he was convinced its future was not just bright but brilliant.

He picked his guitar and headed for Glitta city centre, to a rendezvous with his usual pals. When he came to Vuruta Bar, he found Shaka and Musa outside. They told him there was a special meeting of their cell that they all needed to go to. They crossed the city until they came to Old Garage, which was the venue of the meeting where they found Apunda, the journalists and several others seated on stones and planks of wood. Like any other group of the disinherited, they were discussing the fast-deteriorating situation in Kuzania.

'At this rate, even the elections might not be held. This country is going to explode,' Shaka said.

'Let it explode!' said an elderly man. 'In the olden days, we used to burn forests to ashes in order to create new fields for cultivation. If Kuzania burns, we shall plant new fields and the yields will be high.'

'These are true words,' said Musa.

'Shaka,' the old man continued, 'I came here to meet you and to thank you for all you have done for the Movement. I was with your father on the day he was arrested. I escaped the rope purely because the colonial administration thought they should hang only the leader of our forces. What pains me most to this day is that I was forced to witness the hanging. I was chained and forced to accompany your great father to the gallows and I could not raise a finger to save him. I would have gladly died with him.' The old man spoke with a trembling voice and Shaka looked at him, not knowing what to say.

'My son,' the old man continued, 'I have seen the fire in your eyes and it burns with greater intensity than your father's did. I know you will do him proud and, wherever he is, I believe he is happy he planted this seed on fertile soil.' He took a sip of his drink and continued. 'As we walked to the gallows, your father talked to me, pouring his heart out. The words he told me have remained a secret, guarded in my heart. My days are almost gone and the recipient of the message has not only matured but he has distinguished himself in the new phase of the struggle. I cannot hold them back any longer and that is why I came to see you.'

'Go on,' Shaka said impatiently.

'We removed your father's body from the gallows and loaded it on to an open Land Rover. The authorities drove it away and buried him in the prison yard. The government lies and says it is not known where your father was buried. They fear heroes! I remember that I did not see a good man die, no! I saw a god wasted by the cruel hand of betrayal. If he had lived, Kuzania would not have landed in this mess.' He was silent again.

'Go on, what did he tell you?' Shaka asked again.

'When your father was asked whether he had anything to say before they hanged him, his eyes shone brighter than the brightest star in the sky. They were fire, red hot fire like I had seen in them in battles in the forest. He turned to me and said:

'"Report me fairly to those I leave behind and especially to my young son. I know their love for me is overwhelming and this is mutually shared. This is a cruel separation. I swam across freezing and swollen rivers and scaled the mountains of Kuzania to bring freedom to our people. Our struggle was not racial, it was for the good of mankind. I can see and hear the sound of our cattle grazing in the highlands, but alas, there is also the crazy laughter of hyenas and the owl wail of death! Tell the people to be careful, with independence there is danger lurking everywhere. At last comes the roar of the lion, scattering the agents of bad omen, and it gives me the reassurance that my death is not in vain! The strength lies with the future generations, who will restore dignity to Kuzania.

'"Look into my eyes, do you see any fear? It is the hope for a better tomorrow that gives me the strength to face death courageously. These eyes will burn tyranny to ashes. There should be no mourning, no tears; tell the people to smile, for the day of the restoration of black dignity will come. Grasp my departing spirit and spread it to all the corners of Kuzania. Feed it to coming generations and let it be a light, a guiding star to illuminate the new world. And when they talk about me, let them tell the young ones, 'there once lived a man, who faced death, to set you free'." '

The old man paused. 'Then they hanged him. I have kept my promise to him. It is up to you, Shaka, to set the record straight. Our ideals were distorted with independence and the cause was betrayed by the hyenas and owls or, as you call them today, "pigs" and "demigods". The roar of the lion must be heard to scatter the agents of death.'

Shaka was overwhelmed. All he could see was the image of his father urging him to roar like a lion.

'Those were inspirational words, a beacon to the future,' said Musa.

'Let me tell you, the song I will write out of this message will be sung beyond the boundaries of Kuzania. It will be the universal anthem of the oppressed and the disinherited all over the world, I promise you,' Brother Music said.

Shaka grasped the hand of the old man. 'You can rest assured your words have not fallen on deaf ears and my father's wishes will be fulfilled.' His voice was like the voice of a commander in battle, assured that victory was at hand.

'I do not doubt you, my son,' said the old man.

'The message will be spread through our cells to all parts of Kuzania. We owe it to our fallen hero, and it gives a new sense of urgency and impetus to the work of the Movement. Whatever was said must come to pass,' Apunda said.

'I have recorded the message. We can make copies and distribute them,' said one of the journalists, pointing to a tape recorder by his side.

'I suggest,' said Brother Music, 'that Shaka takes the cassette to the school of journalism. It should be

317

transcribed first and copies made both for records and for distribution. It will be cheaper and we can reach more people that way.' That very day, the distribution started.

In the same room where they had met last, the UK and US envoys were having a serious discussion with the managing director of the local daily. African, who had briefed them on what he knew, including rumours of a possible coup. 'As I told you last time, Tumbo is a dangerous man and an incorrigible fool. He is going to plunge this country into chaos.'

'We know this! We have known it all along! Do you think we are as blind as bats?' The British high commissioner asked.

'God, some of these buffoons! The idiot knows he cannot even get his daughter's vote yet he dreams of leading the nation!' the US ambassador observed. 'But, since he seems bereft of reason, he sure will listen to the big bang.' He smiled to his counterpart.

'What big bang?' the MD asked.

'When Tumbo loses the elections, it will be a big bang on his inflated ego!' lied the high commissioner hurriedly.

'I see,' said the MD, not fully convinced.

'What did you find out about the Movement?' the ambassador asked him.

'The people's welfare is the central focus of the Movement. It has wide support, the general population is angry with the current regime. The people in the slums live in hovels that neither protect them from cold nor rain. Life is not any better in the rural areas. The Movement seeks to clean up the political mess that is pushing Kuzania to the abyss. This is not a communist movement, it is a people's crusade. Hungry people do not have to follow the teachings of Karl Marx or Mao Tse Tung to rise against tyranny. They have set a timetable for change and the deadline is called "the year X".'

'You mean their programme is not immediate?' the ambassador asked.

'Well, in as far as I can read it, the year X is here and now!'

'I think your analysis is very sound. It is true the people have received a raw deal from their government. It is also very true that the masses and their leaders are on the warpath. Haven't you noticed that even the church has joined them? It is people like Tumbo who are standing between the people and democracy. The likes of Tumbo are a danger to themselves, to the people, to the nation and to our interests. If the movement is an alternative, we have to work with it,' the British high commissioner concluded.

'All right, two things will have to be done,' the ambassador told the MD. Firstly you have to lay the ground for the total demise of Tumbo, exposing him for what he has always been. Secondly, through your good offices, put us in touch with the Movement. You will be handsomely rewarded.'

'I have to say no on both counts. In this country, you only report positive things about the leaders, unless you have instructions from higher authorities to do otherwise. Tumbo is still a Cabinet minister and he has powerful connections. I will not stick my neck out. Why don't you use *Time* or *Newsweek*? Secondly, I cannot help you in getting in touch with the Movement. It operates in a clandestine way and it is not easy

319

to penetrate. When they need you, they will come to you.'

'Then of what good are you? If you cannot help over simple matters like these, you are not worth your title!' the British envoy said.

'That's your opinion,' was the terse reply.

'Get out of here!' said the ambassador. The managing director of the local daily left with all his dignity, not caring whether he was going to lose his job or not. He felt that if African dignity had to be restored, he too had to make his contribution.

17

One Hungry African Night

Shaka read the transcript of his father's last words many times. Although he felt it carried a great message of hope, justice could have been better served if it had an introduction, which he now supplied: he gave his father the honour he had been denied by the post-independence leadership. He also established the linkage between the struggle for independence and the struggle the Movement was waging against a corrupt, ineffective and dictatorial regime. Satisfied with what he had done, he took a copy to the vice-president. The big man held back tears as he read the last sentence.

'Shaka, I had known for a long time that the gods have favoured you with special gifts but who could have ever thought that a young brain like yours was capable of a feat like this? You have not only done justice to your father but you have correctly analysed the current struggle and given it a high intellectual profile. What next do you want to do with this wonderful paper?'

'I am going to distribute it far and wide in Kuzania and send copies to leading newspapers in the world,' Shaka replied.

'I want you to post a copy to *Newsweek, Time, The Economist*, the *New Statesman* and all the leading dailies in the world. In Kuzania, it should also be translated into leading vernacular languages. However, judging from the weight of the contents, I do expect some problems with the government. Please be careful. Here, take this money and organise the distribution.'

Shaka got a big bundle of notes for the work and returned to the school of journalism. His father's transcript, now with an introduction, was being printed. He organised the distribution to cells within Glitta and the suburbs but decided to handle personally distribution in the provinces to ensure maximum effectiveness. His mission to the provinces would start early the following morning as there was no time to waste. He walked to the library of Glitta University, where Nzinga was studying. He found her buried in books.

'Hi, love,' he whispered, squeezing her shoulders gently.

'Oh, hi, you look great! Has something very good happened?'

'Yes and no,' he said. 'Let's go for coffee and I will brief you about one or two things.' Nzinga stood up slowly, Shaka holding her hand. She was now very visibly pregnant and not as agile as she had earlier been. Shaka informed Nzinga of his mission to the provinces.

'I understand,' she said smiling. 'But don't stay one minute longer than you have to. The baby is due any day.' She held his hand and squeezed it.

'As soon as I drop off the last bunch, I will board the next minibus. I will be back sooner than soon.' He looked at her warmly, his eyes full of love. 'I need to go home, organise a few items and have an early night. I will be catching the first bus to the Lake province in the morning.'

In the provinces, Shaka moved as swiftly as a gazelle. Wherever he went he found members of the Movement waiting for him. As coordinator of communications, he distinguished himself as a thoroughly efficient man. His father's last words gave fire to the Movement; word was spreading like bush fire that the spirit of the old general had risen and taken the shape of his son. 'Shaka' was the word on people's lips and in their hearts.

After a couple of days, Shaka woke up one morning feeling as if he had fought an elephant all night long. His body ached from head to toe. His first reaction was to wonder if Nzinga was all right, then he thought about his sick mother and old man Agu. Such thoughts weighed heavily on his mind as he sat down to breakfast in a small local hotel. He was down to the last sip of tea when two gentlemen joined him. From the look in their eyes he had no doubt they were policemen.

'Shaka,' one of them said coldly, 'we have orders to take you to the police station.'

'What is the meaning of this? I am not a criminal! Orders from whom?'

'The orders are from a higher authority. The rest will be explained at the police station. Now, if you don't mind, let's go.'

The headlines were splashed across the local daily the following morning: 'Key Dissident Nabbed'. The story read that the government in its usual efficiency had arrested a key member of an underground communist movement bent on causing chaos in Kuzania. The paper went on to say that at the time of his arrest, he was carrying and distributing highly subversive and inflammatory literature that could easily cause bloodshed. The aim of the movement, it was said, was to seize power by unlawful and unconstitutional means. The dissident was assisting with investigations and would be brought to trial as soon as the investigations were complete. The nation was warned to be on its guard.

Early that same morning, there was a knock on Nzinga's door.

'Nzinga, open up, it's me, it's urgent.'

Nzinga recognised the voice of her friend next door. She opened the door and her friend slumped on the bed, handing her the newspaper. 'They have arrested Shaka!'

Nzinga read the first few lines and put the paper down. Her mind raced madly like a computer. 'The bastards! They are going to kill him!'

As the news spread through the halls of residence, students came over to offer Nzinga solidarity. The gathering outside Nzinga's hall soon developed into a large crowd. They requested that a plan of action be mapped out before it was too late. At the back of everybody's mind was the threat on Shaka's life from Tumbo. Nzinga emerged from her room shocked and shaken but with no tears in her eyes. Shaka's father had said, 'No tears...' There would be no tears for Shaka either, not just yet. She knew that Shaka was the bravest man Kuzania had and she was sure he would survive against many odds. She faced the crowd with great courage, her nerves as hard as steel.

'Up with Nzinga!' someone shouted and the crowd

roared back the same in response. 'Up with Shaka!' Again the crowd roared back in deafening unison.

Nzinga could hardly believe her eyes. The multitude was surging forward, each trying to shake her hand, offering words of comfort and solidarity. She knew there had been a complete transformation in her life and in the feelings of the people towards what was happening in Kuzania.

'Nzinga must speak to us,' someone was telling the crowd. 'Let Nzinga give us the order and we will wreck this city.'

People were shouting. Nzinga felt a spirit moving within her urging her to take charge of the situation. What shall I say to these people? she asked the spirit. Slowly, she felt strength and words building within her. She raised her hand and the crowd went silent.

'Brothers and sisters, friends all; at a moment like this when I have just received the shocking news of the arrest of Shaka, I find it hard to express myself freely, and I hope you will bear with me in this agony. I thank you most sincerely for your spontaneous solidarity. All I can say is that may this solidarity live on to the year X and beyond.' There were deafening cheers. 'In my estimation, it would be wise to hold our tempers until we know where Shaka is, and to continue doing so to the days of his trial. If the trial they have promised is a sham, then we shall burn this city to ashes!' There were even greater cheers and whistling.

'Shaka is innocent. What he was distributing was not subversive literature but the last words of his late father, the great freedom-fighter General Jongwe Mkombozi. The general died to set us free; why should his words be labelled subversion, and treachery? His words have exposed the treachery of the current government and that is why they must be hushed!'

'Go on, Nzinga, tell it all,' someone shouted from the crowd.

'In my hands are the last words of our hero. I want you to judge for yourselves whether this is treason...'

'Read them, read them,' the crowd clamoured.

Nzinga read the words, beginning with Shaka's introduction. She was particularly proud to be united with Shaka's father thus, and she felt part of a great nationalist family. She finished reading. 'And they dare call this treason, subversion and treachery?' she asked.

The crowd was hushed, silently digesting the powerful message. Truly Jongwe Mkombozi was a god; Nzinga was a harbinger of salvation, and Shaka was even greater. Why should Kuzania be betrayed twice? 'Shaka will be saved,' the crowd roared. 'General Mkombozi will be avenged.' 'Up with Nzinga,' the crowd roared, incensed, with a sense of an urgent and historic mission.

Nzinga spoke again. 'I share with you your sense of historic duty but, if we all love General Mkombozi, then we must unite to save Shaka, his own blood, his very spirit. The action we take should be guided by reason and maturity. We must not give the demigods an excuse to arrest more people or close the university. I therefore urge that we break up this gathering before the riot squad arrives and keep vigilant, to be reunited as the situation demands. I will find a way of keeping you informed of developments,' she told them.

A rickety minibus stood near the halls of residence. As the crowd began to disperse, an old man wearing a heavy blanket and a sickly woman were helped out. 'It is Agu,' someone in the crowd shouted. They had watched Agu on television and he was now a national hero. 'Up with Agu, up with Agu,' shouted the crowd.

'Give way, give way,' someone was shouting as Nzinga went towards Agu and Shaka's mother. Nzinga embraced Shaka's mother.

'My daughter, you were sent to us by God! We sat in the car to wait for you to finish speaking. May a thousand angels ever guard your life.' As Shaka's mother was speaking, tears rolled down her cheeks.

Agu spoke in turn. 'The things I saw in my dreams were true! I am a living witness to the fight between good and evil. My child, we came to give you courage in this hour of need but instead you have warmed our hearts with your bravery! May the gods and the spirits spread their protection to cover you day and night.' Agu spat on his chest, giving Nzinga more blessings.

'We have come to take you home,' continued Shaka's mother. 'Shaka warned us before he left for the provinces to keep our ears on the ground as the baby is almost due. Let us go home, my daughter,' she pleaded.

The crowd looked on spellbound as Nzinga, Shaka's mother and Agu drove away.

When Shaka's trial opened, the city came to a standstill. People from far and wide thronged the High Court. Crowds sat outside, shouting Shaka's name when he was brought forward. The trial was threatening to shake the nation to the core of its foundations. Shaka had been accused of being an agent of communism in the pay of foreign masters, a key leader of a clandestine movement threatening to overthrow the democratically elected government of Kuzania. It was further revealed that the government had documentary evidence that the

Movement had concealed a large quantity of arms, which were hidden in caches in different parts of Kuzania. Its cadres had been trained in Cuba, Libya, North Korea, Albania and Iraq. The government lamented that, in the face of massive evidence, Shaka had opted to deny the charges and to adopt a stance of total uncooperation. He was withholding vital information necessary to avert bloodshed and chaos. The government appealed to those with information to surrender it freely without fear to the nearest police station.

Shaka spoke in his own defence: 'I am accused of a myriad things, all lies. They tell me this is a trial in a court of law. I ask for justice, not this travesty and mockery of justice in which law is but a toy in the hands of tyranny. There once lived a man who faced death like a god. His name was General Jongwe Mkombozi, my late father, God rest his soul in eternal peace. In his hour of death, he left a message to be a guiding star to the youth of Kuzania. Dutifully I have carried out his wish by distributing his message to all the corners of Kuzania. If in doing so I have committed a crime, then he died in vain. Our independence is a sham and our leaders are despots and demigods!

'For doing what I am doing, I have been chained. I have no apologies to make and no compromises with a regime as sick as this. The small part I have played in opening the eyes of the people I will call my biggest achievement in life, in the service of the motherland. My efforts have not been in vain as I see the people's hunger for their rights grow by the day, to be crowned, with final victory, in the year X.

'My father died in the hands of oppressors. Should I follow the same fate it would be a great honour. Our joint spirits will come back in the final fight between

328

good and evil. Victory is certain, in the year X. I do not plead guilty or not guilty, I plead for the final victory in the year X.' Shaka sat down. He had delivered his defence.

Shaka was given life imprisonment. He walked out of the courtroom smiling and waving to the people, his eyes burning with fire. Overnight, Shaka became a legend throughout the land and beyond. People argued that Kuzania could still be salvaged if only a few more like Shaka would come forward and lead the struggle. People dreamt of victory and full stomachs in the year X. They saw themselves walking with dignity in the streets of Glitta and beyond, as equals with other races. It was as if a new proud race had come into being.

For three weeks after Shaka's trial, the government remained on a state of high alert, waiting for riots. Nothing came. Riot police and paramilitary units remained stationed around all strategic installations. The units also ringed the University of Glitta. A rapport between the units and the students slowly developed.

'When are the riots?' the security forces would ask the students.

'What riots?' the students would ask in return, laughing.

'In support of your hero Shaka!'

'The riots are like the crimes Shaka was accused of. They only exist in the imagination of the political leaders. There are no riots planned, so you should ask them to save you from the heat of the sweltering sun!'

Security men and students would be seen smoking in groups, leaning on the armoured personnel carriers. They were learning a lot from each other as 'comrades'. The Movement took full advantage of the situation and recruited many members of the forces through its university cells. In the end, it was clear to all that something was really rotten in the state of Kuzania, and it could only be changed by replacing the political leadership.

When the security units were at last withdrawn, the parting between them and the students was like the separation of close friends. New and lasting bonds of understanding, friendship and cooperation had been established. They doubted whether, if riots ever came again, they could stand to face one another as enemies.

The first indication of mass action came from the rural areas. Farmers stopped all deliveries to the cooperatives and felled trees across roads. Then came a strike by industrial workers, who planned countryside protests against low salaries and the high cost of living. Leaflets were distributed, calling on workers in all sectors to support the farmers and the industrial workers in a week of demonstrations. This would be followed by an indefinite strike until the grievances of the people were seriously addressed.

The clouds were gathering, announcing the coming of the rains, the season of hailstorms, thunder and lightning, when many things happen in Africa.

WaMwago and Stans were having a very good time. To evade detection by Tumbo and his henchmen, they were consummating their love in top-class tourist camps, using Stans's private plane. WaMwago was full of joy, having discovered how sweet love can be.

Stans was head over heels with his 'sweet octopus'. He knew he loved her and, at the back of his mind, he was happy that the only obstacle that stood between him and everlasting bliss was probably meat for the vultures by now. Operation Black Pig would have dealt with Tumbo for once and for all.

After the love tryst, Stans explained to WaMwago that he had guests at his house and was unable to take her home with him that afternoon.

WaMwago was very disappointed. She had not had enough of her sweet Stans. It struck her like lightning that a solution was already at hand, in her handbag. 'Love, I have keys to Tumbo's suite at the Milton Hotel! He never goes there over the weekends unless I am with him. Let us go and relax there for a while. I haven't had enough of you!' she said sexily.

'Are you sure we will be safe there?' asked Stans.

'Positive,' said WaMwago.

'Brilliant, let's go!'

They parked the car outside the hotel and proceeded to Tumbo's suite. Soon they were on Tumbo's bed, making love, Stans devouring her like fire on dry grass. His 'sweet octopus' wrapped her arms and legs tightly round him, enjoying every second of it. After making love twice, they fell into an exhausted sleep.

Hon. Tumbo was sitting restlessly in the golf club, in the company of Kimondo and a very young woman. He had never felt so defeated in his life. Uppermost on his mind was the fact that his plans for a coup were not working because his American and British allies had refused to give him the support that he had expected. He did not understand them any more. They would come to him once they knew how important he was in the protection of their interests. Had he not bent over backwards to favour their companies for government tenders and establishing industries in Kuzania?

Then there was the president, who did not want to

331

see him either. How much did he know? he wondered. There was William Stans, whom he had built into one of the heaviest investors in Kuzania as his business partner. The man had grown horns and wings and was not responding to his calls. Then there was WaMwago, his sweetheart whom he had transformed from a miserable housewife to an international businesswoman of class. She, too, had developed wings and these days she was out on her own most of the time. Finally there was that scum from the slums, who not only had bewitched his daughter Nzinga into rebelling against him but had got her pregnant and made her run away to the slums with him. Things had gone terribly wrong for Tumbo.

'There are ominous signs in the air,' Tumbo told Kimondo.

'Don't worry, boss, everything will be all right. I know our people. They jump up and down for a week and then collapse in hunger and exhaustion. These demonstrations and strikes are nothing but a passing cloud,' Kimondo consoled him.

'No, it is not them I am referring to. I am talking about our other plans,' said Tumbo.

'You worry yourself too much, boss. Sure, there is some delay but things will work out quickly as soon as the money issue is sorted out.'

'My friends have let me down badly,' said Tumbo. 'But I am a double-edged sword. If one side is not sharp enough, the other is available! I have another plan,' he said enigmatically, refusing to say more.

After a few more drinks Kimondo offered to drive Tumbo home, as Tumbo's driver had been waylaid taking Kimondo's car to the garage to repair a small fault.

'That's a good idea. Drive us to the Milton Hotel.' That said, Tumbo and the young girl sat in the back seat while Kimondo drove them out of the club.

A few yards from the gate of the golf club stood a lanky figure in a raincoat. As Hon. Tumbo's Mercedes appeared, he put his hand in the coat pocket and grasped the cold steel of a .45 revolver. He was expecting Hon. Tumbo to be seated on the back left as usual. He was surprised to see three people in the car and, worse still, Tumbo holding and kissing someone. He loosened his grip on the revolver in disappointment as the vehicle sped past.

In the basement of the Milton Hotel, Tumbo and the young girl got out and Kimondo drove off. Disappointed with the unpredictable behaviour of WaMwago, Tumbo had decided to give himself the treat of Kimondo's young female friend.

Colonel Shabaha was sitting in his car by the round-about between the hotel and Hon. Tumbo's house. He had received word on his walkie-talkie that Tumbo had escaped the attempt at the golf club. If Hon. Tumbo survived all other assassination attempts, he would finish him. His .38 six-shooter was in the shoulder holster. As he waited, he saw Hon. Tumbo's Mercedes approaching in the distance, its tall communication aerial distinguishing it. Colonel Shabaha unzipped his jacket and waited. As the minister's car approached the round-about he saw it had only a driver. Hon. Tumbo must have been dropped somewhere in the city centre. He knew Tumbo would be driven home sooner or later. When the car passed him, he saw that the driver behind the wheel was Kimondo, Tumbo's campaign manager. He decided to recce the route one more time to ensure he had chosen the most appropriate spot. He had assured the Movement he would be successful, and he had to deliver in the face of the earlier failure. He would stay around until the following morning if that was what it took. He rolled down the road a distance behind Kimondo.

Just before the junction that leads to Happy Valley, there was a slope and a small brook. On the other side of the river, partly hidden by the bushes, sat a sports car with two men enjoying the evening breeze. On the rising ground adjacent, another man was lying on the ground, holding a high-velocity rifle with telescopic sight and night vision. Finally he received word on his walkie-talkie that Hon. Tumbo's car was approaching the bridge. He took aim as the car approached, the barrel pointing just before the bridge.

Colonel Shabaha thought he heard the pop of a rifle firing. The next thing he saw was Hon. Tumbo's car losing control, crashing into the bridge and finally resting in the brook below. Then came a sports car speeding in his direction. In it, there were three white men. As he drove across the bridge, he saw the wreck of Tumbo's car in the water. There was nobody stirring. He turned around and began following the speeding car, but soon lost it. He guessed that the three white men were also after Tumbo; presumably they mistook Kimondo for him.

At the airport, the three Americans found Scudulis waiting. They told him the job was done and he gave them their tickets and boarding passes. Scudulis then phoned Stans's house, to collect his share of the blood money. He was told that Stans had flown to the game parks and was expected that evening. He left a message that Stans should call him as soon as possible. Scudulis drove the sports car to his house and parked it in the underground garage, where it was to be dismantled and crated for export as diplomatic cargo.

Hon. Tumbo and his new playmate came to a halt in the lift on the twelfth floor of the Milton Hotel. He was hugging his young victim, wondering what treasures she carried in her warm and tender body. It had been a long time since he last had a *'ndogo ndogo'*, as he used to call teenage girls. Tonight was going to be very special, he thought, with thoughts of WaMwago buried far deep in his subconscious.

'Here we are!' he said excitedly as he pulled out the key to his suite. 'Tonight, I am going to treat you like a queen and tomorrow you will buy yourself an expensive dress and a pair of shoes...' The young girl was giggling, drunk with wine and happy to be associated with an honourable minister.

Tumbo opened the door and led the young girl inside. 'Come this way,' he said, as he headed for the bedroom. Hon. Tumbo's first sight was clothes carelessly scattered on the floor; his next was two naked people lying on his bed. Tumbo stood there, paralysed.

Stans lay frozen on WaMwago, wondering whether he were seeing Tumbo or his ghost. Something must have gone wrong with Operation Black Pig. WaMwago kept her gaze on Tumbo, her mouth wide open in fright unconscious of the weight of Stans, who had gone limp above her. They had both thought it had merely been the maid coming to restock the bar.

The young girl knew something was very wrong. She ran out of the suite, slamming the door behind her, and left the hotel, shaking with fear.

In blind fury, Tumbo threw his full weight on them, shouting, 'Bastards, bastards, bastards!' He rained

335

blows on the couple, biting them furiously like a mad animal. 'Bastards, how can you do this to me?' Tumbo shouted as he worked on them. 'I will kill both of you!'

Stans pleaded with Tumbo, 'Let's discuss ... this ... matter as ... gentlemen! I can ... explain...' but each word was punctuated with a blow or a bite from Tumbo. Deciding it had gone too far, he pushed Tumbo away and jumped out of bed. Tumbo was left lying across WaMwago. He hit her and then struggled from the bed, looking for Stans. WaMwago stood on the bed, holding a loose bedsheet in front of her breasts, too shocked to speak. Tumbo rushed at Stans and grabbed him. They went crashing on the floor. Tumbo sank his teeth deep into Stans's side, and Stans started punching Tumbo. Both in pain, they struggled up and stood in front of each other, each sizing up the other. Tumbo's eyes focused on Stans's exposed genitals. Stans saw the lowered gaze. As Tumbo dived for his genitals, he side-stepped and brought up his knee, catching Tumbo squarely on the nose and mouth. Tumbo fell down bleeding.

'Stop it, stop it, someone is going to get hurt!' WaMwago pleaded with her lovers.

Tumbo stood up and flung himself at Stans. They went crashing on to the bed where WaMwago was standing. All she felt next was a sharp pain at the side of her head as blood oozed from her nose. She fainted as the two men rolled on to the floor. Stans, the ex-GI, came alive. As Tumbo rushed at him once more, Stans's stepped aside, grabbed Tumbo's hand and flung him as hard as he could against the window. There was the sound of breaking glass as Tumbo went through the window. His body was catapulted over the outside railing. The body hit the pavement below with a thud. It twitched for a second or two, then it was still, lifeless. Blood oozed from Tumbo's mouth, nose and ears. It was a ghastly sight.

Up on the twelfth floor from where the fat man had fallen, the figure of a naked white man was seen looking down.

Stans dialled Scudulis and asked him to drive to the airport and refuel his plane to the maximum. He quickly dressed and left the room, leaving WaMwago lying on the bed, unconscious. Driving to his house, he picked up the money the president had given him. He informed his American guests that there had been a terrible accident and he was leaving Kuzania for a while. He urged them to take the next available flight out. They had delivered the gun but Stans was too preoccupied to find out why his plans had not been carried out to the letter.

At the airport, Scudulis was waiting for Stans. 'Boss, we did it! We got rid of him with no trouble at all! The guys have flown out and the car is in the garage.'

'Scudulis, you are the biggest liar the world has ever seen!' Stans shouted angrily.

'Honest to God. The car is —'

'Shut up! If you really want to know, I have just killed him myself.'

'There must be a mix up somewhere! Are you sure, boss?'

'Arrange to have my car stored until you hear from me,' said William Stans, as he opened the cockpit of his Cessna.

'You can't fly now . . . we haven't got clearance,' advised Scudulis.

'Who cares,' replied Stans, as he started the engine.

'What about my payment —' Scudulis shouted in the din of the propellers.

337

'The devil will take care of that!' shouted Stans, as he throttled the engine.

'I don't understand —'

Air-traffic control saw the Cessna leave the parking sheds and head for the runaway. 'What the hell does the fool think he is doing? We have no plane scheduled to take off now!'

William Stans took to the skies, heading west. Scudulis watched the plane as it disappeared into the night. As he stood there, lightning brightened the sky, followed by a huge thunderclap and heavy rain. In the season of gales, hailstorms, thunder and lightning, William Stans was eaten by a hungry African night. Nobody has ever seen or heard of him since.

18

A Day in the Year X

In 'D Block' – 'D' standing for 'death' – of the maximum-security prison in the outskirts of Glitta, Shaka sat on a mattress infested with bedbugs and fleas. He had promised his beloved Nzinga a dance to the beat of tom-toms, bongo drums and the blare of impala horns in the celebrations marking the coming of the year X. He knew he would not keep that promise. However, like his father, he would not die like a dog. He had made his contribution, however modest, in the struggle to rid Kuzania of tyranny. It was up to others to finish the job. He thought of his mother and Agu and wondered how they would manage the new climate of threatening chaos, which would be wrought with danger. He placed his hopes on Nzinga and the Movement to come to their aid. He thought fondly of Nzinga, that special woman who had built a strong bridge across the class divide. She would bear him a child but how would they survive? Then he remembered Nzinga's words, 'The Lord will provide.'

Shaka reasoned that, given the history of state brutality in Kuzania, his life sentence was synonymous with death; it was not a question of *if* he should die in the cells but a question of *when*. Even the unsanitary conditions beckoned death. He knew he would be gone in a matter of months, if not weeks.

Shaka heard the sound of heavy boots outside the cells. He thought it was the guard, bringing him his usual breakfast of half-cooked porridge. Even farmers look after their pigs better, he thought. He compared the taste of the porridge to the life of people in Kuzania, insipid and flat, lacking any sweetness. The guard opened the heavy door to Shaka's cell and beckoned him outside. As the guard led him to the administration building he felt the sun on his body and took a deep breath of fresh air. Such irregular behaviour could only be a bad omen; he feared for his life.

In the building, he was introduced to a senior police officer. As they talked generalities, a prison warden brought him a tray of tea, a fried egg and bread. He wondered why he deserved this special treat. The senior police officer informed Shaka that he had been sent to discuss the possibility of his release. However, it would only be on condition that he agreed to work with the government to smash the Movement. If he consented, he would be granted presidential pardon and be allocated a free mansion in the zones of the affluent in Glitta. He would be free and rich.

'Why do you need my cooperation? The government has powerful machinery to act forcefully without my assistance.'

'Look, young man, don't you value your freedom? We are doing this to help you. As you put it very correctly, the government has a long arm and it is capable of handling any situation. However, we need your help to penetrate the very centre of the Movement. The strikes and the riots are easier to deal with but farmers and peasants need a different approach and this is where you come in. They know you, they trust you and you could be very helpful in breaking their will. There will be a lot of money put at your disposal for the operation. You know what, I really envy your good luck, young man, I wish it were me—' He was cut short by Shaka.

'Officer, the farmers have not been paid their dues for many seasons. At first, the farmers were told exports were fetching peanuts while the prices of machinery and fertilisers were rising too high. But look at what has happened! The directors of the cooperatives are riding around in Mercedes. They chalk up sixty per cent of the value of all produce, while the farmers in their hundreds of thousands share the remaining forty per cent. When farmers rebel against naked exploitation by uprooting cash crops, you call it a rebellion against the government and you blame an invisible movement!' Shaka concluded.

'I did not come here to be lectured and, even if you tried, you cannot convince me the Movement is not behind the rebellion; it has now penetrated the civil service and even the armed forces. You must show your patriotism by helping the government to smash the Movement and save this nation from anarchy. In return, you will have your freedom and you will be showered with wealth.'

The mention of wealth brought back memories of Hon. Tumbo, the people's representative. They were trying to make a small Tumbo out of him! With a broad smile on his face, he replied in a deep low voice: 'You want me to sell my soul? Never! Go and tell your superiors that I am not interested in my personal freedom. Tell them that, like my late father, I would die for the well-being and dignity of my people. If they wish to give me freedom on that basis, I will be for ever grateful. Tell them that I am not a traitor and I cannot betray the cause, for all the wealth in Kuzania. Tell them—'

The senior police officer suddenly and without warning slapped Shaka hard across the face. 'Bloody fool!' he said. 'We offer you freedom and you throw back insults! You demand to be treated like a prince? If you wish to suffer, I will personally take charge of your misery! Put him back in the cell!' he commanded the warden.

Shaka slowly rose from his seat, his nose bleeding from the heavy slap. He did not feel pain, he felt he had delivered a heavy blow against tyranny.

The senior police officer marched angrily to his car. He was on his way to the police headquarters, to report to his superiors that Shaka was a die-hard communist. Shaka was thrown back in the cell.

An hour later, the prison warden, accompanied by the same senior police officer, entered Shaka's cell. They carried with them an assortment of instruments of torture. Without a word, they started punching and kicking him.

Shaka was numb, in shock, but refused to talk. He was stripped naked, handcuffed, then forced to the floor. Needles were inserted in his fingers and a bottle pushed into his anus. Still he refused to give them any information. Undaunted, they worked on his testicles with pliers. Somewhere along the line, he passed out.

On the same Saturday morning, scores of people were streaming into the city centre. A meeting to herald the onset of the campaign of civil disobedience was planned in Freedom Park. Private cars, minibuses and buses were ferrying people to the city without charge. By noon, the huge crowd was singing freedom songs that had not been heard for years. The government had issued a warning that the meeting should not be held and neither should any demonstrations take place. From the huge turnout, the warnings had fallen on deaf ears. The people's defiance had reached a peak.

Those marching in the city centre filed past the offices of the ministry of Commerce, lamenting that they had been denied the chance to burn Tumbo alive in the year X. They marched past the offices of the minister for Internal Security and demanded that Nyoka be hanged in Freedom Square. They marched past the ministry of Justice and demanded that Shaka be released immediately. At three o'clock, they assembled in a huge crowd in Freedom Park. On to the dais came old man Agu. The crowd went wild with cheers. He had become the symbol of resistance and its guiding spirit. As Agu took the microphone, the cheering died down.

He addressed the multitude. 'I greet you all in the name of freedom and dignity. Today, the sun will not go down before we have settled old scores! But I am told that you have planned two weeks of strikes. Let me ask you, if our adversaries sit back and wait for the two weeks to expire, what will you do then? I tell you, this is a bankrupt strategy.

'I have waited for a very long time to enjoy freedom and dignity and I can't wait another day. Because of our patience and silence in the past, we have been taken advantage of. Evil cannot go unchallenged for ever! This is the day patience died, this is the day we found our voice, this is the day we shall settle old scores. The time for action is today!'

There were deafening cheers to Agu's words.

'We are not the cause of the present national malaise,

we are its victims, but we hold the key to the solution, and salvation is at hand.' Agu paused and adjusted the blanket Shaka had bought him. He took a pinch of snuff from his bottle hanging by a string around his neck. He inhaled the snuff and sneezed three times with great pleasure. He smiled widely, visibly relaxed. The crowd roared with laughter, eagerly waiting for him to continue.

'Very early this morning, I received a special message from our service commanders. They asked me to be here this afternoon to break good news to you.'

Freedom Park went silent. The air was pregnant with expectation. Agu smiled broadly, his face shining, his clean-shaven head reflecting the rays of the warm tropical sun.

Before Agu could resume the address, a convoy of military vehicles was seen slowly approaching the park. All the service commanders were standing, each in an open jeep, smiling and waving to the crowd. Behind them followed the police commander and prison commanders. Riot police and the paramilitary, who stood at a distance ready to quell any riots, were taken by complete surprise. They lowered their guard and waited.

The crowd stood silent, waiting. In the past, people had felt only fear when confronted with the might of the organs of state oppression but today they could only feel joy. Someone in the masses started singing an old liberation song and the whole crowd joined in. They were going to start a new life or perish on that day. It was an irrevocable decision.

The convoy came to a halt and the chief-of-staff of the armed forces led his team to the dais. The singing stopped. He saluted, shook Agu's hand very warmly and then they embraced. An alliance, it seemed, had been worked out between Agu, their hero and spirit of resistance, and the armed forces of Kuzania. The stadium went wild with cheers. The other commanders greeted Agu, then stood in a line behind him. Such cheering had not been heard on earth since the world was created.

The commander of the anti-riot forces turned to his colleague.

'What is the meaning of this?' he asked.

'To me,' he replied, 'it looks like a palace coup.'

'Then what do we do? The crowd might turn against us!'

'I suggest we start making ourselves scarce, slowly,' his colleague suggested.

As the crowd focused on Agu and the service commanders, the anti-riot squad thinned out. Nobody paid any attention to them as they retreated in small numbers. They were their own prisoners. Truncheons, rubber bullets, live ammunition, water cannons and whips had been rendered impotent. All of a sudden, the implements seemed too heavy to bear. The squad could hear loud cheers of joy from the multitude they had gone to beat, maim and kill.

Agu motioned the crowd to silence. There was instant hush. 'When I told you that I had a special message from the armed forces, some of you may have thought I was joking. Agu is too old and too serious to play games!' Everybody burst into laughter, including the commanders. He continued: 'When I received their delegation this morning, they urged me to appeal to you for calm and order. What you do not know is that they have put their services at your disposal.' The crowd roared on and on. 'They urged me to do my best to see to it that not a single drop of blood would be shed; Kuzania has bled enough. They assured me their guns would no longer be turned on you, because you are not enemies. Freedom can only be claimed in a climate of peace, trust and cooperation between all groups and institutions. That is why they have joined you here to offer their solidarity in search of solutions to our pressing problems. They tell me that the problem is not with the oppressed people, but with the political leadership. What you have witnessed today, I am told, is a palace coup. I am told there are changes to come in our leadership but they will be brought about peacefully with fair and legal elections. This day, our sons and daughters in the armed forces have done us proud and, if I have ever seen patriotism displayed in all its splendour, this is it! They are not murderers, assassins and mercenaries; they are the people's protectors!'

The crowd shouted in support, 'Our armed forces!', 'Our protectors'. The police force and the prisons were not hailed by the crowd; the two departments had become too notorious to enjoy the praise of the people.

Agu continued: 'I wish to call upon the chief-of-staff to confirm my words. Commander, speak to the people.' Agu sat down in the most dignified fashion, adjusting his blanket. He was beaming with joy.

The chief-of-staff, a towering, majestic and stately figure full of vigour, took the microphone. 'Brothers, sisters, mothers, fathers and all, I salute you in the name of freedom and the fight for dignity,' came his booming voice as the crowd listened attentively. 'Late last night, I summoned the service commanders to a meeting to review the tension in our country. We were greatly concerned with the countrywide demonstrations and strikes. We know the root causes of the problems facing the people and the nation, as old man Agu has told you

346

most ably. We are as much ashamed and concerned with national pillage as you are. We are not a foreign force of occupation and our sacred duty is to protect Kuzania. If events continue unchecked, soon there will be no Kuzania to protect. I want to assure you that our duty is not to safeguard sectarian and class interests at the expense of the survival of the state and that is why we are here today. Down with the Tumbos!'

'Down with the Tumbos!' the crowd responded.

The chief-of-staff continued: 'We wish to enter into an open covenant with the president and commander-in-chief to the immediate effect that, one, the forces of law and order and the judiciary will never again be used to promote injustice and narrow interests; and, two, the political system will be reformed immediately to cater for the wishes and aspirations of the masses of Kuzania, including the registration of new political parties. The details of these demands will be worked out through open national debate involving political parties, pressure groups and other key actors. I hereby command the first tank squadron to roll to State House and bring the president to address the people on these crucial matters.'

As the chief-of-staff sat down, he shook hands with Agu and they exchanged a few lighthearted words. The crowd roared on and on.

People in the crowd climbed on the tanks and others ran alongside them as they rolled up the hill to State House, half a kilometre away. Foreign and local journalists punched their lap-top computers and scribbled on their pads as fast as they could. This was an event the likes of which the world had never seen and they were having difficulty assessing the impact on Kuzania, its neighbouring countries and other countries in the world. The people were singing and dancing, celebrating Agu's prophecy that the sun would not go down before old scores were settled. They were savouring victory. Brother Music was surrounded by a group of university students singing 'The Year X'.

Agu and the commanders sat on the dais chatting and laughing like old friends. All of a sudden, things on the dais went very serious. Agu was hammering home an important point to the chief-of-staff. The chief-of-staff went off and gave instructions to the prison and police officers. Immediately, jeeps and police escort cars took off at high speed, sirens blaring, heading in the direction of the maximum-security prison.

As the tank column came to the gates of State House, the gates were wide open with no sentries in sight. They had fled. A civilian worker informed the commander that the president was alone in his office. When the tank squadron commander knocked on the president's door, there was no reply.

'Your Excellency,' he said, standing outside the door, 'we have been sent by the chief-of-staff and the people to fetch you. Have no fear, they want you to speak to them.' He waited and still nobody stirred. This was repeated a second time to no avail. The squadron commander tried the handle and found the door was unlocked. Slowly and cautiously, he pushed the door open, expecting the worst. He saw the president kneeling in prayer on the floor beside his desk. 'Your Excellency, we have been sent...' He repeated the words but the president did not respond. The squadron commander shook the president by the shoulder. 'Your Excellency, this is no time for prayer! The people are impatiently waiting for you to address them at Freedom Park!'

Slowly, the president stood up, like a man in a trance. There was a strong smell of whisky in the room and pieces of broken glass on the floor. The wall had stains of whisky splashed on it.

'What do you see on my hands?' The president asked the squadron commander, showing him his open palms.

'I see sweat in your hands, Your Excellency, but as I was telling you —' He was cut short.

'No, it is not sweat, it is blood!' the president said, shaking. 'You call yourself a soldier and yet you cannot distinguish between blood and sweat! Tell me, why does Hon. Tumbo keep calling me a fool?'

The squadron commander was even more alarmed. 'Mr Tumbo is dead, Your Excellency, he cannot possibly —'

'You are a liar!' the president fixed a weak but wild gaze on him. 'Tumbo was here just now, laughing and calling me a fool! Doesn't he know that I am the president and commander-in-chief of the armed forces of Kuzania? Doesn't he know that I am His Excellency and I can deal with him very ruthlessly? Am I not a powerful man?'

The squadron commander was convinced that something was very wrong with the head of state. He did not know how to deal with the alarming situation. 'Your Excellency, I was sent —'

'I have heard you, I am not deaf, you know! I am tired, very, very tired and I cannot continue with this any longer. My time has come. With the death of Tumbo, my choice has been made simple. The incumbent vice-president, Hon. Fikira, will be president. Yes, Fikira will be president and he will speak well of me ... '

At first, there were whispers and murmurs outside the office door and then the crowd that had accompanied the tank column to State House broke into wild cheering and jubilation. They started running back to Freedom Park.

'What is that noise?' the president asked the squadron commander.

'It is the people celebrating,' he replied.

'What are they celebrating?'

'They are celebrating your announcement that Fikira is the new president.'

'What? By whose authority? I am the president of Kuzania and the commander-in-chief of—' He was in turn cut short by the commander.

'But, Your Excellency, you have just told us Fikira is our new president!'

'But I did not say he takes over immediately. He will take over after the elections,' the president said, like a man pleading to be understood.

'Well, well, then there was a failure in communication and in the circumstances, Your Excellency, I would let the mistake stand,' the commander advised him, knowing that any moment now the news would be announced in Freedom Park. He knew that the mistake was the best thing to happen to Kuzania, given the mood of change.

'Use your radio and call the stadium. Tell the chief-of-staff there has been a mistake and . . .' As the president spoke, there were deafening cheers coming in long, loud waves from the direction of Freedom Park. The people were overjoyed. Fikira was their man and the president knew it.

'You mean, I was . . . I have been, been . . .' the president was stammering and incoherent. 'It . . . it is another conspiracy! It, it, it is a, a, a . . .' He collapsed in a heap on the carpet, shaking and sweating profusely.

'Someone call a doctor quickly!' the squadron commander shouted. The president had suffered a massive heart attack.

*

When the squadron commander returned to Freedom Park, he found the people singing and dancing. Brother Music was singing for his own freedom and that of Kuzania and he was giving it the very best he had. Agu sat there with the service commanders, chatting and laughing, all tapping their feet to the catchy beat.

The squadron commander reported to the chief-of-staff what had happened at State House. Agu and the service commanders began discussing the report. As they were nodding their heads in agreement, the sound of sirens was heard approaching Freedom Park. The crowd went wild again. They shouted at the top of their voices: 'It is Shaka!', 'Shaka is here!', 'Shaka is free!'

Shaka, standing in an open jeep, was waving to the crowd. He appeared to be in great pain and was helped to the dais. Agu embraced him, and Shaka repeated, 'Thank you, Great-grandpa, thank you, Great-grandpa.'

'You will be fine, my boy, you will be fine,' Agu responded, visibly pained by the condition Shaka was in.

Shaka was embraced by the service commanders and they sat on the dais together. He noticed Brother Music, Musa and Apunda standing close by and his face brightened. He waved at them warmly and they waved back, very touched to be so close to him once again. Shaka sat on the dais, half dazed by pain from the torture, wondering whether what he was witnessing was real or a mirage. He focused his eyes on the huge multitude and saw smiling faces, bright eyes full of joy and hope. He heard their thundering voices and wondered whether at last they had seen a flickering light at the end of the dark tunnel of their miserable history. Thousands of jubilant voices seemed to answer that, at last, salvation was at hand. He smiled. This is a day in the Year X! he said to himself.

There was a booming voice over the public address system. Shaka heard the name of Agu mentioned and the crowd went wild. He heard the name of Hon. Fikira and the crowd cheered even more, then he thought he heard his own name and the cheering became deafening. The three names were called repeatedly and the crowd kept roaring back. He heard them name him a hero, address Hon. Fikira as the president and Agu as the force and spirit of salvation and freedom. He tried to smile but the smile came only momentarily. The pain in his groin was excruciating and the figures around him were losing shape. Nothing was registering in his mind any more except pain. A thousand twinkling stars were fixed on the faces of the multitude and he saw the dark tunnel of their history illuminated from end to end. He felt deep human warmth engulf him totally. He tried to radiate some of the warmth in return. Beads of sweat covered his forehead and he felt ecstatic as he was lifted higher and higher. He wanted to reach out to the people and shake their hands, each and every one of them. He felt his body moving and, as he stretched his hands, he fell from the chair. His buttocks were covered with raw blood.

'The bastards, they have tortured him to death!' the chief-of-staff cursed as the police and prison commissioners looked down in shame. The crowd was silent as Shaka was rushed to the intensive care unit of the armed forces hospital.

When the meeting resumed, the chief-of-staff called on Hon. Fikira to come forward. From somewhere in the multitude, a lanky and energetic man weaved his way forward through the crowd towards the dais. It was when he removed the long overcoat and broad hat that the crowd knew for sure that the man was none other than Hon. Fikira. He had marched in their midst incognito. Such humility was not common; people were astounded, and most grateful. He was sworn in there and then without either a tie or a suit. He was the most dignified man Kuzania had ever seen, a man from the breed of angels. If the world had cared that day, it would have realised that from the descendants of angels of the Royal Celestial Forces who had settled in Kuzania after the ancient crash of a celestial UFO, there were four people who had graced the dais. They were Fikira, Agu, Shaka and the chief-of-staff. The only one missing was Nzinga, who was a direct descendant from her mother's side. But that is a long story dating back to the first Armageddon in heaven. Suffice it to say that, after many millenniums, good had the upper hand over evil in Kuzania.

After the swearing in, the chief-of-staff addressed Hon. Fikira. 'Your Excellency, Mr President and commander-in-chief of the armed forces of the Republic of Kuzania, please address the nation.' He saluted and sat down. The crowd went wild again.

President Fikira lifted his hand and the crowd was silent. 'Fellow citizens, the joy I feel in my heart today is hard to express. It is the joy of one who has waited for years to see the birth of freedom in Kuzania.' The crowd cheered again. 'I will let you into another secret! When the chief-of-staff reached me yesterday and asked what should be done to save the explosive situation in Kuzania, I told him without hesitation that only one man could answer that question, and that man was none other than old man Agu. You know the rest of the story. We have bottled up anger in the face of tyranny for too long. We have endured hardship like mindless robots. Were we not all born equal with a mandate from nature to fulfil our God-given potential and to enjoy life? Then what happened? Along came the demigods, descendants of devils, and we were condemned to misery, despair and death.

'We have been hounded like wild beasts and locked up in cages called detention camps. Why? Because we wanted our God-given rights restored. The voice of reason was branded dissent and high treason. You have seen what they have done to Shaka, a young man who has hardly tasted life. We salute his bravery and sacrifice and, above all, his invaluable role in the Movement, which has contributed immensely to the success of this great day. Our victory is his victory, his victory our victory. Did these demigods and their demons of torturers have any human feelings? I leave you to make the judgement. Who are the beasts with twin heads of evil? We or they?'

'They are beasts,' the crowd roared back.

'For how much longer were we to serve their diabolical whims? Is this the freedom we fought for?'

And the crowd answered in one voice; 'No! No! No!'

President Fikira continued: 'Today marks a new beginning in the lives of the citizens of Kuzania. Today marks the first day in "the year X", as Brother Music puts it. Let our toil, energies and sweat bring forth abundant fruits and joy to all. We shall soon settle old scores with the demigods. Those who have died in the throes of their own folly will answer for their sins on the day of judgement. How can they face our ancestors and those who died in the fight for freedom? Their greed for money, power and lust will haunt them eternally.

354

Those who have ears let them hear now. Such a breed of evil will never haunt Kuzania again!

'We were living in the dungeons of hell but, today, we have scaled the walls and savoured freedom and dignity. The old world is dead and, in its place, a new one is rising, based on humanity and justice. The demigods who have been manufacturing and spreading tyranny have a price to pay and the trials will be based on the rule of law and justice. There will be no vengeance, but justice will be done as a deterrent and a warning. When Satan rebelled against God in heaven, he was banished to hell.

'I call upon the new leadership to revisit our past and correct the glaring gross imbalances in order to give each and everyone a chance to do their best, for their own good and for the good of Kuzania. I also propose that old man Agu be nominated to sit in parliament for life.' There were deafening cheers of approval from the crowd.

'I call upon the incoming leadership to select an appropriate site in the capital for the erection of a towering monument in honour of this day and in memory of those who have lost their lives over the years fighting for independence and dignity in Kuzania. Let the people look upon the monument as an inspiration and guarantee that tyranny will never reign again in this land.' The new president was silent for a while.

'Speak on, speak on!' the crowd urged.

'I wish to thank the patriots in our armed forces for their maturity and valour. Today, they have risen to the occasion in a most commendable manner. I also want to thank the nation for the burden of leadership that has been placed on my shoulders. I give the assurance that we have buried dictatorship this day.

Other political parties will be registered without hindrance and national and presidential elections will be held within a year. I declare here and now that I will be offering my candidature under the National Redemption Party, which will rise out of the Movement. If anybody within the Movement wishes to oppose me, let them be free to do so without fear. Ours will be practical democracy and not the farce we have suffered in the past.

'In the meantime, I promise to do my best to steer the ship of the state out of the current storm, with your support and under your scrutiny, to ensure that posterity will remember this day as the day of our salvation and freedom, our beginning. We fought for dignity, freedom and land and the three issues will be addressed most vigorously. Those who have stolen public lands and plots will answer for their sins. In this nation, we have big Tumbos and small thieves. The days of thieves are only forty and their time has come.

'We shall build a well-fed and dignified nation on the fertile land of Kuzania, the land that history tells us was home to the garden of Eden. We shall plant good on this land and its seeds will find their way to all the corners of the earth. Long live Kuzania.'

'Long live Kuzania,' the crowd roared back, and cheered him long after he had left the stadium in the company of the service commanders and Agu. They were going to the army hospital to check on Shaka.

The crowd did not want to leave Freedom Park. Brother Music was singing 'The Year X' and the crowd was responding wildly. A people who had long forgotten how to be happy had found their voices at last. Their cheering soared to the heavens while they shook the foundations of the earth with the stomping of their feet in dance. They discovered that they could sing and dance and be happy like other human beings. It was a sweet discovery after years of feeling numb. They now knew that you couldn't imprison the soul, only the body, and that an imprisoned body could be released, at a stroke, with struggle and sacrifice. There they were, faces that had long lost the touch of human warmth, now radiating with fresh humanity; tears that in the past had signified deep anguish, helplessness and death now signified joy and happiness. With chains and shackles removed, they were a new and free people, celebrating the assurance and rekindled hope of a better tomorrow, a better life.

Nzinga was rocking her hours-old baby at the Glitta Maternity Hospital. He was strong, healthy and wonderful, like the new nation. She had just received news of events, including Shaka's release, at the Freedom Park. She wished she had been there to witness the birth of a new Kuzania, as she wished that Shaka had been there to witness the birth of their son. She consoled herself that he would soon be there. She was happy she had voted with the people, for it was they who had given her, Shaka and their son a new lease of life. Tears of joy rolled down her cheeks and she felt the urge to shout 'Freedom at last!' for the world to hear. She thought of her father's huge mansion with a two-acre compound and she resolved it would be turned into a home for the rehabilitation of street urchins and parking-meter boys. Overcome with fatigue she returned the baby to his cot, lay on the bed and fell into a deep sleep, with a smile on her face.

* * *

357

When Jenny WaMwago was released from the hospital, she was a thoroughly battered person, both physically and mentally. Age seemed to have suddenly caught up with her. She was a very different creature from the tantalising 'sweet octopus' who had held hearts spellbound with her gorgeousness.

The story of Tumbo, WaMwago and Stans was a big hit and many people volunteered information to journalists, Stans's house keeper included. The story was used to hit hard at corruption and immorality in Kuzania, especially in the political leadership. The picture painted was one of a breed of devils corrupt in the extreme; insensitive, greedy and lustful. WaMwago was said to have played the game very successfully by acquiring the financial and material favours of several of the demigods. Most worryingly, had Tumbo succeeded in his presidential ambitions, WaMwago would have had a fair chance of becoming the first lady.

WaMwago went home in a taxi. Nobody had come to visit her in hospital. She had plans to be alone for a while before deciding what to do next. Her dream of settling down in Vermont with Stans had evaporated, so she was going to make a new start in life – or was it going to be a continuation of the old, with new faces? Of her recent past, nothing registered but memories of lost opportunities.

On arrival at her flat, she found a guard at the door. Inside the house, there were carpenters and painters busy refurbishing the house. She was baffled, but was advised to address her enquiries to the National Housing Credit and Loans. She was informed that Hon. Tumbo had defaulted in repayments and, now that he was dead, the company had no choice but to repossess the flat. WaMwago remembered that she had given Tumbo some money to assist with the initial deposit. Thereafter she had assumed Hon. Tumbo was meeting the necessary financial obligations. She recalled also that Tumbo had kept the agreement papers and she had nothing to show that she owned the place – if she ever did. She was told that the furniture and other household goods were auctioned to recover some of the debt. In a flash, she recalled that the logbook for her car was never given to her. She had heard of foolish women who were easily cheated by men in a similar manner but this was the limit. She had very little savings left and a huge medical bill to settle. She thought of Tumbo and cursed him.

WaMwago stood on the driveway, motionless. The world had become a big pit, a void into which she was falling. What was she going to do? Where was she going to go? Whom could she turn to in this hour of need? She was alarmed by her desperation and scared of the world around her. Half dazed, she felt something warm escaping from her body, as she urinated on herself under the gaze of surprised labourers.

Musa was closing his business for the day when a battered and haggard woman came to him.

'Excuse me sir,' said the woman. 'Could you tell me where I can find cheap accommodation around here?'

'Sure, sure,' replied Musa, the man with a solution to each and every problem except his own. He recognised WaMwago at once. Her picture had been in the papers several times by courtesy of Rev. Mwago, in the serialised story of her life. 'I will take you to a place nearby.' He took WaMwago to a hotel where the occupants were women who traded their bodies for money and who sang a song called 'The Milk Song'.

'Ambrosia, come over here.' Musa called a young woman. 'Take your sister to the manager, she is looking for a place to stay.'

'This way please. You will like it here,' Ambrosia assured her as they walked to the manager's office.

'I am sure I will. The place looks quite comfortable,' lied WaMwago, who was already dreading the stale smell in the air. She was no longer a snake in the jungles of the Amazon, trying to fly like a bird. She was standing on very firm ground, among her professional colleagues. Her survival was guaranteed.

Uncertain times arouse a myriad possibilities, as divergent groups fish in troubled waters. The catch must be made before the water settles, and each expects to surface with a prize winner. The plunge is not dictated by reason but by wild dreams. If reason and common sense had anything to do with it, political transition in Africa would not be the nightmare it is today. Like snow sculptures, the dreams are transient, their duration dictated by the weather. In Europe in winter, grand snow sculptures of the wonders of the world, crystal clear, adorn open spaces. The Taj Mahal, the Leaning Tower of Pisa and the Pyramids of Egypt are translocated by imagination. With time they melt, along with African dreams of democracy, development, prosperity and security. They are washed away in the season of thunder, hailstorms and lightning when many things happen.

The evil hydra rejuvenates itself like the tail of a lizard. In the junior quarters of the main barracks in the outskirts of the city of Glitta, a master sergeant was outlining the final details of a coup d'état. The justification of the imminent putsch was that the old political leadership had handed the ship of state to a bunch of communists and anarchists on a silver platter. The coup plotters were a collection of malcontents from different wings of the armed forces, most of them visibly drunk. In their clouded minds, they viewed themselves as saviours of Kuzania.

They had a list of those to be eliminated. The new president, Shaka and Agu were at the top of the list. In particular, Shaka was said to be a disciple of Osama bin Laden and that he had received military training in Libya, Sudan and Afghanistan. It was through this training that he had learnt how to hypnotise multitudes, including the daughter of the late Hon. Tumbo, into joining the Movement. He was said to be a very dangerous man. They were all raring to save Kuzania and, if they succeeded, Africa would have another name to add to the list of countries ruled by generals, colonels and master sergeants grappling with complex and un-fathomable state matters in State House, guided by ignorance and incompetence.

A corporal who had been recruited by the Movement during the occupation of the university following Shaka's arrest intervened.

'This makes me sick! There is no threat of communism and anarchy in Kuzania! The bin Laden connection is bullshit! The time has come to move forward. Let us give democracy a chance. The days of the military in power are gone; you only have to look at what is happening in West Africa. Why do we want to make fools of ourselves?'

The master sergeant drew his pistol.

'You are a traitor!' he screamed at the corporal. In the scuffle that ensued the gun went off; the corporal lay sprawled on the floor, blood oozing from his chest. His body shook violently momentarily and then he lay still.

'It was an accidental discharge! Honestly! Believe me, I had no intention of shooting him!' the master sergeant pleaded with his officers. Nobody believed him. They were not ready to give their loyalty to a bloodthirsty fool. The master sergeant was taken to the central police station. The coup died with the corporal.

The old guard under Hon. Nyoka was also on the prowl, much weakened and fearful of the future. In Africa, whatever the constitution says, the old guard will invent reasons to justify the need for the continuation of the status quo. Entrenched in power for decades, the old guard, bankrupt in ideas and incoherent except to itself, issues a catalogue of imaginary achievements and creates excuses for glaring past failures. Under threat, failures are blamed on saboteurs, dissidents and their foreign masters. When the clamour for change becomes a crescendo and the momentum is irreversible, the old guard issues threats and warns of a fight to the death. Although these are the kicks of a dying horse, they can be lethal.

Fortunately for Kuzania, the old guard had over-exposed itself and its credibility was long gone. The clique was disintegrating, like the morning dew when the sun rises. The moribund bunch of self-seeking opportunists was no longer a factor in the evolution of a new Kuzania. Maybe another hydra would emerge but, for the moment, Kuzania looked safe to chart a new future.

A couple of days later, Shaka and Nzinga were seated in the back seat of an army saloon car. Apunda sat in the front with the driver. Shaka had been discharged from hospital and he was going home, to Kawempe.

The three were talking excitedly about recent events in Kuzania, which offered a new lease of life for the citizens. Shaka had his arm around Nzinga's waist and Nzinga's arm was resting on his thigh. He looked at Nzinga.

'I can't wait to see our boy! Nzinga, you are an angel!' He kissed her passionately.

'When Agu told the chief-of-staff to give orders to have you released...' Apunda was trying to say, but Nzinga interrupted excitedly.

'When I moved in with your mother, we extended the house and got electricity connected. It is quite cosy. We sit there with Mother watching television. Our favourite is always Agu's star show on video! He comes to see us quite often and at times I go to chat to him. Then there is my favourite song that I always play in your honour!'

'Which one is that? I thought "The Year X" had not been recorded yet!' Shaka joked.

'That, too, we shall play, but the song devoted to you is one by the Four Tops and it goes: "If I were a carpenter and you were a lady, would you marry me anyway, would you have my baby!"' Nzinga's voice was beautifully melodious as she happily sang the verse to Shaka.

'So tell me, would you?' Shaka asked her.

Nzinga turned to him, looked at him straight in the eye and kissed him on the lips. 'Yes! Yes!'

Soon, they were in Kawempe. In the yard, they found a huge crowd waiting. Shaka waved at them and shook hands until his arm ached. Women were ululating and others were singing his praise.

'He is going to be our member of parliament!' one said.

'He will be a minister in the new government,' another suggested.

'Why not the vice-president?' asked another.

At last Shaka found Agu: 'Great-grandpa, last but not least!' He embraced him. 'The earth has not your equal, you are the greatest man on earth and history will never forget you! You have moved mountains. Thank you, Great-grandpa, you have saved our lives!'

'No, no, you have saved mine! I now can face my Maker with pride. I have a great story to tell those who went before. I have a special one for your father. I will tell him that his son has become a fearless fighter. What do they say? "Like father like son." He will be very proud of you, Shaka – they all will be. Now I am ready for death. My mission is accomplished, thanks to you and Nzinga and the others, but remember every word I said about the fight between good and evil...'

'Don't talk about death, it is time to start a new life!' Shaka told him.

'Not for me. The end has come. You don't need me, the nation has matured.' Agu released himself from Shaka and retreated to his stool under the shade. He looked happy but visibly much weaker. The public limelight had taken a heavy toll on him.

Nzinga watched them from a distance, not wishing to interfere with their reunion. She joined Shaka as he entered their new home. His mother was waiting in the sitting-room. In her arms was Shaka's son.

'Mother! My son!' Shaka held both in his arms, 'Welcome home, my son,' cried his mother. Shaka felt Nzinga's presence close behind him and he pulled her into the circle. They stood there, tears of joy rolling freely down their cheeks, united in love.

Eventually Shaka took Nzinga's hand and went outside to talk to the people. The crowd, full of warmth and friendship, was a sight to behold.

Agu watched them. Privately he knew that the world was only beginning to witness the power of good over evil. The young couple in front of him were the guardians of good, as celestially deigned. He felt privileged to have been associated with them so closely.

That evening, a big welcome celebration was planned in the local park. The Movement had made very elaborate arrangements. Several committees had been charged with the task of the preparations and all had reported that everything was in top gear. What surprised the Movement were the generous donations of food and drink from all the corners of Kuzania. Lorry-loads of cows, goats, sheep and chicken had arrived at the park grounds without prior announcement. Butchers and roasters emerged from the people, offering free services and a local charcoal dealer organised the donation of bags of charcoal from his tradesmen. The local people brought huge amounts of food from their kitchens.

When Shaka and Nzinga arrived at the park later in the evening, they were welcomed by a huge crowd of people. Teams of traditional dancers from different parts of the country were performing and each had its own large crowd joining in. Musa, Apunda and Brother Music were all there. The celebrations began with speeches, followed by food. Everyone ate to the full. Then came the highlight of the evening, music and dancing, Brother Music at the forefront, with tom-toms, bongos and impala horns. Reverend Mwago was in the thick of it, dancing energetically.

Shaka and Nzinga took to the floor. The sky was clear with a full moon, while a million stars were twinkling to the music's rhythm. It was a night free of devils, as they say. Nzinga, her eyes shining like two twinkling stars was dancing very close to Shaka, their strong thighs moving in unison. With a warm smile on her face, her sweet lips parted and she kissed him. He responded passionately. In the beauty of a day in the year X, they were enjoying feelings of dignity and splendour hitherto unknown. It was not just they: the whole nation was caught in the magic of rebirth, the beginning of a future that would release the worth and potential of its citizens.

Brother Music, the self-made music maestro, was leading the band with the meticulousness of a seasoned conductor. His guitar fused with bongo drums, tom-toms and the wail of impala horns to a sweet harmony, yielding music from the bowels of time, authentic, melodious and wonderful. When the song 'The Year X' was played, the crowd went wild. It was the song of triumph of good over evil. It was the people's song. Shaka and Nzinga danced closely, melting into each other.

As the song ended, to the cheers of the crowd, Shaka turned to Nzinga.

'The evening is not complete.'

Surprised, Nzinga fixed her gaze on him.

'What else would you have wished for?'

'I wish the crippled woman who was bulldozed to death in Komoro was here to share in the celebrations and to add her sweet voice to the music.'

'Not all who deserve a better tomorrow live to see the day, Shaka,' replied Nzinga. 'Think of your own father and other patriots who went before their time. Our big challenge now is to give life to the living and not to mourn the dead. Come, let's dance, such good music should not go to waste!'

With a smile, Shaka took Nzinga by the waist and the two joined the crowd, losing themselves in the vibrant rhythm of a soul rekindled. The healing process had begun.

High in the heavens, the band of cherubs and seraphims was rendering the tune, 'A Dream Come True' in their own celebration, marking the triumph of good over evil in Kuzania, the land that the Good Lord had created as a living symbol of his majesty and perfection on earth.

Old man Agu and Shaka's mother were seated in the moonlight, enjoying the late-night breeze of a most warm and extraordinary evening. Agu, looking to the heavens, could see a bright star, whose light fell on Kawempe stadium. He smiled to himself. Shaka's son was soundly asleep in his grandmother's lap.

'Do you think our people have crossed the valley of despondency for good?' Shaka's mother asked Agu.

Agu thought for a while, his eyes fixed on the calm face of Shaka's son. 'It is too early to say but we have certainly crossed the line of despair. The dark tunnel of our history is too long to traverse in a single motion. People can now see the light at the end, but it is still faint.'

'Your assessment is very sound,' said Shaka's mother. 'We cannot undo age-old evils within a day. The joy I have is that I lived to see the beginning of the journey to the promised land and, for that, I am most grateful to the Good Lord.'

'You've spoken for both of us!' Agu responded. 'The future of this nation is now secure in the hands of the youth, who have proved themselves mature beyond their age. By and by, the world will borrow a leaf from Kuzania on how to build a new garden of Eden without serpents.'

As they sat, music from Kawempe park came seeping through the night. They heard the sound of traditional instruments fill the air and their blood warmed, their hearts full of joy.

'There is a new song for my people!' Agu declared.

Shaka's mother did not reply. She was rocking the baby to the beat of the new sound in the air, as if cajoling the rhythm to enter into his heartbeat.

At last my story must come to an end but, let me tell you; as I watched the joy in Kawempe park, I wondered whether the night and its agents of evil would ever be so unkind again. In the soul of men such as Tumbo and his ilk, the centre is black. Their nature, like a black hole, eats all that is good in man and thrives on chaos, on despair, on dehumanisation. Guard yourself and be warned that, whatever your station in life, the two mighty forces of good and evil will sway you, now this way, then that way, in the flow and ebb of time. Weigh your choices wisely as you drift through life. Such is the predicament of man, some say from a curse in the garden of Eden. Now you know better.

Satisfied, I joined the dancing as Brother Music belted out the popular song, 'The Year X' once again, by public demand.

Perhaps we will meet again. Adieu.